Cornelius Van Til's Doctrine of God and
Its Relevance for Contemporary Hermeneutics

Cornelius Van Til's Doctrine of God and Its Relevance for Contemporary Hermeneutics

Jason B. Hunt

WIPF & STOCK · Eugene, Oregon

CORNELIUS VAN TIL'S DOCTRINE OF GOD AND ITS RELEVANCE FOR CONTEMPORARY HERMENEUTICS

Copyright © 2019 Jason B. Hunt. All rights reserved. Except for brief quotations in critical publications or reviews, no part of this book may be reproduced in any manner without prior written permission from the publisher. Write: Permissions, Wipf and Stock Publishers, 199 W. 8th Ave., Suite 3, Eugene, OR 97401.

Wipf & Stock
An Imprint of Wipf and Stock Publishers
199 W. 8th Ave., Suite 3
Eugene, OR 97401

www.wipfandstock.com

PAPERBACK ISBN: 978-1-5326-8287-2
HARDCOVER ISBN: 978-1-5326-8288-9
EBOOK ISBN: 978-1-5326-8289-6

Manufactured in the U.S.A.   08/30/19

Dedicated to my wife, Laura,

My parents, Charles and Karen Hunt

In memory of Cornelius Van Til
(1895–1987)

Contents

Preface | ix

Part I: What Does Van Til Have to Do with Hermeneutics?

Chapter 1: Introduction | 3
Chapter 2: Surveying the Field, Part I | 41
Chapter 3: Surveying the Field, Part II | 61

Part II: Van Til's Doctrine of God

Chapter 4: Creator-Creature Distinction | 103
Chapter 5: Incomprehensibility | 133
Chapter 6: Ontological Trinity | 158

Part III: Van Til's Doctrine of God Applied

Chapter 7: The NT Use of the OT | 185

Conclusion | 211

Bibliography | 217

"From where, then, does wisdom come? And where is the place of understanding? It is hidden from the eyes of all living and concealed from the birds of the air. Abaddon and Death say, 'We have heard a rumor of it with our ears.' "God understands the way to it, and he knows its place. For he looks to the ends of the earth and sees everything under the heavens. When he gave to the wind its weight and apportioned the waters by measure, when he made a decree for the rain and a way for the lightning of the thunder, then he saw it and declared it; he established it, and searched it out. And he said to man, 'Behold, the fear of the Lord, that is wisdom, and to turn away from evil is understanding.'"

—Job 28:20-28

"Whoever trusts in his own mind is a fool, but he who walks in wisdom will be delivered."

—Proverbs 28:26

Preface: Cornelius Van Til and Hermeneutics

CORNELIUS VAN TIL (1895–1987) was a theologian and apologist who served on the faculty of Westminster Theological Seminary (1928–1972). He was, apart from Calvin, strongly influenced by the Dutch reformed tradition (Kuyper, Bavinck, and Vos). However, he was also controversial in the sense that he wrote polemically, and he creatively summarized reformed doctrines in new ways to meet the challenges of his day. This led to a strong polarization among those who interacted with his work, both positively[1] and negatively.[2] This was, in part, due to his interaction with philosophy and borrowing philosophical concepts, which he redefined according to the Christian worldview. His ideas have often been misunderstood and even misapplied.[3] Yet, he saw his own work as merely presenting and applying "generic Calvinism," and confronting opposition to Christ and his church.[4]

Perhaps his most significant contribution to the field of apologetics was his self-conscious determination to construct a biblical, full-orbed Christian worldview, which did not merely focus on proximate arguments but ultimate commitments. He sought to present a Christian system of truth in terms of *metaphysics, epistemology, and ethics*. Moreover, he saw a great need to evaluate apologetic methodology in order to discern whether one's method was consistent with this system of truth. Underlying his apologetic method and worldview was a strong emphasis on the doctrine of God. This emphasis has often been overshadowed by misunderstanding, terminological confusion, and idiosyncrasies in his thought.

1. Roberts, "Van Til," 73; Frame, *Van Til*, 44; Muether, *Cornelius Van Til*, 16.

2. Robbins, *Cornelius Van Til*; Lewis, "Van Til," 361; Pinnock, "Philosophy," 422; Clark, *Trinity*, 88.

3. See White, *Van Til*, 14.

4. Van Til's "generic Calvinism" and "reformed tradition" consisted of the summary of doctrine found in the following creeds: Belgic Confession, Heidelberg Catechism, Canons of Dordt, and especially the Westminster Confession of Faith (Van Til, *Defense of Faith*, 1, 277). References to "Reformed tradition" in this work are consistent with this notion.

Sharing the same theological heritage with Van Til, expressed primarily in the Westminster Confession of Faith (along with the Larger and Shorter Catechisms), I share the same fundamental theological presuppositions. I see his work largely as a positive and fruitful contribution to articulating a Christian worldview. That said, his work does display some areas of weakness. Two particular areas stand out in this regard and will be touched upon in the pages that follow. First, he is unclear at points and begs further elaboration. Second, he can tend to paint some of his opponents in an unfair light (even if his criticism has some merit), creating a "straw man" of sorts. In the end, however, I find his work to be fertile soil for exploring theological consistency in a number of fields.

In what follows, we will attempt to apply Van Til's logic to hermeneutics and investigate potentially fruitful applications. Just as Van Til evaluated apologetic methodology in terms of the doctrine of God, hermeneutical methodology can also be evaluated along the same lines. A distinctly *Christian* hermeneutic should be consistent with a Christian doctrine of God.

In part I, we will examine three important foundational matters in order to establish Van Til's relevance for contemporary hermeneutics. First, we will evaluate how Van Til has been perceived in relation to the hermeneutical discussion (chapter 1). Second, we will examine how "hermeneutics" has come to be defined and understood today (chapter 2). Third, we will look at how the relationship between metaphysics and hermeneutics has been articulated in terms of being compatible with a Christian worldview, especially as it relates to the doctrine of God (chapter 3).

Part II will introduce Van Til's doctrine of God as a self-conscious Christian response to the issues raised in part I. His doctrine of God will be discussed along three main contours emphasized by him in his work in apologetics: the Creator-creature distinction (chapter 4); incomprehensibility (chapter 5); and the ontological Trinity (chapter 6). From our discussion of each, we will consider general hermeneutical implications for the contemporary scene.

In part III, we will apply Van Til's doctrine of God to a particular contemporary issue within evangelical[5] hermeneutics: *the NT use of the OT*

---

5. This term has become increasingly hard to define in terms of consensus. This is due to differing criteria and tools used to measure whether one fits the pre-constructed category of "evangelical." Perhaps the most helpful definition of "evangelical" involves a biblical-theological approach, which is tied to scriptural emphases related to the gospel (e.g., Christological, biblical, historical, theological, apostolic witness, and personal), going back to the first century (cf. Stott, *Evangelical Truth*, 13–34). This is opposed to more sociological approaches which tend to see "evangelicalism" as a late development in the history of the church. A biblical-theological approach to defining "evangelical" would distinguish between and affirm the formal principle (authority of

(chapter 7). This will provide a brief case study of how Van Til's theological emphases speak to questions of meaning and method. Our aim will be to assess gaps in the debate related to worldview considerations at the level of presupposition.

The concern throughout is to probe the level of consistency that exists between theology and method in hermeneutics. The content of Scripture should be used to establish method, if we take that content seriously. It is hoped that this study will stimulate further consideration of Van Til's thought for hermeneutics.

Scripture as the "norming norm") and the material principle (what is considered as the content of the gospel). *My* references to "evangelical" and "evangelicalism" have this biblical-theological approach in mind, as well as an awareness that some claim to be "evangelical," though they do not actually fit into this definition. Incidentally, Van Til had a much narrower working definition of "evangelical." He used this term to refer to non-Calvinistic (sometimes referred to as "inconsistent Calvinism") protestants, often pairing them together with Romanist apologetics in contrast to Reformed apologetics (Van Til, *Defense of Faith*, 54, 93, 277, 309–10, 322, 340).

Part I: **What Does Van Til Have to Do with Hermeneutics?**

Chapter 1: Introduction

Introduction

IT WAS THE EARLY apologist Tertullian who uttered the famous words, "What indeed has Athens to do with Jerusalem?"[1] He penned those words in the context of opposing all attempts which he saw as muddying the waters of Christianity through an unstable hybrid of Greek philosophy and the gospel. Van Til certainly acknowledged an appreciation for his emphasis on the distinction between believing and unbelieving thought.[2] Not surprisingly, the sole formal *festschrift* for Van Til bears the very title, *Jerusalem and Athens*.[3] The title of the present chapter points us in a different direction, though the underlying issues associated with it remain.

What does Van Til have to do with hermeneutics? Taking a cursory glance at his body of work, one will find only one book directly devoted to the issue of hermeneutics—*The New Hermeneutic*.[4] Yet, this work, while dealing with the new hermeneutic of Ernst Fuchs and Gerhard Ebeling in particular (among others), will perhaps disappoint those looking for a more direct and extensive treatment of the hermeneutical issues raised—at least according to the standards of more contemporary work in the field.[5] For example, Gadamer, who many consider a giant in philosophical hermeneutics, is given a mere *seven* page treatment, largely taken up with his philosophical influences (R. G. Collingwood in particular).[6] Gadamer is seen not as an innovator, but as merely being symptomatic of deeper philosophical undercurrents—hence, his brief treatment. Van Til's treatment takes on much of the same form and tenor of his forays into the field of

---

1. Tertullian, *Prescription against Heretics* 7.
2. Van Til, *Theory of Knowledge*, 83–109.
3. E. R. Geehan, ed., *Jerusalem and Athens*.
4. Van Til, *New Hermeneutic*. An example of a more indirect treatment can be found in his evaluation of Jewish interpretation of Christ and the Old Testament (*Christ and the Jews*).
5. E.g., Thiselton, *Two Horizons*; Vanhoozer, *Is There?*
6. Van Til, *New Hermeneutic*, 82–88.

apologetics. These forays demonstrate his characteristic presuppositional/ transcendental method. In short, Van Til argued for the truth of Christianity from the impossibility of the contrary.[7] The only "proof" for the Christian position is that unless its truth is presupposed, there is no possibility of proving anything at all.[8] God *himself* is the source of possibility, intelligibility, and applicability.[9] Van Til remarks elsewhere that "unless one offers at the outset the totality interpretation of all reality as given in Scripture as the presupposition of the possibility of asking any intelligent question, one has not really offered the Christian position for what it is."[10] In spite of appearances, Van Til appeals to an inner-logic in his evaluation of the philosophical currents active in and around the new hermeneutic. His assessment reveals a different emphasis, if not an expected one. Writing about his general presuppositional approach, he says: "to argue by presupposition is to indicate what are the epistemological and metaphysical principles that underlie and control one's own method."[11] Clearly, he is engaging in this type of argumentation in the *New Hermeneutic*. Rather than arguing according to the emphases as dictated by hermeneutical philosophy, it is primarily the *doctrine of God* which drives his critique of such figures as Heidegger, Bultmann, Gadamer, and the new hermeneutic.

Macro-Hermeneutics

Van Til, while directing his attention elsewhere in terms of apologetic method, often makes *macro*-hermeneutical[12] assertions throughout his works which have potentially vast implications for biblical interpretation. However, many of these implications are left unnoticed and undeveloped.

Consider the following cross-section of statements scattered throughout Van Til's works. First, in introducing the doctrine of God for his theology and apologetic method, he emphasizes that *who* God is precedes *that* God is.[13] In other words, we must know something of the nature of God in order to discuss and reason concerning his existence in the proper

---

7. Van Til, *Christian Epistemology*, 204–5; Bahnsen, *Van Til's Apologetic*, 6.
8. Van Til, "My Credo," 21.
9. Van Til, *Doctrine of Scripture*, 131.
10. Van Til, *Systematic Theology*, 13.
11. Van Til, *Christian Apologetics*, 128. "Christianity not only has its own methodology, but also that only its methodology gives meaning to life" (*Case for Calvinism*, 106).
12. I.e., a broader philosophical description of what constitutes understanding versus merely focusing on particular interpretive rules.
13. Van Til, *Defense of Faith*, 30; *Christian Epistemology*, 118.

manner.[14] Hence, *who* God has revealed himself to be must necessarily affect how we think about him (i.e., ontology informs epistemology).[15] Van Til argues that:

> Christianity offers the triune God, the absolute personality,[16] containing all the attributes enumerated . . . the conception of God is the foundation of everything else we hold dear . . . For us *everything depends for its meaning upon this sort of God.*[17]

All our interpretive efforts are ultimately rooted in our notion of the nature of God.[18]

Second, he often emphasizes God's *pre-interpretation* of all created things as they exist in the plan of God. Consider the following statement in his discussion of God's omniscience:

> God's knowledge of the facts[19] comes first. *God knows or interprets the facts before they are facts.* It is God's plan or his *comprehensive* interpretation of the facts that makes the facts what they are.[20]

The category of interpretation *precedes* existence. In other words, for God, interpretation precedes creation. The reality of God's pre-interpretation of all things necessarily makes man's interpretation, "correspond to the interpretation of God . . . our thought is receptively reconstructive" of God's thoughts (to be correct).[21] "God is the ultimate category of interpretation."[22] Man's interpretation is a *response* to God's pre-interpretation. Indeed, the

---

14. Van Til, *Christ and Jews*, 4.

15. Van Til, *Defense of Faith*, 55. He insightfully points out that, in the fall narrative, Satan, in effect, said that Eve should decide the question, "*How* do we know?" without asking the question, "*What* do we know?" (*Defense of Faith*, 57).

16. I.e., God is both absolute and personal.

17. Van Til, *Defense of Faith*, 34 (emphasis mine).

18. Van Til, *Christianity and Idealism*, 85.

19. Van Til generally regards a "fact" in two important, but differing, senses. First, in a positive sense, referring to created, revelatory facts pre-interpreted by God—which combines both the universal and particular—making them ultimately intelligible. Second, in a negative sense, referring to what he called "brute facts"—uninterpreted by God, man, or both—making them unintelligible (Van Til, *Christian-Theistic Evidences*, 54–58; *Christian Epistemology*, 1–10, 118; *Systematic Theology*, 37, 40; *Defense of Faith*, 140–41, 167; *Theory of Knowledge*, 34–37; Frame, *Van Til*, 77–78, 180–83, 272–75, 308, 313, 314). In this particular case, he is referring to "facts" in the positive sense.

20. Van Til, *Defense of Faith*, 32 (emphasis mine).

21. Van Til, *Christianity and Idealism*, 9, 127.

22. Van Til, *Defense of Faith*, 67.

Bible needs to be interpreted by man, yet only with divine enablement (Holy Spirit) and according to divine pre-interpretation. Elsewhere, Van Til expresses this principle in terms of the self-attesting Christ—"In all things, and in every field, man must live by the *previous interpretation of Christ as God* . . . The *self-attesting Christ is the presupposition* of all intelligible predication."[23] In the words of Bahnsen, "According to Van Til *only Christ* can *testify* to himself and *interpret* His acts and words."[24] Since the fall, there are essentially two opposing interpretive principles at work:

> The Christian principle of interpretation is based upon the assumption of God as the final and self-contained reference point. The non-Christian principle of interpretation is that man as self-contained is the final reference point.[25]

Human autonomy "distorts the doctrine of Scripture itself by finding the ultimate exegetical tool in the subjective experience of human freedom" rather than acknowledging the authority of Scripture and the Holy Spirit to confront the souls of men.[26] The real issue is whether sinful man will recognize and submit to God's pre-interpretation as original or not.

Third, he often speaks of the nature of Scripture in the very terms he uses to describe the nature of God. Rather than seeking a general concept of revelation from which to reason back to God, "When we seek to determine the nature of the Christian-theistic concept of revelation we turn again to our concept of God."[27] With a view to special revelation, for instance, he relates the self-attesting nature of Scripture to "the self-sufficient and self-explanatory character of the Triune God."[28] When setting forth a distinctively Christian epistemology concerning the necessity of Scripture for illuminating both the object and subject of knowledge, he states that:

> . . . the concepts of an *absolute God*, an *absolute Bible*, and absolute regeneration go together. The concept of *absolute Scripture* as a necessity for the illumination of the object of knowledge and of the subject of knowledge go together.[29]

---

23. Van Til, *Is God Dead?*, 39, 41 (emphasis mine); *Evolution and Christ*, 32, 38, 44. By "predication," he simply means making an assertion (attaching a predicate to a subject).

24. Bahnsen, "Socrates or Christ, 237 (emphasis his).

25. Van Til, *Theory of Knowledge*, 44; Van Til, *Psychology of Religion*, 145, 150.

26. Van Til, "My Credo," 9.

27. Van Til, *Systematic Theology*, 117.

28. Van Til, *Theory of Knowledge*, 19.

29. Van Til, *Christian Epistemology*, 167 (emphasis mine), 221.

Tied to the absolute nature of both God and the Bible is the absolute authority with which God speaks to us in and through Scripture. Van Til is quick to point out that dealing with an absolute authority necessarily involves circular or spiral reasoning on man's part.[30] Interestingly, this creates a situation which parallels discussion in contemporary hermeneutics concerning the hermeneutical spiral and the nature of reading and interpretation as a dialogue. In terms of the subject-object relationship (another key issue in hermeneutics), Van Til observes that since nothing has "existence and meaning independently of God, it is impossible to think of the object and subject standing in fruitful relation to one another that they actually do unless God is back of them both."[31] In another place, he addresses the issue of allowing men to interpret "facts" without God as the Achilles' heel in apologetics, and argues to the contrary:

> The *real issue is whether God exists as self-contained*,[32] whether therefore the world runs according to his plan, and whether God has confronted those who would frustrate the realization of that plan with a *self-contained interpretation* of that plan. The fact that Christians ... can never do more than restate *the given self-contained interpretation* of that plan approximately does not correlativize that plan itself or the interpretation of that plan ... the *self-contained* circle of the ontological trinity is not broken up by the fact that there is an economical relation of this triune God with respect to man. No more is *the self-contained character of Scripture* broken up by the fact that there is an economy of transmission and acceptance of the word of God it contains.[33]

I will address particular emphases exhibited in this lengthy quote in later chapters, but at this point it is sufficient to highlight how Van Til speaks of God, Scripture, and God's interpretation almost seamlessly, with a view to their unique shared quality of complete *self-sufficiency*, even as they come into contact with man and man's interpretation. At the same time, he maintained a nuanced understanding of the unity and interplay between general and special revelation, both being revelation of the same God:

> it is, according to Scripture itself, the same God who reveals himself in nature and in grace ... *revelation in nature and*

---

30. Van Til, *Christian Epistemology*, 12.
31. Van Til, *Systematic Theology*, 123.
32. I.e., completely self-defined, self-sufficient, and self-interpretive; independent of creation (Van Til, *Reformed Pastor*, 74, emphasis mine).
33. Van Til, "Introduction," 22–23 (emphasis mine).

> *revelation in Scripture are mutually meaningless without one another and mutually fruitful when taken together.*[34]

For Van Til, both general and special revelation exhibit corresponding qualities of: necessity, authority, sufficiency, and perspicuity.[35] As far as special revelation is concerned, these attributes are so important that if any were missing, we would have none of them. "The whole matter centers on an absolutely true interpretation that came into a world full of false interpretation."[36] A genuinely Christian philosophy of history must not only recognize a distinction between the two (general and special), but also must not separate them. Indeed, history is not properly self-interpreting but, rather, needs special revelation (even more so, since the fall) in order to complement and interpret it. Again, he explicitly ties these corresponding attributes of general and special revelation to the nature of God who reveals both.[37] God is self-interpreting and so is Scripture.[38] If Scripture was dependent upon any other principle for its own interpretation, then it would not be ultimately authoritative. Likewise, if God were dependent on anyone or anything other than himself for his own self-explanation, he would cease to be the ultimate authority.

Fourth, Van Til often speaks of the necessity of Scripture after the fall,[39] with a view to redemptive history. Consider the following statement:

> *no valid interpretation* of any fact can be carried on *except* upon the basis of the authoritative thought communication to man of God's final purposes in Scripture, as this Scripture sets forth in final form the redemptive work of Christ. *Every fact must be interpreted Christologically.*[40]

---

34. Van Til, "Nature and Scripture," 266, 269 (emphasis mine); 266–77; *Paul at Athens*.

35. Van Til, "Nature and Scripture," 264, 269.

36. Van Til, *Systematic Theology*, 227.

37. Van Til, "Nature and Scripture," 265–67. Elsewhere, he states that "only on the basis of a world in which every fact testifies of God can there be a Word of God that testifies of itself as interpreting every other fact" (*Systematic Theology*, 179).

38. Van Til, *Case for Calvinism*, 104–5; *Great Debate*, 33; *Systematic Theology*, 60; *Christian Epistemology*, 123; *Scripture*, 40; "Introduction," 34–35.

39. Though, in many places, Van Til follows his mentor, Geerhardus Vos in affirming the presence and necessity of special (verbal) revelation prior to the fall (Vos, *Biblical Theology*, 27–40; Van Til, *Common Grace*, 69; *Systematic Theology*, 126; *Theory of Knowledge*, 30; *Reformed Pastor*, 69, 71; Jue, "Theologia Natural," 168–70).

40. Van Til, *Reformed Pastor*, 98 (emphasis mine). Elsewhere, in a sermon on "Christ and Scripture," he argues that Christ placed "himself before the Jews as the one through whom their Scriptures alone received their meaning" (Van Til, *God of Hope*, 8).

In particular, he presupposes the storyline of Scripture as the context for understanding its message as a whole, implying that this message functions as an interpretive lens through which fallen man must view interpretation in general. Interpretation must be exercised in light of the *telos* of the redemptive-historical message of Scripture.[41] He urges that "Scripture must be interpreted in analogy with Scripture itself . . . all interpretation must be subordinated to Scripture as a whole."[42] In response to an essay by Richard Gaffin on the hermeneutical value of Vos' *The Pauline Eschatology*, he says that after receiving revelation from God, man must submit all his reasoning "at every point to the teleology of Scripture."[43] Moreover, opposing the claim of Howard Roelofs and Jesse De Boer that the facts and redemptive-historical interpretation recorded in Scripture are inherently ambiguous pointers to the Christ, Van Til affirms that "Scripture gives an infallible interpretation of the events it records."[44] In the same context, he makes reference to the "interpretation found in the canon of the Old and New Testaments," which men (like Roelofs) wrongly seek to stand above and judge by the criterion of their own reason.[45] This speaks of a distinct *canonical* awareness in Van Til's interpretive approach.

Fifth, he emphasized the exhaustively personal and covenantal environment in which man exists and interprets.[46] Likewise, God's revelation, both general and special, is exhaustively personal and covenantal.[47] As we shall see later, this idea is rooted in his doctrine of the Trinity, in which the three persons are covenantally related.[48] However, for now, consider the implications for biblical interpretation. For example, Van Til insists that "covenant theology furnishes the only completely personalistic interpretation

---

41. Discussing pre-redemptive special revelation, Van Til makes the same point that "history cannot be seen for what it is at any stage, except when viewed in relation to its final end" (*Systematic Theology*, 126).

42. Van Til, *Systematic Theology*, 240.

43. Geehan, *Jerusalem*, 243; *Christ and the Jews*, 35.

44. Van Til, *Defense of Faith*, 218; Van Til, "Christian Scholar," 172; *Systematic Theology*, 225. Van Til, discussing verbal inspiration, also makes mention of the Spirit's necessary and authoritative role in giving the correct interpretation of the facts of redemption. He also asserts this point in opposition to Roman Catholic interpretation which he sees as seeking an infallible interpretation in the human interpreter rather than in Scripture itself (*Systematic Theology*, 233, 250).

45. Van Til, *Defense of Faith*, 219;*Psychology*, 148–49.

46. Van Til, *Defense of Faith*, 176

47. Van Til, *Doctrine of Scripture*, 24, 27, 67; *Defense of Faith*, 113–14.

48. Tipton, "Triune Personal God," 141; Van Til, *Christian Epistemology*, 78, 96, 102; *Theory of Knowledge*, 207; "Introduction," 28.

of reality."[49] This means that a biblical ontology is ultimately personal and covenantal—and must inform one's epistemological approach to interpreting Scripture. Hence, reflecting the Trinity, theology and hermeneutics are inherently *ethical* activities. Either one interprets as a covenant keeper or as a covenant breaker in relation to the triune Creator.[50] All of this resonates with issues in contemporary hermeneutics which center on whether the reader has an ethical obligation to the original author,[51] and if so, what is the nature of that obligation?

Lastly, and closely related to the previous category of statements, there is a persistent concern in Van Til's writings that men must submit to the pre-interpreted word of God or else it will only mean what they want it to mean.[52] He vividly brings this point home when discussing the room left open for human autonomy in the hermeneutics of Bultmann, Fuchs, and Ebeling. Ultimately, these theologians, regardless of their particular emphases, are "following the example of Adam . . . modern theologians demythologize the voice of God and reduce it to ventriloquism."[53] It is clear that his concern parallels that of many contemporary evangelicals in response to postmodern trends in hermeneutics.[54]

Many more statements like these, appearing in various apologetic contexts, could be added to the list. However, my immediate concern here is not to be exhaustive but, rather, suggestive of macro-hermeneutical trajectories in his thought. As the above quotations show, Van Til repeatedly made reference to the concepts of *meaning* and *interpretation* in his writings, albeit in ways uncommon to most contemporary treatments.

Hermeneutical Response to Van Til

The general hermeneutical response to Van Til's ideas has been lackluster to say the least. He has either received decidedly short and mixed reviews among some scholars, or from others, no review at all. Most fall into the latter

---

49. Van Til, "Covenant Theology," 306; *Christian Epistemology*, 98, 100; *Common Grace*, 69–70.

50. This is a characteristic Van Til uses to depict the ethical antithesis between believing and unbelieving thought (e.g., *Defense of Faith*, 257–60; *Apologetics*, 62–63; *Systematic Theology*, 161, 189, 274).

51. E.g., Vanhoozer, *Is There?*, 81, 367–78, 383, 436–37.

52. Van Til, *Reformed Pastor*, 75.

53. Van Til, *New Hermeneutic*, 69. He speaks of a similar tendency in Western philosophy (e.g., Spinoza) which he labels as "monological" (versus man inherently in dialogue with his Creator) (*Christ and Jews*, 38).

54. E.g., Osborne, *Hermeneutical Spiral*, 480.

category. In what follows, we will mention how Van Til has been spoken of and attempt to provide a succinct evaluation and response. Our aim here is not to be exhaustive, but to paint a picture in broad but accurate strokes.

First, let us consider a few examples of those who bring Van Til's name up in hermeneutic discussion, yet are quick to dismiss his relevance for one reason or another. At the outset of his seminal work, *The Two Horizons*, Anthony C. Thiselton seeks to defuse possible objections to his explicitly philosophical approach to hermeneutics. He argues that such an approach is fitting due to the wider issues that have become part of the hermeneutical discussion.[55] Curiously, after helpfully providing examples of this significant shift, he singles out Van Til as one who would *oppose* "any attempts" at such an endeavor. While agreeing that Christian revelation must have preeminence for all aspects of life, Thiselton warns against rejecting philosophical categories (apparently including Van Til as a proponent of such a view) in New Testament interpretation.[56] He argues that to borrow certain conceptual tools from philosophy does not necessarily entail a subscription to a philosopher's particular worldview.[57]

In response to Thiselton, it would seem that his fears, though understandable, are ultimately unfounded. Even a cursory glance at Van Til's writings reveals a thorough working knowledge of philosophical categories and actual *use* of many "conceptual tools," as Thiselton calls them. In particular, Van Til borrows largely from idealism in service of his theological formulation—e.g., concrete universal, limiting concept, implication, and linear inference.[58] One example of a philosophical emphasis found in idealism which he found to be particularly helpful was that there needs to be comprehensive knowledge *somewhere* for there to be any true (partial) knowledge *anywhere*.[59] He even articulates an interesting corollary to this thought related to the issue of dialogue between God and man in discussing the thought of Martin Buber: "One cannot find signs of God's address to man anywhere unless one finds them everywhere and unless one finds them as controlling the whole of history from its very beginning."[60] To be sure,

---

55. Thiselton, *Two Horizons*, 5.

56. Thiselton, *Two Horizons*, 3, 9, 47; Thiselton, "Philosophical Categories," 87–100.

57. Thiselton, *Two Horizons*, 10, 47.

58. Frame, *Van Til*, 21. One clear example of this is found in Van Til's unpublished essay, "Evil and Theodicy," in which he explicitly borrows Hegelian terminology (overcoming "through negation of the negation to the affirmation") in order to argue for both election and reprobation as means to God's glorification (Bristley, "A Guide.")

59. Van Til, *Christianity and Idealism*, 15-16; *Defense of Faith*, 65; Oliphint, "Van Til's Methodology," 27–33.

60. Van Til, *Christ and Jews*, 36.

Van Til self-consciously re-defined such terms and concepts on the basis of a Christian worldview, but if anything, he sought tirelessly after a comprehensive Christian philosophy, covering the same ground as any nuanced secular system in terms of metaphysics, epistemology, and ethics.[61] After all, in order to challenge unbelief at every point where it is found and function consistently with the precedent set in Scripture (1 Pet 3:15; 2 Cor 10:5), the apologetic method must address *all* legitimate categories. He even defined apologetics in the following manner, "the vindication of the Christian philosophy of life against the various forms of the non-Christian philosophy of life."[62] He argued that due to the comprehensive nature of what is involved in stating and vindicating a Christian theology, one necessarily must state and defend an entire Christian *philosophy*.[63] Van Til did emphasize the antithesis between Christian and non-Christian thought, yet not in a way which ignored conceptual tools but, rather, in a way that involved the very *use* of them. He explicitly states that it is not wrong to make formal use of categories of thought from any thinker.[64] Van Til did not shy away from philosophy, even as he confronted it. Due to his extensive interaction and borrowing of philosophical terminology, he was often accused of following and endorsing those very schools he opposed. For example, he has been labeled by his critics as Kantian,[65] an idealist,[66] and a follower of Kierkegaard.[67] This at least shows that he truly engaged philosophically with differing views, even to the point of being accused of following them.

In discussing the rise of postmodernism and its impact on the field of hermeneutics, D. A. Carson considers various Christian apologetic responses. He mentions Van Til as coming out of a form of the fideist school, which he associates with Kuyper, Dooyeweerd, and more generally, with all forms of reformed foundationalism. He cites the classroom experience of John Cooper's presuppositionalist attack on modernism as evidence of the practical futility of such an approach in a postmodern world. In short, Cooper's impassioned focus on presuppositions is met by an unimpressed Paul Ricoeur, who merely asks Cooper to validate his own presuppositions.[68] Carson goes

---

61. Van Til, *Christian Epistemology*, xiv-xv.
62. Van Til, *Christian Apologetics*, 17.
63. Van Til, *Christian Apologetics*, 55-56.
64. Van Til, *Christian Epistemology*, 57.
65. Anderson, *Benjamin B. Warfield*, 46, 48; Daane, *Theology of Grace*.
66. Buswell, "Fountainhead," 48; DeBoer, "New Apologetic," 3; DeBoer, "Van Til's Apologetics," 7-12; Pinnock, "Philosophy of Christian Evidences," 423; Knudsen, "Crosscurrents," 308-10.
67. Evans, *Faith Beyond Reason*, 103.
68. Carson, *Gagging of God*, 95-96; Cooper, "Reformed Apologetics," 108-20.

on to say that in light of the unique challenges of postmodernism, standard apologetic approaches (e.g., evidentialism and presuppositionalism) "simply do not touch the committed deconstructionist."[69]

What is ironic about Carson's dismissal of the usefulness of Van Til's approach is that he proceeds to articulate a number of reflections on the strengths and weaknesses of postmodernity which evoke certain Van Tillian emphases. For instance, he applauds postmodernity's concern with modernism's disregard for the finitude of man and the noetic effects of sin which distort data and make the data fit into our self-serving grids.[70] Carson observes that *both* Christians and non-Christians are under the influence of their own interpretive communities.[71] In addition, in the face of the new hermeneutic and deconstructionism, he insists that true knowledge of the meaning of the text and intent of the author is possible, even if exhaustive knowledge is not.[72] Later, he highlights how often deconstructionists "insist on *either* absolute knowledge or complete relativism."[73] Van Til repeatedly made reference to this very point. He emphasized the limits of human knowledge in terms of the Creator-creature distinction.[74] Without such limits, man either seeks to know everything or claims to know nothing. In the end, Carson wants to assume God's existence from a Christian worldview and to "explore how God's existence affects our understanding of understanding."[75] In doing so, he argues that from a Christian view of finitude there are valid insights to be appreciated from both modernity and postmodernity, yet is careful not to succumb to the worldview of either one.[76] These points explicitly fall in line with Van Til's primary concerns in apologetics.

There is another striking parallel between Carson's emphases and that of Van Til regarding the *doctrine of God*. Even in his evaluation of Descartes'

Carson does recognize that Cooper's expression of presuppositionalism might not satisfy some presuppositionalists.

69. Carson, *Gagging of God*, 96.

70. Carson, *Gagging of God*, 98; Van Til, *Christian Apologetics*, 129; *Systematic Theology*, 56. Carson calls for a proper corrective to the dispassionate and impersonal approach of modernity to "truth" (*Gagging of God*, 101–2). This mirrors Van Til's own concern (Van Til, "Covenant Theology," 306; *Scripture*, 24, 27, 67; *Common Grace*, 69–70; *Christian Epistemology*, 98, 100; *Defense of Faith*, 113–14).

71. Carson, *Gagging of God*, 126–27; Van Til, *Why I Believe*.

72. Carson, *Gagging of God*, 102–3, 121; Van Til, *Systematic Theology*, 65–66, 268–70.

73. Carson, *Gagging of God*, 107 (emphasis his).

74. E.g., Van Til, *Theory of Knowledge*, 47–51.

75. Carson, *Gagging of God*, 130.

76. Carson, *Gagging of God*, 132.

epistemological influence in hermeneutics, Carson underscores that the Cartesian disjunction between subject and object stems from not taking God into account. A view which includes an omniscient God from the start would understand that from God's view, "all human beings are 'objects,' and all their true knowing is but a subset of his knowing."[77] Elsewhere, he affirms the essential relationship between biblical theology and systematic theology and the fact that everyone assumes a systematic theology (a doctrine of God in particular) as they begin to employ any method of theology or use of critical tools in the process. All of this affects, among other things, what data is permitted and on what basis it is permitted, which is also tied to the issue of authority.[78] In discussing the bible's plot-line and the importance of interpreting Scripture according to a redemptive-historical framework, he highlights particular attributes of God—consciously following John Frame's emphases:[79] the *Creator-creature distinction*,[80] God as *absolute personality*,[81] and the *Trinity*, showing God to be inherently personal.[82] The fundamental "I-thou" relationship is found in God himself.[83] Citing Colin Gunton, he argues for pairing the ontological "otherness" of God to his "relationality." God is both other than creation and in crucial relation to it at the same time.[84] Granted, there is much overlap here between these emphases, but they are mentioned with a view to combating religious pluralism.

Three important observations can be made about Carson's treatment. First, he brings the doctrine of God into an *interpretive* discussion, involving redemptive history and its contemporary hermeneutic relevance. Second, like Van Til, he argues that approaching Scripture *depends* on who God is.[85] Third, his emphases happen to be very similar to those of Van Til,[86] who also was interacting with and combating unbelieving philosophy and inconsistent methodology, albeit in the realm of apologetics. Perhaps, Carson may have some use for Van Til after all.

---

77. Carson, *Gagging of God*, 59.
78. Carson, "Unity and Diversity," 77–79, 91.
79. Carson, *Gagging of God*, 194; Frame, *Apologetics*, 34–50.
80. Carson, *Gagging of God*, 194, 201, 202, 204, 223, 229.
81. Carson, *Gagging of God*, 223–24.
82. Elsewhere, he argues that God is not merely an impersonal "ground of being" (Carson, *Collected Writing*, 19, 21).
83. Carson, *Gagging of God*, 226–28.
84. Carson, *Gagging of God*, 229.
85. Carson, *Collected Writings*, 22.
86. Frame, *Van Til*, 51–88.

More recently, Kenton Sparks has brought Van Til's name into his discussion concerning the relationship between hermeneutics and epistemology. He argues that there have been essentially two modern responses to postmodernism among evangelicals: *presuppositionalism* and the *propositional* approach.[87] In each case, there is an epistemic optimism which outstrips both the pessimism of antirealism and the optimism of practical realism. "Practical realism," which Sparks seems to endorse, is characterized by a postmodern awareness (e.g., value of tradition and limits of human knowledge) yet also by a guarded optimism.[88] With regard to *Presuppositionalism*, especially of the Van Tillian variety, Sparks particularly objects to the notion that "the only healthy way to interpret anything is via a *special hermeneutic* that presupposes the truth of Christian belief."[89] He argues that epistemologically, presuppositionalists are "strong Cartesian foundationalists" in that they start with basic beliefs necessary to reach truth, which are supernatural gifts only available to Christians.[90] In the end, he sees Van Til's ideas as endorsing a view of interpretation in which God miraculously gives Christians success and that *only they* are able to provide the right interpretation.[91]

Though much could be said in response to Sparks' accusations, I will restrict my comments to the following. Again, we have a mixture of misunderstanding and later endorsement of ideas which mirror Van Til's own. As for misunderstanding his ideas, it will suffice to say that Sparks has completely ignored the basis for the epistemological ideas he cites—namely, Van Til's two-level ontology (i.e., Creator-creature distinction). This is an integral aspect of his thought which cannot be missed. It is directly related to the idea of the need for comprehensive knowledge in order to have true partial knowledge. Without this grounding, Sparks understands Van Til as setting up an unstable rule by which man must decide between pure rationalism and pure irrationalism (i.e., either man knows all, or he knows nothing in reality). Ironically, this is Van Til's persistent critique of all non-Christian

---

87. Curiously, he says in passing that *both* are inspired by the common sense realism of Thomas Reid, who, he argues, was more nuanced in his thought than representatives of either of these approaches (Sparks, *God's Words*, 44). However, Sparks provides no evidence in support of such a claim (especially with regard to Van Til). In fact, Reid's influence appears in varying degree, consistently or inconsistently, in two apologetic approaches which Van Til argued explicitly *against*, namely Old Princeton and that of Joseph Butler (Frame, *Van Til*, 134n7, 273; Hunt, "Bavinck," 330–31; Van Til, *Systematic Theology*, 162).

88. Sparks, *God's Word*, 44–47.
89. Sparks, *God's Word*, 45.
90. Sparks, *God's Word*, 45.
91. Sparks, *God's Word*, 46.

epistemology, certainly not something he himself endorsed. In a footnote to the accusation of Cartesian foundationalism mentioned above, he faults Van Til for what he sees as an inconsistency in claiming that we must think God's thoughts after himself, but that we must also think analogically.[92] Sparks argues that these two are mutually exclusive ideas—*either* God tells us everything in order to think God's thoughts after him *or* we think analogically, which means we approximate them but do not *really* think them.[93] However, one need not look any further than the immediate context of the very passage that he cites (in favor of driving a wedge between true and analogical knowledge) for correction. Van Til states that:

> The system that Christians seek to obtain may, by contrast, be said to be *analogical. By this is meant that God is the original and that man is the derivative. God has absolute self-contained system within himself.* What comes to pass in history happens in accord with that system or plan by which he orders the universe. *But man, as God's creature, cannot have a replica of that system of God. He cannot have a reproduction of that system.* He must, to be sure, think God's thoughts after him; but this means that he must, in seeking to form his own system, constantly be subject to the authority of God's system to the extent that this is revealed to him.[94] . . . *If one does not make the human knowledge wholly dependent upon the original self-knowledge and consequent revelation of God to man, then man will have to seek knowledge within himself as the final reference point.* Then he will have to seek an exhaustive understanding of reality. Then he will have to hold that if he cannot attain to such an exhaustive understanding of reality, he has no *true* knowledge at all. Either man must then know everything or he knows nothing. This is the dilemma that confronts every form of non-Christian epistemology.[95]

Sparks makes a glaring omission here. It is *God alone* who has comprehensive knowledge of creation—rooted in his exhaustive self-knowledge.[96] This same God reveals truth to man in part, alleviating any instability in terms of man's finite capacities. As for his contention that Van Til's presuppositionalism leads to affirming that *only* Christians are able to provide the right interpretation, there seems to be an oversimplified straw man present. Van Til

---

92. Basically, Van Til's notion of "analogy" emphasized the ontological and epistemological differences between God and man, based on the Creator-creature distinction.
93. Sparks, *God's Word*, 45n55 (citing Van Til, *Theory of Knowledge*, 16).
94. Van Til, *Theory of Knowledge*, 16 (emphasis his).
95. Van Til, *Theory of Knowledge*, 17 (emphasis his).
96. Van Til, *Systematic Theology*, 371–75.

explicitly recognizes that "followers of the self-authenticating Christ always disclaim infallible interpretation."[97] Rather, only the self-authenticating Christ has the infallible interpretation as God. As for his comments citing a disregard in Van Til for what he calls *general* hermeneutics (i.e., interpretive practice, Christian or not),[98] he displays a very superficial understanding of Van Til's nuanced view of the unbeliever's knowledge of God, general revelation, and common grace.[99] Space will not permit an extensive treatment here but, in short, unbelievers cannot help knowing truth about God, being in the image of God and living in God's world, and can arrive at truth, even if ultimately inconsistent with their own unbelieving commitments.

Not unlike Carson, Sparks ends up mirroring Van Til's emphases later in his discussion. There are two particular examples in which this is seen. First, he argues that the fall narrative underscores the Creator-creature distinction. The Creator alone knows all and the creature does not. The serpent essentially tempted Adam and Eve to subvert this distinction, which has important implications for epistemology and hermeneutics.[100] Indeed, the fall narrative functions significantly in Van Til's works, as he sees this as the origin of all unbelieving epistemology, especially in light of the Creator-creature distinction.[101] However, as Sparks nuances certain implications of the fall for epistemology, he also *diverges* from Van Til at certain key points.[102] However, he at least sees the need to consider these issues in relation to epistemology and hence, interpretation. Second, he emphasizes that man, being in the image of God, has the ability to succeed as an interpreter. This seems to mirror Van Til's notion of analogy, though again, not without its divergences.[103]

---

97. Van Til, *Case for Calvinism*, 145.

98. This is Sparks' definition.

99. Van Til, *Defense of Faith*, 190–99; *Common Grace*, 5; *Systematic Theology*, 117–89; Bahnsen, "Crucial Concept," 1–31; *Van Til's Apologetic*, 442–60. For example, using a helpful and creative illustration, Van Til refers to the unbeliever's faculties functioning like a "buzz saw"—which may work efficiently but in the wrong direction, making faulty use of his created equipment (Van Til, *Defense of Faith*, 97, 105).

100. Sparks, *God's Word*, 49.

101. E.g., Van Til, *Theory of Knowledge*, 47–49; *Christian Epistemology*, 20–23; *Defense of Faith*, 36–37; *Christian Apologetics*, 33–34, 42–43, 79, 154–55.

102. Sparks, *God's Word*, 49–50. For instance, Sparks exaggerates what Adam and Eve did *not* know and seems to confuse finitude with sin. The latter confusion is expressed in saying that, "only an infinite being—God himself—is able to perceive reality without distortion . . . our epistemological success is limited by finitude" (*God's Word*, 50). This raises questions concerning what is epistemological "success" for finite man and whether man's thinking is inherently distorted due to his finitude.

103. Sparks, *God's Word*, 50–51. This seems to contradict his earlier dismissal of Van Til's concept of analogy (*God's Word*, 45n55).

However, Sparks' rightful concern for man's ability to have interpretive success is plagued by confusing finitude with sin and rooting epistemology in the reliability and probability of *man* to get things right, even if imperfectly so. While Sparks exhibits obvious misconceptions regarding Van Til's epistemology, he does show concern for issues he sees as having an important relation to hermeneutics, which mirror Van Til's own.

Our brief survey of Thiselton, Carson, and Sparks' interactions with Van Til has ironically highlighted his *relevance* for contemporary hermeneutics rather than providing reasons for his dismissal. Rather than succeeding in downplaying his relevance, each has actually opened the door for a further investigation into it.

There are others, however, who have seen the *positive* relevance of Van Til for hermeneutics and have explicitly mentioned him in their work. Rather than proceeding in a chronological fashion, we will begin with those who give indirect, passing attention and then progress to those who give more direct attention.

D. Clair Davis, in an essay on inerrancy and Westminster Calvinism, argues that Van Til brought a helpful shift in apologetics at Westminster Theological Seminary, from focusing merely on detailed refutation of liberalism to a focus on the integrity of a Christian *methodology*. This is due to Van Til's self-conscious aligning of method with theology—specifically, God as *Creator*.[104] While no theological model can exhaust the revelation of the triune God, our model and method should seek to approximate God's system set forth in Scripture. He specifically cites John Frame, Vern Poythress, Edmund Clowney, and Richard Gaffin as deriving from Van Til's theological emphases and methodology, and expanding their application beyond his own scope, including hermeneutics. For example, Gaffin delves into Berkouwer's criticism of Van Til's lack of exegesis by providing explicit exegetical support for the latter's emphases in epistemology, which have significant implications for interpretation.[105] This coincides with the fact that while Princeton and Westminster's focus was on the doctrine of Scripture, the current focus has become biblical hermeneutics. He suggests that Van Til would have welcomed this shift and applied his distinctive approach accordingly.[106]

Vanhoozer, a key contributor to the current hermeneutical discussion, mentions Van Til briefly in an essay on the interplay between theology and

---

104. Davis, "Inerrancy," 44.

105. Gaffin, "Epistemological Reflections," 103–24; Berkouwer, "Authority of Scripture," 197–204.

106. Davis, "Inerrancy," 45–46.

hermeneutics in interpreting not only the Bible, but culture.[107] He apparently commends Van Til for stressing that "created reality does not exist as brute, uninterpreted fact . . . it is already meaningful because it is interpreted by God."[108] Hence, the task of the human interpreter is to "think God's thoughts after him."[109] After such an endorsement, it is surprising that he makes no further mention of Van Til. This is even more peculiar as he proceeds to discuss such topics as presuppositions and conflicting worldviews, even concluding his discussion with the observation that "culture is the fruit of a theology or worldview."[110] Whatever the reasons for not giving Van Til a more prominent place in the dialogue,[111] Vanhoozer does employ a few important ideas in Van Til's thought in service of the interplay between theology and hermeneutics.[112]

Richard Pratt mentions Van Til when discussing the *personal* dimension of interpretation. Elsewhere, he more explicitly endorses Van Til's approach to apologetics,[113] but here, in this context, he is very brief.[114] However, what he speaks of is significant. Earlier he had argued that sanctification and interpretation are interdependent.[115] In the midst of that discussion, Pratt says that we must "'think God's thoughts after Him' if we are to interpret properly."[116] In other words, sanctification involves not only our behavior and emotions,

---

107. Vanhoozer, *First Theology*, 309–36.

108. Vanhoozer, *First Theology*, 322.

109. Vanhoozer, *Frist Theology*, 322.

110. Vanhoozer, *First Theology*, 326.

111. The only other mention of Van Til appears in another essay entitled "The Trials of Truth" on Christian epistemology in the face of postmodernism. Vanhoozer cites an article by John Cooper, who reminds us of the contributions of twentieth-century Dutch-Calvinists, including Van Til. In particular, he mentions their attack on the alleged neutrality and autonomy of man's reason (Vanhoozer, *First Theology*, 343n16). Vanhoozer uses this to support his notion of "expository epistemology" (i.e., the need to uncover one's ultimate presuppositions).

112. Another idea congruent with Van Til's thought is Vanhoozer's treatment of the questions of God, Scripture, and hermeneutics as one problem. Each is part of the "hermeneutical circle" in which our understanding of God informs hermeneutics and our hermeneutics informs our understanding of God (*First Theology*, 9–10; Van Til, *Christian Epistemology*, 1–13).

113. Pratt, *Every Thought Captive*.

114. This is not to say that Van Til's ideas are not in the general backdrop throughout his work on hermeneutics (Pratt, *He Gave Us*, 1, 66–67). For example, he expresses appreciation for Van Til's assessment of the influence of Kant in the history of western philosophy, citing *The New Hermeneutic* in the very context of discussing his *definition* of "hermeneutics" (Pratt, *He Gave Us*, 1, 409n1).

115. Pratt, *He Gave Us*, 43–52.

116. Pratt, *He Gave Us*, 47.

but our thinking as well.[117] His direct mention of Van Til expands on this earlier reference in the form of a quotation summarizing the point that our whole being (mind, emotions, and will) must be in submission to God in a manner of consistency found in God himself.[118] Man's interpretation of Scripture involves applying it to our whole existence. This *holistic* thrust is in keeping with contemporary hermeneutical concern for both the horizon of the text and of the *interpreter* as it relates to meaning.

Michael Horton discusses the legacy of Van Til's apologetic in terms of the present context of postmodernism. He highlights Van Til's all-encompassing vision which governs our view of reality (ontology) and our access to it (epistemology).[119] He applauds Van Til's emphasis on a *covenantal* epistemology which shows that the deep problems of apologetics "are not final intellectual, but ethical."[120] Horton sees these points to be especially relevant to a contemporary situation where rationalism and empiricism have crumbled. Postmodernity has now adopted the myth of neutrality as a by-word and assumed the stance of truly coming to grips with *horizons*, *language games*, and *paradigms*. One will recognize these terms as regular verbiage in contemporary hermeneutics. In Horton's opinion, Van Til's approach is uniquely equipped to deal more adequately with such issues and to confront the ethical rebellion lurking behind unbiblical notions of them.[121]

More directly, albeit much more briefly, William Edgar introduces the second edition of Van Til's *Christian Apologetics* with the call for not only providing more detailed applications of Van Til's pioneering work, but also to apply his thought to *other* fields besides apologetics. In particular, he believes more work must be done in the area of philosophy in order to engage contemporary issues. He specifically asks, "How does [Van Til's] approach work its way into discussion . . . with *hermeneutical* philosophies?"[122]

In a critical discussion of Van Til's concept of *analogy*, James Emery White raises the question of how one is supposed to "determine the correct analogical correspondence in light of the subjective interpretation of the text?"[123] He claims that particular weaknesses in Van Til's ideas, such as a lack of clarity in knowing how and when our interpretation coincides with

---

117. Van Til emphasized this very point, citing Charles Hodge in support (Van Til, *Christian Apologetics*, 94–97; Hodge, *Systematic Theology*, 2:99–101, 244; 3:16, 35–36).

118. Pratt, *He Gave Us*, 395; Van Til, *Systematic Theology*, 387.

119. Horton, "Consistently Reformed," 144.

120. Horton, "Consistently Reformed," 145.

121. Horton, "Consistently Reformed," 148.

122. Van Til, *Christian Apologetics*, 14–15 (emphasis mine).

123. White, *What is Truth?*, 59.

God's and a general neglect of the hermeneutical problem of subjective interpretation, contribute to endorsing an infallible hermeneutic for the regenerate (similar to Sparks). Again, there seems to be some confusion present throughout his argument, evidenced by the fact that White at one point associates Van Til with Gordon Clark[124] (an outspoken opponent of Van Til's epistemology), and at other points cites and endorses accusations of fideism[125] and Kantianism.[126] Regardless of these particular misconceptions, what is interesting for our purposes is that all of this leads White to conclude: "Put simply, Van Til leaves no room in his concept of truth for the *serious hermeneutical issues his system generates*."[127] Even if White ultimately disagrees with Van Til's system and his ability to provide adequate answers for the issues raised by it, there remains at least the acknowledgment of its relevance for hermeneutics.

J. I. Packer, in an essay for Van Til's *festschrift*, speaks of the inherent relations between biblical authority, inerrancy, and hermeneutics. He observes that "it appears also from the fact that every hermeneutic implies a theology . . . where a false hermeneutic operates the Bible will not in fact have authority, whatever is claimed to the contrary."[128] This observation clearly parallels Van Til's own insistence upon apologetic method assuming either the truth or the falsity of Christian theism as its starting point.[129] More specifically, "every bit of exegesis of Scripture already involves a view of the nature of Scripture."[130] Packer laments the tendency of latter-day evangelical separation of interpretive principles and the conditions and means of understanding.[131] Again there is a similar concern in Van Til's emphasis on deeper philosophical presuppositions and preconditions related to knowledge and method.

Krabbendam comes to many of the same conclusions Van Til does in his work on the subject.[132] He also locates the new hermeneutic within the larger hermeneutical stream running from Schleiermacher, Heidegger,

---

124. E.g., he confuses Van Til with Clark's notion that all truth is propositional and must be deduced from the Bible in order for it to be knowable (White, *What is?*, 60, 169; Clark, "Bible as Truth," 158, 167; *Trinity*, 85).

125. White, *What is?*, 51–58. For a discussion of how Van Til repudiated fideism, see Bahnsen, *Van Til's Apologetic*, 72–78.

126. White, *What is?*, 44.

127. White, *What is?*, 59 (emphasis mine).

128. Packer, "Biblical Authority," 141.

129. Van Til, *Christian Apologetics*, 129.

130. Geehan, *Jerusalem*, 204.

131. Packer, "A Response," 565.

132. Krabbendam, "New Hermeneutic," 535–58.

Gadamer, and theologians, such as Bultmann and Barth. It is Krabbendam's "transcendental appraisal of the New Hermeneutic" which particularly resonates with Van Til's own critique. He sees the fundamental failure of the new hermeneutic, and modern hermeneutics in general, in an assumed Kantian dualism which provides its basic framework.[133] This nature-freedom dialectic of Kant is expressed in terms of the subject-object relation (nature) and a transcendence of that relationship (freedom). There exists a fundamental opposition between the two realms, while at the same time a presupposing of one another. There is a necessary subject-object relationship, yet that relationship must necessarily be transcended in order for true hermeneutical understanding to be achieved.[134] The new hermeneutic's failure comes into focus amidst the backdrop of such dialecticism. It is not interested in traditional rules or techniques of interpretation because such things are merely carried out in the realm of nature. Epistemologically, it seeks understanding in the non-objectifiable realm of freedom. Yet no matter how much they try to achieve such understanding via the so-called *language event*, objectifying assertions remain inescapable. True understanding remains a perpetual mirage. It allows higher critical methods to have final authority in the nature realm regarding Scripture and assumes that the language of the Bible is "metaphysically deficient," failing to transcend objectification (i.e., the language of Scripture is inadequate and incapable of expressing its own subject matter.) Seeking to bridge the gap between objectifying and non-objectifying understanding, the new hermeneutic only succeeds in further objectification.[135] Krabbendam insists that it is this assumed and unquestioned dialectic which must be confronted in order to expose its true nature—rebellion against the God of Scripture.[136] Specifically, this presupposed dialectic is symptomatic of fallen man in general, who seeks to interpret creation from an autonomous vantage point—one not in submission to Scripture but rather one which suppresses it.

It is important to note how Krabbendam brings Van Til's own critique of the new hermeneutic into view, while endorsing the scope of its application beyond it. First, he seeks to confront a presupposed framework of metaphysics and epistemology underlying the more salient features. Second, he seeks to expose the unstable mix of rationalistic and irrationalistic elements of the dialectic which undermine its own claims and goals. Third, he identifies the new hermeneutic with the ethical rebellion of the would-be

---

133. Van Til, *New Hermeneutic*, 22–23.
134. Krabbendam, "New Hermeneutic," 549.
135. Krabbendam, "New Hermeneutic," 546, 551–52.
136. Krabbendam, "New Hermeneutic," 553, 555.

autonomous man against the God of Scripture. He and Van Til both understand the search for the transcendence of the subject-object relation as a sinfully evasive move.[137] Fourth, he argues that the dialectic underlying the new hermeneutic is merely symptomatic of fallen man's attempt to conceive of reality and knowledge *apart* from Scripture. Hence, the critique leveled at the new hermeneutic by Van Til, it is argued, *is* fit for biblically evaluating other hermeneutical approaches and philosophies.

Bahnsen has identified a search for epistemological *certainty* among twentieth-century philosophers.[138] He surveys three key figures representing the schools of both pragmatism and linguistic analysis: Dewey, Wittgenstein, and Austin. The latter two are particularly notable because of their association with contemporary hermeneutics. Wittgenstein's concept of language games and Austin's speech-act theory have become common parlance in the field. None of the three is ultimately able to escape skepticism regarding certainty, because, according to Bahnsen, they never started with the only presuppositions fit for the task.[139] After noting the necessity of addressing epistemological problems, justification, objectivity, and the need for a self-attesting worldview which will ground certainty, he turns to Van Til for clarity.[140] The key issue boils down to the *relation* of the human mind to the divine mind and with respect to *how* the human mind attempts to interpret reality.[141] Perhaps more pointed is the question: "Which mind, man or God's, is to be taken as original and epistemologically ultimate?"[142] Christian epistemology, he argues, is "*revelationally transcendental* in character."[143] Bahnsen asserts that modern philosophy is encumbered by a phenomenalism wherein all methods of interpretation have become anchored in the mind of man as an autonomous thinker, who seeks to *impose order* on an ultimately chaotic, irrational reality.[144] What of Dewey, Wittgenstein, and Austin? In spite of helpful emphases in terms of epistemological awareness, they too are entangled in the dialectical tensions between

---

137. Krabbendam, "New Hermeneutic," 554–55; Van Til, *New Hermeneutic*, 101–9, 116–17, 207–8.
138. Bahnsen, "Pragmatism," 241–43.
139. Bahnsen, "Pragmatism," 243–84.
140. Bahnsen, "Pragmatism," 285.
141. Bahnsen, "Pragmatism," 287.
142. Bahnsen, "Pragmatism," 289; Van Til, *Christian Epistemology*, 15, 107, 133.
143. Bahnsen, "Pragmatism," 291 (emphasis his).
144. Bahnsen, "Pragmatism," 291; Van Til, *Defense of Faith*, 148.

rationalism and irrationalism, leading to ultimate skepticism.[145] Clearly, Bahnsen sees the relevance of Van Til's thought for broader issues which necessarily affect hermeneutics.

In a different, but relevant context, Beale brings up Van Til in his interaction with Peter Enns concerning his book, *Inspiration and Incarnation*. Beale asks whether we should allow extra-biblical ancient Near Eastern texts to dictate the genre of Genesis or let it speak for itself. Beale opts for the latter, for only then can we rightly seek to understand its relation to extra-biblical texts. He criticizes Enns' use of these texts as a *lens* through which to understand the Old Testament, as well as his endorsement of Second Temple Jewish hermeneutics as a *lens* through which to understand the hermeneutics of the New Testament authors.[146] Ironically, Enns claims to be coming from a "reformed, specifically presuppositional, theological, and epistemological starting point."[147] Beale acknowledges his own indebtedness to Van Til and argues that Enns has got it all backwards. Van Til would first start with Scripture and judge all things by Scripture.[148] He would seek to understand the self-interpretation of Scripture first and then judge all ancient Near Eastern texts and Second Temple Jewish methods accordingly. What is intriguing is that Van Til is considered relevant to a hermeneutical discussion of which he never directly wrote about.[149]

Somewhat perplexing, however, is Beale's mention of Van Til in another, yet related hermeneutical context. This time he is dealing with postmodern questions regarding the New Testament use of the Old Testament. Beale seeks to explain a biblical epistemology in which "we can sufficiently, but not exhaustively, understand the meaning of the biblical authors' writings."[150] Specifically, he is responding to Moyise's view that what is important is not *whether* the New Testament author respected the Old Testament context, but *how* the Old Testament context interacts with the New Testament context, sometimes creating new understandings which can redefine and distort the original context by placing it in a new one.[151]

---

145. Bahnsen, "Pragmatism," 292; Van Til, *Theory of Knowledge*, 50; *Reformed Pastor*, 89.

146. Beale, *Erosion of Inerrancy*, 77–78.

147. Enns, "Response," 315n6.

148. Beale, *Erosion of Inerrancy*, 78n45.

149. However, Van Til did write about Philo Judaeus' hermeneutical method and treatment of the Old Testament, which would fall in the latter part of the Second Temple period (*Christ and Jews*, 3–22).

150. Beale, *Erosion of Inerrancy*, 224.

151. Contra Moyise, Beale sees these two questions as inherently related (*Erosion of Inerrancy*, 225).

Contrary to Moyise's subjectivist hermeneutic, Beale favors N. T. Wright's "critical realism,"[152] which seeks to avoid the extremes of objectivism and subjectivism.[153] Beale seems to adopt an epistemology which is essentially based on *probability* and a horizontal frame of reference, rather than one consistently in relation to God.[154] Yet, this is clearly something that he wants to avoid, as is evident later, when he grounds his epistemology and meaning in the transcendent God of Scripture.[155] He then suggests that Wright's epistemology of "presuppositional verification" as being very close to that of Kuyper, *Van Til*, and Gordon Clark, as well as the common sense hermeneutical validation of E. D. Hirsch.[156] The key observation to be made at this point is twofold. First, Beale lumps Van Til in with some strange bedfellows—namely, Wright, Clark, and Hirsch.[157] This will become more apparent later, but there seems to be some over-generalization and a neglect of epistemological differences among these individuals, especially in relation to Van Til. Second, Beale has rightly underscored the need for a distinctively *Christian* epistemology in order to clarify and properly evaluate a key issue in contemporary hermeneutics (i.e., New Testament use of the Old Testament). In doing so, he brings Van Til into consideration, yet in a way which begs for more elaboration. Moreover, he has recognized that the stability of meaning can only be found in an omniscient, sovereign, and transcendent God. This implies that not only do we need a distinctively Christian epistemology for hermeneutics, but a *Christian ontology* as well.

McCartney and Clayton have also cited Van Til favorably in their work on biblical interpretation.[158] Much of their general approach *implicitly* resonates well with many of Van Til's particular emphases. There is a clear emphasis on the doctrine of God and its relevance for interpretation. For instance, they see God's comprehensive knowledge, among other things, as the ultimate solution to many of the common postmodern objections

152. Wright, *New Testament*, 31–144. For a helpful, balanced critique of Wright, see: Moritz, "Critical but Real," 172–95.

153. Beale, *Erosion of Inerrancy*, 253.

154. E.g., Wright, *New Testament*, 34, 42, 45–46. Interestingly, shortly after this endorsement, Beale again highlights the Van Tillian ideas that some knowledge can be known, even if not exhaustively or perfectly understood, and that some presuppositions are good and necessary (*Erosion of Inerrancy*, 255). However, he fails to ground these statements in something more stable than at least the appearance of mere common sense pragmatism mediated through a moderate form of hermeneutical syncretism.

155. Beale, *Erosion of Inerrancy*, 257, 259.

156. Beale, *Erosion of Inerrancy*, 254–55.

157. Beale acknowledges his primary influences to be: Hirsch, Vanhoozer, and Wright (*Erosion of Inerrancy*, 260).

158. McCartney and Clayton, *Let the Reader*.

against absolute truth. Our knowledge is limited and partial in relation to this comprehensive knowledge, yet *grounded* in it.[159] God provides the basis for interpretation which is both truly objective and subjective. God's horizon comprehends all horizons in the interpretive process.[160] They also emphasize both God's personal nature (in terms of the ontological Trinity) and his ultimate authority in determining meaning.[161] They clearly root the goal and method of hermeneutics in God. He must point us to the goal of interpretation primarily in terms of the Bible's own interpretation of itself, from which method naturally flows. This involves having sensitivity to both systematic and biblical theology.[162] Since methods are determined by the hermeneutical goal, there is no neutrality in interpretation,[163] not only with respect to the presuppositions we bring to the text, but also *their relation to God* as the determiner of the goal.

However, they *explicitly* make reference to Van Til when discussing the foundations of understanding. Unbelievers, in seeking to make an absolute judgment concerning truth yet denying the Christian system of truth found in Scripture, must essentially put themselves in the place of God as omniscient.[164] They argue that human reason can only function effectively as a tool to comprehend language and other created things if it is conceived of according to the Creator-creature distinction. This is also rooted in how Scripture speaks of man's constitution and the created world around him (Rom 1:19–21).[165] When discussing the relationship between general and special revelation as it relates to interpretation, they argue that facts only have meaning in relation to other facts. Hence, there are no *brute* facts (i.e., no fact exists apart from the meaning the Creator has given to it). "No fact or predication about reality can be known, let alone stated, without a framework of understanding."[166] Similarly, when discussing the underlying issue in using Scripture in evangelism, they bring up the deeper issue of epistemology. Any use of Scripture involves applying it to particular situations. This is a part of interpretation or seeking its modern meaning. They stress that we must acknowledge God as *the* self-existent, original, and

---

159. McCartney and Clayton, *Let the Reader*, 12, 30, 34, 36.

160. McCartney and Clayton, *Let the Reader*, 300–1.

161. McCartney and Clayton, *Let the Reader*, 14, 30, 34, 35, 37–38, 301.

162. McCartney and Clayton, *Let the Reader*, 61–63.

163. McCartney and Clayton, *Let the Reader*, 68.

164. McCartney and Clayton, *Let the Reader*, 7–8; Van Til, *Theory of Knowledge*, 14–15.

165. McCartney and Clayton, *Let the Reader*, 8.

166. McCartney and Clayton, *Let the Reader*, 53–54; Van Til, *Christian Epistemology*, 6.

complete fact which makes sense of all other created facts. God is the starting point for understanding and argumentation.[167] Though rather esoteric at first glance, these points are brought up in such practical contexts as the relationship between general and special revelation in interpretation and use of Scripture in evangelism.

Moisés Silva, in two outstanding essays concerning issues related to contemporary hermeneutics, cites Van Til in support of a number of significant points. First, in evaluating the debate over whether Scripture is essentially clear or obscure (and its effect on hermeneutical method) in the history of interpretation, Silva asserts that we must bring any hermeneutical approach "under the searching light of Scripture itself," whether evangelical or not. No matter how scientific methods or tools appear, none are completely neutral with respect to faith commitment.[168] He says this in the immediate context of the discussing the role of scholarship related to the historical gap between the time and culture of the biblical writers and that of the contemporary reader. Indeed, the bulk of the history of biblical interpretation could be described as an attempt to bridge this gap in terms of meaning.[169] Silva explicitly mentions his influences here—namely, Kuyper and Van Til, both of whom insisted on the differing starting points of believing and unbelieving science.[170] Though both types can appear to have the same general character, they actually move in different directions based on their assumed starting point.[171] However one seeks to traverse the historical gap in biblical interpretation, it must be done in submission to Scripture, *as it is being traversed*.

In another essay, Silva argues that in order to apply linguistic principles to biblical hermeneutics, one must not only ask *what* the Bible says about language in general (e.g., its relation to creation, sin, and redemption), but also must submit to its authority.[172] In other words, we need a meaningful framework shaped by God's revelation in order to evaluate linguistic theories and methods appropriately.[173] He cites both Kuyper and Van Til in support of this point, even quoting the latter with respect to facts being ultimately defined in the context or system in which they are found, either Christian

---

167. Van Til, *Theory of Knowledge*, 12–13.
168. Silva, "Has the Church?," 70.
169. Silva, "Has the Church?," 69–70.
170. Silva, "Has the Church?," 70n20.
171. Van Til typically articulates this in terms of ultimacy. Either man is ultimate in his interpretation or God is ultimate (e.g., *Theory of Knowledge*, 22).
172. Silva, "God, Language," 204.
173. Silva, "God, Language," 204.

or non-Christian. Both systems claim all the facts.[174] Silva helpfully reminds us that a distinctively Christian hermeneutic should be in submission to Scripture *even as* it seeks to interpret it. A distinctively Christian hermeneutic should not rely on notions of ontology and epistemology *in general*, but rather on how they are defined in Scripture.

In another essay, Silva addresses the often maligned and fractured relationship between theology and exegesis.[175] He stresses the close, mutually informing relationship between biblical interpretation and systematic theology. His appreciation for Calvin's hermeneutics includes an awareness of *common grace*, which enabled him to draw from other branches of secular learning, such as philology and literary analysis, and put them to use in service of interpretation and theology.[176] He specifically cites how the Dutch tradition helpfully worked out the implications of Calvin's notions of common grace, epistemology, and sin. He mentions Van Til's relevance for biblical hermeneutics in three ways. First, his emphasis on presuppositions and the denial of neutrality has obvious value in light of contemporary concerns. Second, Van Til stressed that man, far from being a detached neutral observer, actually suppresses the truth in unrighteousness (Rom 1:18–23) and that the fallen condition finds its characteristic expression in seeking to subvert the Creator-creature distinction. Third, unbelievers make true intellectual progress only on "borrowed capital," taking advantage of the very truths which contradict their own unbelieving presuppositions.[177]

In light of these realities, Silva argues that "it is not feasible to separate biblical interpretation from theology . . . systematics *should* influence our exegesis."[178] Later he says plainly, "my theological system should tell me how to exegete."[179] There are three important implications stemming from these conclusions. First, the very nature of systematic theology is that of contextualization. In other words, theology involves seeking to formulate the teaching of Scripture in ways that *apply* that teaching to our present

---

174. Silva, "God, Language," 204n1; Van Til, *Theory of Knowledge*, 36–37.

175. Silva, "Calvinistic Hermeneutics," 251–69.

176. Silva, "Calvinistic Hermeneutics," 254–55.

177. Silva, "Calvinistic Hermeneutics," 257.

178. Silva, "Calvinistic Hermeneutics," 259–60 (emphasis mine); Poythress, "Presuppositions and Harmonization," 508–9; Vanhoozer, *Is There?*, 455.

179. Silva, "Calvinistic Hermeneutics," 261. Silva makes the perceptive point, contrary to the objection that such a method is indefensibly anachronistic, that the very use of modern English to explain the biblical text requires the use of subsequent formal expressions. Hence, contemporary theological explanation of the bible's message demands contemporary theological categories ("Calvinistic Hermeneutics," 262).

context, categories, and concerns.[180] Hermeneutically, theology involves traversing the gap between what a text *meant* and what it *means*. Second, the evangelical presupposition concerning the unity of Scripture requires that the whole Bible be the ultimate context for any one part. This, of course, is based on the conviction that the whole of Scripture comes from one divine author. Lastly, whether explicitly stated or not, all interpret the Bible with theological presuppositions. Better to recognize and evaluate them in light of Scripture than to proceed in a naïve fashion, blind to the exegetical assumptions involved in the process.[181]

So we see that in Silva's hermeneutical considerations, Van Til's influence can be detected across a number of important issues, mirroring Van Til's own use of systematic theology as the basis for his apologetic method and his primary critique of other rival methods.[182] First, presuppositions are not only to be acknowledged and recognized, they are to be evaluated and *used* properly—according to Scripture. Also, we need biblical categories for understanding unbiblical presuppositions in relation to the doctrines of sin and common grace. Secondly, he stresses that whatever hermeneutical method is used to bridge the historical gap between the text and the interpreter, it must be evaluated in terms of its *starting point* (i.e., presuppositions related to ontological, epistemological, and ethical questions).[183] Thirdly, whatever hermeneutical concepts we are dealing with, they must be defined according to the Christian system of truth. Lastly, systematic theology not only has significant influence on exegesis (whether one admits it or not), but it also *should* influence it.

Graeme Goldsworthy reiterates many of Silva's observations and extends the application of Van Til's ideas in the direction of biblical theology.[184] In doing so, he explicitly makes the connection between the fields of apologetics and hermeneutics in terms of presuppositions and starting points.[185] He rightly points out that the varying definitions of hermeneutics that scholars have offered over the years carry with them differing theological stances and presuppositions, which are not neutral in nature.[186] More-

180. Frame, *Doctrine*, 276.

181. Silva, "Calvinistic Hermeneutics," 261–63. Here, Silva again cites Van Til as one who, before Bultmann and Kuhn, emphasized the role of pre-understanding and questioned "neutrality" in scientific method, exposing the role of presuppositions.

182. E.g., Van Til, *Christian Apologetics*, 17–54; *Defense of Faith*, 27–44.

183. Van Til, *Theistic-Ethics*, 1–37.

184. Goldsworthy, *Hermeneutics*.

185. Goldsworthy, *Hermeneutics*, 42. He cites Van Til and Thiselton as particularly significant figures in these respective fields.

186. Goldsworthy, *Hermeneutics*, 21–25, 43.

over, these assumptions regarding the key elements in communication (i.e., sender, message, receiver)[187] "either directly or indirectly deal with the question of God."[188] *Who* God is affects one's conception of the sender, the nature of the message, and the nature of the receiver—every important aspect of communication involved in interpretation. The Bible itself provides not only the proper presuppositions required for a full-orbed worldview, but it also supplies its own hermeneutical principles. He recognizes the challenge of maintaining evangelical presuppositions amidst potentially conflicting ones found in modern philosophical hermeneutics.[189]

What are the basic evangelical presuppositions that Goldsworthy suggests are integral to a biblical hermeneutic? They are essentially *theological*. They are best summarized by four of the Reformation *solas*: grace alone, Christ alone, Scripture alone, and faith alone.[190] What is even more significant, however, is that these four "really take their essential characteristics from God as Trinity." None can exist without the others. They are what they are "only because God is the kind of God he is." Goldsworthy particularly highlights the nature of God in terms of the *ontological Trinity*.[191] He summarizes that the basic presupposition which affects the way we think of every fact available to us "is thus an ontological one concerning the being of God that establishes the ontology of the universe and every creature in it."[192] This resonates with Van Til's own emphasis on the doctrine of God as the basic presupposition in developing and evaluating apologetic method.[193] In sum, "basic Christian doctrine, then, becomes the presupposed basis for the evangelical interpretation of Scripture."[194] Granted, there is a hermeneutical *spiral* involved in which presupposed doctrine influences interpretation and interpretation refines doctrine. Scripture, however, as *God's* word, is the ultimate authority in this dialogue. Presupposing doctrine, argues Goldsworthy, necessarily involves the redemptive-historical character of that doctrine in interpretation. Indeed, this is the main thrust of his book—biblical theology is particularly suited, as a hermeneutical model, to fit the worldview of

---

187 These correspond to the common hermeneutical categories of author, text, and reader.

188. Goldsworthy, *Hermeneutics*, 43 (emphasis mine), 44, 47.

189. Goldsworthy, *Hermeneutics*, 22.

190. Goldsworthy, *Hermeneutics*, 46–50.

191. Goldsworthy, "Ontological," 161–62; *Hermeneutics*, 258–72.

192. Goldsworthy, *Hermeneutics*, 50–51.

193. Van Til, *Systematic Theology*, 59, 124, 197, 283, 367n51.

194. Goldsworthy, *Hermeneutics*, 53; Van Til, *Defense of Faith*, 27.

Christian theism.[195] At the same time, there are what he calls "ground rules" for communication established by God, consisting of a biblical ontology and epistemology. There is an ontological priority of God properly expressed in the Creator-creature distinction and as Trinity. This means that we cannot simply set this priority aside and ignore it while engaging in interpretation. Epistemologically, who God is and who we are in relation to him brings both objectivity and subjectivity together in harmony—as opposed to one trumping the other as seen in forms of modern and postmodern hermeneutics. In sum, Goldsworthy has brought in Van Til's ideas in service of formulating a distinctively *Christian* hermeneutical model.

Vern Poythress has probably brought Van Til's thought to its widest and most creative application in the field of hermeneutics. He does this in at least four main ways. First, he acknowledges the value of Van Til's general presuppositional approach for hermeneutics. In particular, Poythress has highlighted the insights of Thomas Kuhn in the history and philosophy of science[196] which has helpfully drawn attention to the role of presuppositions and lack of neutrality, paralleling Van Til's own insights in apologetics.[197] Kuhn claimed that progress and change in knowledge comes not through mere piecemeal addition, but primarily through the use of frameworks, composed of basic assumptions, standards, and values.[198] These insights, if biblically defined, are of particular relevance in evaluating hermeneutical methodologies, such as the historical-critical method,[199] forms of literary criticism,[200] and Speech Act theory.[201] However, he also points out that the primary subject matter is different between science (creation) and biblical interpretation (Creator). In the case of biblical interpretation, due to God's infinity and the nature of his relation to creation, no one analogy, theory, or model could ever define or capture him.[202] This idea of capturing God in a theoretical framework involves reducing God to the limits of creation, thereby confusing the Creator-creature distinction.

In discussing different types of biblical theology and its relationship to exegesis and systematic theology, he argues that, rather than hindering, all

195. Goldsworthy, *Hermeneutics*, 68.

196. Kuhn, *Scientific Revolutions*.

197. Poythress, "Science and Hermeneutics," 503–5, 528–9; *Symphonic Theology*, 84, 122.

198. Poythress, "Science and Hermeneutics," 473, 478–79.

199. Poythress, "Science and Hermeneutics," 438, 441–42, 465–68.

200. Poythress, "Philosophical Roots," 165–71; "Structuralism," 221–37; Conn, "Historical Prologue," 22–23.

201. Poythress, "Canon and Speech," 337–54.

202. Poythress, "Science and Hermeneutics," 500; Van Til, *Case for Calvinism*, 145.

three disciplines enrich one another. He mentions that Van Til *and recent philosophical hermeneutics* have recognized that "'circularities' are inevitable for finite human beings." For example, exegesis necessarily involves making assumptions about the nature of reality and the presence or absence of God in the Bible. If presuppositions are inevitable, the question becomes, *where are they taken from*, from systematic theology or secular philosophy? Here, Poythress expresses a distinctly Van Tillian concept of *antithesis*. The only alternative to systematic theology influencing exegesis is the "corrupting influence of hermeneutical assumptions rooted in human rebellion against God and desire for human autonomy."[203]

Besides presuppositions, other related Van Tillian ideas appear in various interpretive contexts. Poythress brings up his idea of brute facts to argue that no event or reality as a whole exists prior to and independent from any perspective, knowledge, or interpretation of it. All reality and events are ultimately meaningful to God *prior* to creation and hence, our knowledge is dependent on this backdrop of divine knowledge.[204] Interestingly, this comes up in the context of a hermeneutical discussion of the fourfold Gospel account of the person and work of Christ. In another related context, the idea that there could be such a thing as mere events of history "without God's word commanding them and interpreting them" is a counterfeit illusion, imposing our meaning upon that which is assumed to have no previous meaning.[205] Historical investigation cannot avoid prior commitments about the nature of reality and meaning.[206] The question becomes, *which god or metanarrative is assumed?*

Discussing God's relationship to language, he mentions that unbelievers actually depend on God in order to rebel against him.[207] He sees Van Til's ideas of *antithesis* and *common grace* as helpful in making sense of the effects of sin on language and communication. The former refers to allegiances between believers and unbelievers, which manifests itself in ultimately different worldviews. The latter refers primarily to the fact that unbelievers are not as bad as they could be—holding onto fragments of truth, though

---

203. Poythress, "Kinds," 134.
204. Poythress, *Symphonic Theology*, 49; Van Til, *Theistic Evidences*, 40–65.
205. Poythress, *In the Beginning*, 239.
206. In context, Poythress mentions postmodernism, modernism, and "critical realism." Each, he argues, to one degree or another exhibits "autonomous criticism" of which there is no "autonomous escape."
207. Poythress, *In the Beginning*, 79–80. This is an example of Van Til's notion of "borrowed" or "stolen" capitol (Van Til, *Systematic Theology*, 152–53; *Case for Calvinism*, 147–48).

inconsistently so (at least according to their unbelieving assumptions).[208] Both ideas are used by Satan to endorse counterfeits of truth, having formal similarity yet meaning something very different. These counterfeits are rooted in and aided by a faulty view of the Creator-creature distinction, expressed in terms of a false transcendence (God is unknowable), false immanence (God identified with creation), or an unstable combination of the two. Modernism tends toward a false immanence, whereas postmodernism tends toward a false transcendence, though both feed off one another and display an unstable mixture of both.[209]

In addressing key tenets of postmodern deconstructionism, he cites Van Til in opposition to Derrida, who infamously asserted that, concerning meaning, "There is nothing outside the text."[210] Though not absolutely denying the existence of things outside a text in principle, deconstructionists emphasize that all we have are processed and assimilated human constructions. All we have access to with regard to God are such constructions. However, from a biblical worldview, meaning is not ultimately generated by man, but by God. God, as Creator, defines reality and there is no meaning that doesn't come from God—"no existence that does not depend on his signifying word . . . we never get outside God's meanings."[211] Here, Poythress explicitly employs Van Til's emphasis on all facts and meanings of those facts being derived from being in relation to God and his all-encompassing plan. Indeed, there are no brute facts, but only that which exists in the "text" of God's plan.[212] Ironically, deconstructionism does have some affinity with Van Til's transcendental apologetic. Both are interested in critically examining assumptions. However, deconstructionism seeks to undermine a text through exposing assumptions made concerning background issues of language and thought. These background assumptions, it is argued, are of an unfathomable, universal nature, of which man cannot have comprehensive knowledge.[213] Hence, these assumptions undermine explicit assertions made in the text. Van Til, to the contrary, would argue that the grounding of all so-called unfathomable knowledge is the comprehensive knowledge that God has of his creation, in relation to his own comprehensive self-knowledge. Texts are only undermined insofar as the

---

208. Poythress, *In the Beginning*, 114–15.

209. Poythress, *In the Beginning*, 320–25; Frame, *Knowledge of God*, 14–18.

210. Poythress, *In the Beginning*, 371; Derrida, *Of Grammatology*, 158.

211. Poythress, *In the Beginning*, 372.

212. Poythress, "Christ," 312; Van Til, *Defense of Faith*, 59–69; *Christian Epistemology*, 12–18; 34–37.

213. Poythress, *In the Beginning*, 374.

author (or reader), through the text, assumes an autonomous epistemological stance, independent of God.

Second, he endorses his own brand of *perspectivalism*, which he consciously derives from Van Til, Frame, and Kenneth Pike.[214] That said, we will focus primarily on his more conscious use of Van Til.

Poythress argues for the triune character of meaning, relying on both Van Til's formulation of the doctrine of the Trinity and his concept of analogy (based on the Creator-creature distinction, with human knowledge as derivative, dependent, and genuine).[215] Similarly, he emphasizes that the *nature* of God affects *how* we know him and his revelation.[216] Moreover, Poythress, like Van Til, speaks of the nature of God and Scripture in similar terms. One may view the meaning of Scripture as tri-perspectival, analogous to aspects of the Trinity. He suggests a triad of attributes of God which reflect the diversity, relational communion, and deity of each person as a perspective on the entire Godhead.[217] They can be seen as corresponding to certain attributes of Scripture with regard to meaning: *instantiational* (particular text), *associational* (connections or relations with other texts), and *classificational* (stable meaning). While each person of the Trinity has all three of these attributes, each is particularly associated with an attribute: the Father with classificational, the Son with instantational, and the Spirit with associational.[218] In sum, when seeking the meaning of a text of Scripture, it is important to appreciate the Trinitarian qualities of it as the word of the triune God.

Poythress goes on to argue that various non-Christian philosophies are guilty of exalting one particular perspective at the expense of others. In terms of ontology, he observes that the realist-nominalist categories have suffered from an unbiblical exaltation of unity (tendency of realism) and diversity (tendency of nominalism), which are actually equally ultimate in the doctrine of the Trinity. Furthermore, he argues for other philosophical tendencies: rationalism exalts the classificational aspect, empiricism exalts the instantational aspect, and subjectivism exalts the associational aspect.[219]

---

214. Frame, *Knowledge of God*; *Christian Life*; Pike, *Linguistic Concepts*.

215. Poythress, "Reforming Ontology," 187–219; *Redeeming Science*, 25–26; *God-Centered*, 16–20, 38–43, 52–58, 63–76.

216. Poythress, "Why?," 96–98.

217. Here, Poythress and Frame rely on Van Til's previous formulation of his own latent perspectivalism with regard to the doctrine of the Trinity (Poythress, "God's Lordship," 29n4; Frame, *Van Til*, 119–23, 170–72).

218. Poythress, "Reforming Ontology," 191–93, 197; *God-Centered Interpretation*, 72–74.

219. Poythress, "Reforming Ontology," 198–200. Similarly, Torres has seen a

Each is ultimately an assault on the triune nature of God. Van Til's notion of the non-Christian rationalistic and irrationalistic tendencies is used to expose ontological assumptions present in unbelieving philosophy which subvert the Creator-creature distinction.[220] He sums up his argument for Trinitarian logic by admitting and embracing its circularity, in accordance with Van Til.[221] He uses Trinitarian logic in order to argue for it. This is something unavoidable in light of the ultimate authority and ontological status of the triune God. There is no possibility of neutral reasoning in this respect.[222] Van Til's ontological emphases are used to evaluate various philosophies relevant to hermeneutics.

Another relevant way in which Poythress applies his Van Tillian-influenced Trinitarian ontology to hermeneutics is through its relation to another triad, concerning verbal communication.[223] In redemption, the persons of the Trinity perform particular roles analogous to roles seen in God's verbal communication: the Father as *author*, the Son as *text*, and the Spirit closely associated with the *reader*. The practical effect is that the ultimate archetype behind all human communication, in terms of its key categories (author, text, and reader), is the Trinitarian being of God. This accounts for seeing an ultimate unity *and* diversity concerning all three. Consequently, we must avoid Trinitarian heresies present in certain conceptions of the communication triad. For example, Unitarianism would evidence itself in collapsing author, text, and reader into one meaning, thereby stripping away the essential complexity of human communication. Polytheism, on the other hand, would evidence itself in multiplying meanings related to each aspect of the triad, thereby driving a wedge between each, resulting in at least three *separate*, potentially contradictory, meanings.[224]

Third, Poythress uses Van Til's ideas in articulating the *fullness* of meaning found in biblical interpretation. Seeking to do justice to the divine meaning of Scripture, he considers the relationship between the God and the human authors in terms of the incarnational analogy. Just as in the Chalcedonian definition regarding the two natures of Christ, the human and the divine

---

multiperspectival approach as a useful tool in order to evaluate the strengths and weaknesses of postmodernism (Torres, "Perspectives," 123–36).

220. Poythress, "Reforming Ontology," 215–17.

221. E.g., Van Til, *Defense of Faith*, 123.

222. Poythress, "Reforming Ontology," 218.

223. Poythress appreciates the Trinitarian nature and function of each triad while, at the same time, acknowledging that no one triad captures the Trinity, nor his Trinitarian word. Rather, like his view of perspectives, multiple triads are needed in order to appreciate the inherent complexities involved.

224. Poythress, "Why?," 97–98.

must not be identified or separated in terms of meaning. Ultimately, meaning is what *God* intended through the various human authors to their intended hearers.[225] However we conceive of this complex process, we must keep the Creator-creature distinction intact when considering the roles of the human and divine author in the interpretation of Scripture. For example, the divine message cannot be trimmed down to the limits of human reason.[226] God's speech is, *at the same time*, propositional, personal, and perspectival.[227] It is rooted in God's triune nature and knowledge.

Since the fullness of meaning is rooted in *God*, it follows that the meaning of Scripture, whether looked at narrowly or canonically, is *infinite in its fullness*.[228] Unless this fact is recognized, there is a tendency toward reductionism, especially if comprehensive precision is sought in such areas as historical understanding,[229] language, or philosophical theology.[230] As we are confronted with the divine author at every point in interpreting the Bible, we must avoid the false ideal of exhaustive comprehension of meaning, either in the human interpreter or human author.[231] Only in this way will we preserve the Creator-creature distinction. It is important to recall the necessity of perspectives as Poythress sees it. They are necessary because no single human model or viewpoint can exhaust or capture God's intended meaning through Scripture, since it is rooted in his infinite self-knowledge. Multiple perspectives are needed to appreciate its fullness. Hermeneutical techniques do not exhaust this meaning. God is not a "prisoner of mechanism," nor can he be reduced to mechanical calculation.[232] After all, even the most apparently sterile scientific study is not mere technique, but involves many vital assumptions.[233] After surveying such modern theories of meaning as symbolic logic, structural linguistics, and translation theory, he concludes that reductionism is present wherever scientific rigor (undergirded by unbiblical

---

225. Poythress, "Divine Meaning," 241–56.

226. Poythress, "Divine Meaning," 256.

227. Poythress, "Truth and Fullness," 212; "Divine Meaning," 252–54.

228. Poythress "Presence of God," 87–103; "Divine Meaning," 241–79; *God-Centered*, 20–25, 32–36, 43–47, 75–76; *Symphonic Theology*, 16–17, 45–51.

229. Poythress invokes Van Til's notion that one must have complete comprehension in order to begin to reason with one piece intelligibly. In this case, the piece is an historical event ("Presence of God," 98).

230. Poythress, "Truth and Fullness," 223–24, 227; *Symphonic Theology*, 55–91

231. Poythress, "Divine Meaning," 241, 243–47, 256; *Symphonic Theology*, 85.

232. Poythress, *God-Centered*, 89.

233. Poythress, *God-Centered*, 89, 94. At this point, he cites Van Til's *Theistic Evidences*, along with others, such as, Polanyi, *Personal Knowledge*, and Kuhn's influential work.

presuppositions) is enforced.²³⁴ If human language and communication are intelligible only against the backdrop of intra-Trinitarian communication, then "the category of mystery accordingly belongs to meaning and to hermeneutical reflections on meaning," and reductionistic approaches must be critically evaluated.²³⁵

Lastly, Poythress discusses hermeneutics in terms of God's *Lordship* and Christ's *redemption*. The Enlightenment desire for neutral, self-sufficient interpretation is impossible in understanding the Bible's message (or anything else for that matter). God is sovereignly and personally present in all interpretive endeavors. Consequently, our thoughts in these matters are *ethically* related to God, under his authority.²³⁶ "We ought to have God as the standard in judging all rules in interpretation." Without *his* standard, our interpretation is unintelligible.²³⁷ Moreover, his communication to us is *inescapable*, as it is expressed through general and special revelation, a point Van Til also emphasized.²³⁸ In short, our interpretation of the Bible must be a re-interpretation of God's interpretation, according to his standard of that interpretation.

A key characteristic of non-Christian hermeneutics is a denial of God as the stable source and standard of all aspects of the communication process, which not only contributes to interpretive difficulties and alienations, but also opens the door for hermeneutical idolatry.²³⁹ Without God behind the communication process as the authority, sovereignly in control, and present in all, there is no way to hold its vital components together.²⁴⁰ Whatever approach is taken, there is an inevitable deification of creation, where one aspect of the communication process is emphasized in order to ground the whole thing.²⁴¹ By leaving God out of the equation, this grounding is done merely on a human level. The end result is reductionism, in which one aspect of the process (e.g., interpreter) is deified as the autonomous ground of meaning, trumping

234. Poythress, "Truth and Fullness," 213–27.

235. Poythress, "Why?" 97–98.

236. Poythress explicitly states that both he and Frame are indebted to Van Til with regard to these points, citing six of his works in particular (Poythress, "God's Lordship," 29).

237. Poythress, "God's Lordship," 30.

238. Poythress, "God's Lordship," 32; Van Til, *Systematic Theology*, 117–22.

239. Poythress, "Christ," 312.

240. In this portion of his article, he employs Frame's epistemological triad (control, authority, and presence), summarizing God's Lordship (Frame, *Knowledge of God*, 109–22).

241. Poythress highlights three general movements in his discussion: rationalism, empiricism, and subjectivism ("God's Lordship," 37–39).

the others. Yet, "each must fail because none can exist without the others."[242] By ignoring God's role in the interpretive process, there is an inevitable blurring of the Creator-creature distinction. However, by acknowledging God's lordship over interpretation, one can avoid this tendency. The various pitfalls associated with each component in terms of success in communicating truth can only be established on the bedrock of the Trinitarian communication of God, who is infinite.[243] Poythress concludes: "God's Lordship is the necessary presupposition not only of the interpretation of the Bible but interpretation of all human communication."[244]

Emphasizing the *redemption* of interpretation, Poythress argues that Christ alone is the savior of the author, discourse, audience, and the hermeneutical circle. From a biblical worldview, interpretation cannot be separated from redemptive history. The effects of sin must be recognized and its solution taken seriously, even in the realm of hermeneutics. Poythress sums up the situation well:

> Just as there is no metaphysical interpretive standpoint free of the Lordship of God, and just as no moment in interpretation escapes his exhaustive mastery, so no human standpoint is free of the conflict of sin and redemption, and no moment in interpretation escapes the penetrating influence of our relation to Christ's life, death, and resurrection. There is no neutrality. There is no "objectivity" even, in the sense of which Enlightenment rationalism dreams. The only ultimate objectivity is also an exhaustively personal subjectivity, namely the eternal objective fact of intra-Trinitarian communion in truth, power, and personal fellowship.[245]

For both Van Til and Poythress, these theological realities necessarily direct hermeneutics.

I will close this survey of Van Til's influence on those explicitly using his ideas in hermeneutics with Royce G. Gruenler. Though neither as extensive nor as innovative in his application as Poythress, he nonetheless provides a fitting conclusion to our discussion. In his response to Krabbendam's article on the new hermeneutic, he affirms Krabbendam's assessment and proceeds to apply what he calls "Van Til's presuppositional *hermeneutic*" to Gadamer and representatives of the new hermeneutic.[246] In short, there is nothing

---

242. Poythress, "God's Lordship," 37.
243. Poythress, "God's Lordship," 43–58.
244. Poythress, "God's Lordship," 63.
245. Poythress, "Christ," 321.
246. Gruenler, "A Response," 575–76.

new about the new hermeneutic. He describes in broad strokes what this Van Tillian hermeneutic entails. First, we do not impose a set of dogmatic assumptions upon brute or unknowable facts, following Kant. Rather, God has already pre-interpreted and created the facts and their relation to his redemptive plan in Christ. "Common grace and special grace find their union in him."[247] He affirms Van Til's assessment of the new hermeneutic, noting the value in his presuppositional approach, exposing the underlying assumptions being made by Fuchs and Ebeling. Various forms of human autonomy are detected and exposed as non-Christian. There is an "axe to grind"[248] among non-Christian hermeneutics in which hidden agendas stack the deck in favor of certain interpretive outcomes. Only an explicitly Christian hermeneutic is sufficient for this task. Any attempt to separate one's Christian faith from a purely descriptive, historical interpretation will fail to do justice to the content of Scripture. Gruenler explains:

> This is precisely Van Til's point and the awesome challenge of his hermeneutic. Only in humble acceptance of God's own special interpretation of history in Jesus Christ can one properly use the tools of historical research . . . the search for the real meaning of facts in the created world of nature and history can only be achieved by the aid of God's own "canonical" interpretation of those facts.[249]

God's self-disclosure in Jesus Christ and the inscripturated word "is his own interpretation of the deep grammar of nature, history, and of human existence."[250] It is paramount to evaluate hermeneutical method on the level of presuppositions regarding these matters, getting them out in the open, in order to evaluate them from a Christian worldview.

Elsewhere, Gruenler calls this Van Tillian hermeneutic, "Biblicial Realism."[251] He makes it clear that interpretation cannot be isolated from how one broadly interprets the world.[252] Macro-level concerns press in at every point. Ultimately, this involves God and his pre-interpretation of the world. This pre-interpretation is shared among the persons of the Trinity.[253] As he puts it, "It is my conviction that hermeneutics is first of all the enterprise of God . . . truth-bearing ideas are always underwritten by the reality

---

247. Gruenler, "A Response," 576.
248. Van Til, *Defense of Faith*, 257, 302; Bahnsen, *Van Til's Apologetic*, 442.
249. Gruenler, "A Response," 587.
250. Gruenler, "A Response," 588.
251. Gruenler, *Meaning and Understanding*, 169–73.
252. Gruenler, *Meaning and Understanding*, xiii–xiv.
253. Gruenler, *Inexhaustible God*.

of God."[254] Not only has Gruenler brought Van Til and his ideas into the hermeneutical discussion, he has also identified Van Til's approach *as a hermeneutic*—one that has great value in effectively evaluating and diagnosing hermeneutical methodologies.

Conclusion

Because of Van Til's controversial reputation in some circles, he has often been dismissed without sufficient consideration. Therefore, it was necessary, albeit at some length, to demonstrate his relevance for contemporary hermeneutics for those who have tended to dismiss him, and for those who have used his ideas in the field. For the most part, Van Til has been relegated to a mere footnote in the contemporary discussion. In light of the above survey and evaluation, perhaps he should be allowed to have a more prominent voice. If so, *what is his place in the current discussion*? In order to establish the place where his voice can be heard most clearly and helpfully, we need to survey the current field. It is to this that we now turn.

---

254. Gruenler, *Meaning and Understanding*, xvi.

Chapter 2: Surveying the Field, Part I

Introduction

IN ORDER TO UNDERSTAND the appropriate intersections between Van Til's thought and contemporary hermeneutics, it is necessary to get an initial lay of the land. What are the issues and gaps in the hermeneutical literature which Van Til can most appropriately speak to? Admittedly, this is a daunting task. The prospect of trying to engage in a large-scale analysis of even one aspect of the contemporary landscape, due to the complexity and diversity involved, according to Craig Bartholomew, is "like trying to do analysis with a club, where one requires a scalpel."[1] Presuming to provide a detailed analysis of contemporary hermeneutics (1960 to present)[2] would be largely reductionistic.[3] Hence, our aim and scope will be tailored according to particular criteria. First, any mention of key figures and movements will be presented according to scholarly consensus regarding their thought and distinctive contributions. Subtle differences and variations among interpreters of such figures will only be noted if relevant to the discussion.[4] Second, the primary focus will be on contemporary hermeneutics according to the degree of its influence on *biblical* hermeneutics. Third, the survey will be conducted with an eye toward Van Til's emphases in order to make appropriate connections. In this chapter, we will highlight particular trajectories concerning the shifting nature of how hermeneutics has come to be defined.

---

1. Bartholomew, "Babel and Derrida," 306.

2. Admittedly, the boundary here is a bit arbitrary, considering *prior* influences and their bearing on the present-day scene. Hence, we will not restrict the discussion to only this particular period, but the emphasis will be on this period.

3. For more comprehensive treatments, see: Thiselton, *Two Horizons*; *New Horizons*; Palmer, *Hermeneutics*; Howard, *Three Faces*; McKim, *A Guide*; Vanhoozer, *Is There?*

4. This does not preclude general consensus regarding significant *shifts* in the thought of various figures.

Defining "Hermeneutics"

One general trend present in the literature is a shift in how *hermeneutics* has come to be defined. It must be said from the start that the terminology used and distinctions made by various scholars present a unique challenge. For example, more ancient writers tended to treat *exegesis* and *hermeneutics* as overlapping concepts.[5] Some treat *interpretation* and hermeneutics interchangeably,[6] while others distinguish between *exegesis*, *interpretation*, and *hermeneutics*.[7] Thiselton prefers to lump *exegesis* and *interpretation* together as interchangeable and sees *hermeneutics* as a deeper-level discipline.[8] Rather than getting lost in these various distinctions, the following discussion will concentrate on concept-level considerations in order to avoid confusion.

Earlier definitions generally reveal a narrower conception in terms of their scope and aim. For example, Berkhof, though more nuanced than others exhibiting this earlier notion, states that "hermeneutics is the science that teaches us the principles, laws, and methods on interpretation."[9] Similarly, Ramm defines it as a *science* and an *art*—the former because it is guided by systematic rules and the latter because those rules are applied with a certain skill (not mechanically).[10] The same focus on *hermeneutics* as a set of rules for interpretation is still endorsed among many contemporary evangelicals, although for perhaps different reasons. For instance, Thomas, self-consciously relying upon two older works,[11] argues for *hermeneutics* as a set of principles which are to be used in exegesis. He does so in *opposition* to what he sees as confusion in evangelical hermeneutics, due to the adoption of newer and different principles which unnecessarily expand its scope.[12] Porter and Stovell suggest that one could divide the literature on biblical interpretation into two main categories—those which give step-by-step instruction and tools for interpretation and those which introduce a variety of methods, usually involving a diachronic look at the history of interpretive method.[13] In sum,

---

5. Corley, Lemke, and Lovejoy, *Biblical Hermeneutics*, 3.
6. E.g., Tate, *Biblical Interpretation*, 1.
7. E.g., Westphal, *Whose Community?*, 17–26.
8. Thiselton, *An Introduction*, 4; Marshall, "Evangelicals and Hermeneutics," 11–12; Briggs, "What Does?," 55–74.
9. Berkhof, *Principles*, 11.
10. Ramm, *Protestant*, 1, 11; Virkler, *Hermeneutics*, 16; Mickelsen, *Interpreting*.
11. Terry, *Biblical Hermeneutics*; Ramm, *Protestant*.
12. Thomas, *Evangelical Hermeneutics*, 27; "Hermeneutical Trends," 241–42.
13. Porter and Stovell, "Introduction," 10–11.

the general consensus is that earlier evangelical treatments of hermeneutics at least emphasized methodology and rules by which a proper interpretation of a text could be obtained.[14]

These earlier definitions do not necessarily ignore larger questions related to the interpretive endeavor, but they often do not explicitly state their presuppositions. These presuppositions function to determine what questions and what issues are considered relevant to the interpretive task. Many of these assumptions revolve around two key questions: *Where is meaning found? What is the goal of biblical interpretation?*[15] These questions indeed involve a host of other important questions as well. For instance, what *authority* determines where meaning is found and the goal of interpretation? Earlier works on biblical interpretation tended to assume certain categories and distinctions to one degree or another. Such issues as the subject-object distinction between the reader and the text,[16] meaning found in the original author's intent, the goal of allowing the author to speak through the text, and readers inductively allowing the meaning of a text to emerge were often assumed rather than discussed.

In some cases, these older treatments proceeded on certain modernist assumptions and goals.[17] This of course does not mean that in older works a modernistic agenda was pursued. Rather, certain criteria were assumed and seen to be consistent with a Christian approach. The question is whether consistency is present and to what degree. Perhaps most indicative of this type of thinking are those with an especially strong polemical thrust to their work, who sought to guard against certain pitfalls in interpretation. Two examples will suffice. In *The History of Interpretation*, Farrar argues that the history of biblical interpretation, from its rabbinic roots onward, is largely a sad affair, often darkening the true meaning of Scripture rather than elucidating it.[18] He reserves his highest praise for aspects of the grammatical-historical and, especially, the historical-critical method of the Enlightenment.[19] It is here that interpretation reaches its zenith and comes into its own, where scientific and historical precision trump diluted eisegesis. Farrar's emphasis is clearly

14. Kaiser and Silva, *Introduction*, 17; Osborne, *Hermeneutical Spiral*, 21; Vanhoozer, *Is There?*, 19, 23; Thiselton, *Two Horizons*, 11; Scott, "Some Problems," 67; Provan, "How Can I?," 2–3.

15. Klein, Blomberg, and Hubbard, *Introduction*, 6; McQuilkin and Mullen, "Impact," 71; Stein, "Benefits," 454; Goldsworthy, *Hermeneutics*, 25.

16. Carson, *Gagging of God*, 64.

17. Grenz, *Primer*; Bartholomew, "Post/Late?," 25–38.

18. Farrar, *History of Interpretation*, 8–9. For a helpful corrective to Farrar's conception, see: Silva, "Has the Church?," 17–87.

19. Farrar, *History of Interpretation*, 397–437.

horizontal—the level of human history and scientific methodology. Overall, he prefers Enlightenment methods, yet endorses Christ's interpretation of the OT.[20] However, *are these two approaches compatible?*

More recently, Thomas has argued for so-called "traditional" hermeneutics (i.e., focused on propositional truth) in opposition to what he sees as postmodern subjectivism.[21] In particular, he faults various contemporary scholars for redefining hermeneutics to include such elements as theological presuppositions and modern meaning. To the contrary, we must set aside any pre-understanding of doctrine until the exegetical task is *finished*. He goes on to cite works on hermeneutics prior to the 1970s where he sees the traditional quest for objectivity in interpretation—a quest similar to his own. Like Ramm, he is against allowing subjective considerations to become part of the interpretation process.[22] With Terry, he is opposed to any pre-conceived hypothesis, *whether it is correct or not*. This would include one's own dogmatic conceptions, *whether or not* they are seen as an essential part of divine revelation.[23] He claims that Terry's only assumption was that he was dealing with an inspired book.[24] Concerning objectivity, it seems as though Thomas equates objective certainty with *knowability*.[25] Believers have a "divinely-enabled objectivity" via the Holy Spirit.[26] According to Thomas, saying that neutral objectivity is nonexistent (i.e., acknowledging understanding to be subjective and partial) is to affirm that *God* is non-objective.[27] Westphal argues that this type of hermeneutical objectivism (which he sees running through the work of Betti, Habermas, and Hirsch) seeks an *absolute* in reaction to any notion of *relative* which borders on forgetting the difference between Creator and creature.[28] Throughout Thomas' discussion, there is an emphasis on detached objectivity and precision, especially as it relates to the historical side of hermeneutics, for there to be true understanding in interpretation.[29] Moreover, one might add that

---

20. Farrar, *History of Interpretation*, 434–36.

21. He lays much of the blame on Thiselton's work for endorsing such subjectivism (*Evangelical Hermeneutics*, 18, 124).

22. Thomas, *Evangelical Hermeneutics*, 46–47.

23. Thomas, *Evangelical Hermeneutics*, 48; Terry, *Biblical Hermeneutics*, 171–72, 583–84.

24. Thomas, *Evangelical Hermeneutics*, 48. This, however, is no small assumption.

25. Thomas, *Evangelical Hermeneutics*, 48–49.

26. Thomas, *Evangelical Hermeneutics*, 53.

27. Thomas, *Evangelical Hermeneutics*, 53.

28. Westphal, "Philosophical/Theological View," 82.

29. "Precision," as a concept, is highly subjective and complex (e.g., how much "precision" makes it "precise"?) (Frame, *Doctrine*, 171–74; Poythress, *Symphonic Theology*,

even amidst such a supposedly detached approach, assumptions about the morality of knowledge are unavoidable. In such an enlightenment-like pursuit, doubt is considered a virtue and credulity a vice.[30] Hence, neutrality is undermined. Granted, both Terry and Thomas are on the more extreme end of the spectrum. They more self-consciously exhibit certain modernist notions and values present in some older work in the field.

Another highly influential work in evangelical hermeneutics is E. D. Hirsch's *Validity in Interpretation*.[31] Hirsch was a secular literary-critic[32] who argued for the existence of objective meaning in literary works. Perhaps most significant and influential is his distinction between *meaning* and *significance* and its effect on the nature of meaning and relevance for the contemporary reader.[33] For our present purposes, it is important to point out two influential aspects of Hirsch's work. First, his stated goal is to achieve *validity* in interpretation, which he defined as probable consensus regarding the intent of the author. This is opposed to the notion of certainty.[34] Second, his work has a strong polemical thrust, seeing anything less than an unchanging meaning found in the author's intent alone as necessarily relativistic. He particularly takes Gadamer to task for confusing the original meaning (intended by the author) and modern meaning of a text.[35] Hirsch's main focus is rooting validity in the intent of the *human* author and finding objective meaning with definite boundaries, yet through a process of probability and consensus, not certainty. Lundin sees a certain irony in how evangelicals have embraced Hirsch's work, with its modernist premises. "In trying to counter the rationalism and subjectivism

---

55–68; Carson, *Exegetical Fallacies*, 45–47). Thomas' concept of *precision* is such that it rules out ambiguities and perhaps even legitimate uses of imprecision in everyday language. He claims that there is more precision in the Bible than in everyday language use. Not appreciating this, he says, leads to a loss in recognition of "propositional" truth. Again, "propositional" is a difficult term to define when considering the complexities of how language is used, especially in different genres and varying levels of what is considered literal and figurative in a given context (Poythress, *Understanding Dispensationalists*; Packer, "Fundamentalism").

30. Vanhoozer, *Is There?*, 23.

31. Hirsch, *Validity*.

32. He cites his own influences as being: Saussure, Dilthey, Husserl, Keynes, Popper, Reichenbach, and Schleiermacher (*Validity*, xi).

33. Hirsch softened this distinction in later years (Hirsch, "Meaning and Significance," 202–25; "Transhistorical Intentions," 549–67; Leschert, "Change of Meaning," 183–87; Blue, "Hermeneutic," 253–69). However, his earlier distinction still remains his primary influence in biblical hermeneutics.

34. Hirsch, *Validity*, ix–xi.

35. Hirsch, *Validity*, 255.

that threaten their faith and its sacred texts, Christian scholars turn for aid to the very source of the ideas and practices they so strenuously oppose."[36] This at least raises questions concerning the compatibility of Hirsch's views with a consistent, Christian hermeneutic.

How has the emphasis in defining *hermeneutics* shifted in more recent years? The general trend has been a movement toward a more all-encompassing definition rather than focusing merely on rules and practical methodology. To Gadamer, hermeneutics is not a method for understanding but an exploration of the conditions under which understanding takes place.[37] Understanding always involves interpretation.[38] Earlier evangelical treatments have a perceived lack of sophistication in light of this more recent shift. Noll observes that:

> Evangelicalism . . . has not regularly promoted sophisticated hermeneutics. While many elaborate systems are at hand for extracting meaning from the biblical text, few are available for understanding the interpretive constraints brought to the text, or more specifically the cultural presuppositions which often hide under the guise of commonsensical interpretive techniques.[39]

Accordingly, many have adopted an expanded definition reflective of current philosophical questions. Soulen suggests that the older definition (prior to what he calls the "modern" period) became unworkable in light of the erosion of certain theological premises.[40] He goes on to say that:

> In its modern form, hermeneutics seeks not merely to describe rules for appropriate interpretation but more basically to provide a general theory of human understanding that can support continued claims for the contemporary meaningfulness and possible truth of biblical (and other ancient) texts.[41]

Some evangelical scholars have also followed suit, though not all would go as far as Soulen. Thiselton sees the root of this expanded definition to be "the recognition that historical conditioning is two-sided." The text *and* the interpreter both stand in an historical context and tradition and are

---

36. Lundin, "Interpreting Orphans," 37–8n79.
37. Gadamer, *Truth and Method*, 263; *Philosophical Hermeneutics*, 3–17.
38. Gadamer, *Truth and Method*, 358.
39. Noll, *Between Faith*, 179–80; Wenkel, "A Survey," 113–27; Scott, "Some Problems," 69.
40. Soulen and Soulen, *Handbook*, 73.
41. Soulen and Soulen, *Handbook*, 73; Jeanrond, *Text and Interpretation*, 7; Barr, "Theology," 6.

so conditioned by that standing.[42] Following Gadamer, he concludes that the nature of the hermeneutical problem is shaped by this dual conditioning so that "for understanding to take place, two sets of variables must be brought into relation with each other."[43] Ultimately, this requires a fusion of two horizons, wherein "the interpreter's own horizon is re-shaped and enlarged."[44] For this to take place there must be an awareness of larger philosophical issues involved. J. B. Torrance, in his preface to Thiselton's seminal work, *The Two Horizons*, suggests that "we cannot raise the question of interpretation without raising questions about the nature of knowledge, the use of language, and the scientific and ontological presuppositions operative in the mind of the exegete."[45]

It may be noted at this point in our discussion that certain labels put on the various stages of development in the history of interpretation must be given an honest assessment in order to avoid caricature. This can be seen in relation to the shift in defining hermeneutics. In some treatments, using the *pre-modern* (or pre-critical),[46] *modern*, and *postmodern* schema, the pre-modern phase is almost invariably dismissed for lacking the sophistication of later phases. This criticism differs from that of Noll's cited above in that Noll is exposing the refusal to acknowledge complexity, while here there is a refusal to acknowledge at least an implicit awareness of complexity in pre-modern hermeneutics. Upon closer examination, this dismissal is unfounded. Richard Muller has objected to the term *pre-critical* as a label for pre-Enlightenment hermeneutics due to the fact that medieval and Reformation commentators were readily aware of and actually addressed issues of philology and context. The real issue is a difference over critical *presuppositions*, not critical method.[47] Zimmerman has helpfully provided a corrective to such a tendency.[48] Perhaps most helpful is his point that pre-modern theologians not only had worldview awareness (in terms of epistemology, ontology, and ethics), but also saw hermeneutics as *involving the interpreter*.[49] In fact, Zimmerman contends that the arrival

---

42. Thiselton, *Two Horizons*, 11.
43. Thiselton, *Two Horizons*, 16.
44. Thiselton, *Two Horizons*, xix.
45. Thiselton, *Two Horizons*, xi. Wright, "Interpreting," 49.
46. E.g., Frei, *Eclipse*; Davis, "Critical Traditioning," 750.
47. Muller, *Divine Essence*, 337; Adam, "Poaching on Zion," 26.
48. Zimmerman, *Recovering*; Steinmetz, "Superiority," 65–77; Treier, *Theological Interpretation*, 54–55.
49. Zimmerman, *Recovering*, 17–46. E.g., Calvin, *Institutes*, 1.1.1. Similarly, Thiselton recognizes similarities between pre-modern and post-modern interpretation in terms of hermeneutical awareness (*New Horizons*, 143–46); Grondin, *Introduction*.

of a more universal scope in hermeneutics is actually "a return to interpretation as worldview thinking that pre-Enlightenment theology already possessed to a great measure."[50] Space will not permit a detailed analysis of his argument in support of these points. However, it is a helpful reminder that in the midst of a shifting definition of hermeneutics, recent emphases are not necessarily *new* ideas.

In sum, hermeneutics has generally shifted from an emphasis on techniques and principles of interpretation to seeking to provide a general theory of understanding. The implications of the latter necessarily go beyond merely interpreting texts, but touch upon *all* areas of human awareness.[51] This widened scope has simultaneously brought about both rationalistic and irrationalistic tendencies among scholars who seek to address the Pandora's box of complexity. This shift raises an important question: how can one offer a general theory of understanding while still exercising an appropriate humility which takes into account human limitations?

Reasons for the Shift?

Dissatisfaction with Objectivity and Neutrality

So, *what accounts for this shift in defining hermeneutics?* Surely, the answer to this question is complex and involves a multitude of factors. We will briefly mention some identifiable, interrelated trends that at least contributed to it. It is possible to conceive of these particular factors as perspectives on the overall trend. These will include ones which have both indirect and direct bearing on biblical interpretation.

First, growing dissatisfaction with the overall pursuit of a detached objectivity and neutrality in interpretation has led to a consideration of a wider range of factors, including presuppositions. Unacknowledged presuppositions are actually *more* dangerous than those expressly stated. For example, in what Bartholomew calls the "classic liberal move"—one sets up a fictitious objectivity obscuring philosophical presuppositions under the veil of neutrality which in turn disallows *any* presuppositions (at least from opponents).[52] Consequently, such presuppositions lie outside the sphere of critique and are assumed to be necessarily true. The focus on *rules* of interpretation was not in and of itself incorrect, but incomplete. A growing philosophical awareness in hermeneutics may be traced back, at least more

---

50. Zimmerman, *Recovering*, 21.
51. Porter and Robinson, *Hermeneutics*, 5–6.
52. Bartholomew, "Uncharted Waters," 12, 25; Rogerson, *W. M. L*, 267.

systematically, to the work of Schleiermacher (notwithstanding Zimmerman's observations stated above), who argued that even rules of exegesis presupposed an answer to the question of how any understanding was possible to begin with.[53] Moreover, an explanation of a text using "tools" already involves a *selection* of those tools, which is in itself an interpretive task of understanding *prior* to working with textual data.[54] In fact, Gadamer criticized Helmholtz and Dilthey for not recognizing that scientific method *itself* is a tradition of sorts—a case of modernity invoking tradition in order to free us from tradition.[55] The inevitability of presuppositions was captured bluntly by Bultmann, who said, "There cannot be any such thing as presuppositionless exegesis."[56] Poythress argues that this point would be made with greater clarity if certain distinctions were made. For example, the necessity of a reference point *outside* the system of analysis used in addition to reference points within a system. We must not merely ask, "Which analysis is valid?" but "Which analysis is *useful for what purposes? . . . according to what standards?*"[57] Such considerations help to expose the hermeneutical situation as inherently presuppositional.

Rather than being considered a hindrance to interpretation, many have argued that pre-understanding and presuppositions *must* be embraced in order for understanding to be possible. Gadamer expressed dissatisfaction with the Enlightenment ideals of a perfected, comprehensive, and certain knowledge which is somehow detached from prejudice or tradition.[58] He goes to great lengths to establish that "to stand within a tradition does not limit the freedom of knowledge but makes it possible."[59] Gadamer was opposed to what he saw as futile attempts to root understanding in empathy through an imaginative identification with an historical author (e.g., Schleiermacher and Dilthey), or to somehow neutralize prejudice (e.g., Husserl) in order to achieve understanding.[60] Rather, understanding involves *using* our prejudice *positively*.[61] Along the same lines, one could

---

53. Thiselton, *Two Horizons*, 5; "New Hermeneutic," 82.

54. Palmer, *Hermeneutics*, 23.

55. Gadamer, *Truth and Method*, 270; Westphal, *Whose Community?*, 83–84; Weinsheimer, *Gadamer's Hermeneutics*, 258–59; Maier, *Historical-Critical Method*.

56. Bultmann, *Existence*, 343–44; "Problem of Hermeneutics," 255; *History and Eschatology*, 113; Heidegger, *Being and Time*, 191–92.

57. Poythress, "Analysing Biblical Text," 331 (emphasis mine).

58. Gadamer, *Truth and Method*, 185, 306–7, 324, 336, 340, 446.

59. Gadamer, *Truth and Method*, 324.

60. For a critique of forms of "psychologism" in hermeneutics, see: Wolterstorff, *Divine Discourse*, 93.

61. Browning, *Fundamental*, 37–38; Westphal, *Whose Community?*, 78–79;

also ask the question, *what pre-understanding is necessary to understand a given text?*[62] Polanyi contends that "all knowledge is either tacit or rooted in tacit knowledge."[63] By *tacit*, he means that which is indemonstrable and cannot explicitly be stated. Rather, it is based on one's conception of the nature of things.[64] Scientific measurements are always tacitly personal and theory-laden.[65] Coming from a different angle, Voelz argues that a purely objective reading is not only impossible, it is undesirable, due to the fact that an interpreter should understand a text in light of the expectations of the author and the assumptions of the text.[66] In other words, if the goal is to understand the intent of the author and text, then there should be an awareness of the *presuppositional* intent as well. To summarize, presuppositions should be acknowledged to avoid clandestine bias and as an unavoidable necessity in order for understanding to take place. It is not that presuppositions are a necessary evil to be overcome, but are actually *required*. All of this raises an important question helpfully highlighted by Gadamer: *what are the pre-conditions of true understanding in hermeneutics?*

Historical Awareness

Another aspect of the interpretive endeavor which undermines an emphasis on objectivity and neutrality is the *contextual* nature of interpretation. There has been growing appreciation for the *historical-situated-ness* of both the author or text and the reader in which man's relationship to history and the world is not as a user, but as a *participant*.[67] Porter and Robinson claim that "a study of hermeneutics, like ourselves, belongs to history—to understand means to be historical."[68] In earlier treatments, the historical situation of the original author(s) and text received much of the attention, yet to the neglect of other historical aspects. Indeed, one characteristic tendency of modernity is a general uneasiness concerning history and tradition.[69] As one writer put it, modernity's approach has been "not so much out of the past, indeed

---

Thiselton, *New Horizons*, 146; Thiselton, *Two Horizons*, 235–36.

62. Palmer, *Hermeneutics*, 25.

63. Polanyi, *Knowing and Being*, 144.

64. Polanyi, *Knowing and Being*, 76–77, 141. He argues that "a wholly explicit knowledge is unthinkable" (*Knowing and Being*, 144).

65. Carson, *Gagging of God*, 87–88.

66. Voelz, *What Does?*, 219–20.

67. Palmer, *Hermeneutics*, 242–43, 253; Vanhoozer, "Lost?," 91–93.

68. Porter and Robinson, *Hermeneutics*, 299.

69. Green, "Modernity, History," 308–29.

scarcely against the past, but detached from it."[70] In other words, it sought to study historical objects of the past from a place *outside* history. Much contemporary literature, however, is focused on the historical-bound *reader* and the question of how understanding can take place between the author or text and reader, *both* being limited by their historical vantage points. "The modern interpreter, no less than the text, stands in a given historical context and tradition."[71] "There is no privileged access to a work of literature, no access that stands outside history and outside one's own horizon of understanding."[72] Any notion of a timeless author, text, or reader is considered utterly naïve, labeled by one as a "view from nowhere."[73] Contrary to being a barrier to understanding, it is argued that one's historical horizon provides the necessary pre-understanding to interpret an historical text.[74]

In light of these concerns, Gadamer's aforementioned *fusion of horizons* has become highly influential. In order to move toward a proper fusion, one must first engage in a *distancing* in order to do justice to the historical context of the endeavor. One must take into account the particularity of a text before seeking to fuse with its horizon. However, this distancing and fusing does not take place through detachment from the text, but in *dialogue* with it.[75] Akin to the issue of presuppositions, ignorance of historical distance is tantamount to ignoring pre-understanding.[76] In Gadamer's terminology, "temporal distance" (*Zeitenabstand*) is not an obstacle to be overcome, but rather helps "the interpreter to distinguish between fruitful and unfruitful pre-judgments."[77] Another important concept for Gadamer is "effective-history" (*Wirkungsgeschichte*), from which the interpreter cannot escape. By this, he means "the actual operation of history on the process of understanding itself."[78] He explains that "understanding is not to be thought of so much as one's subjectivity, but as the placing of oneself within the process of tradition, in which past and present are constantly fused."[79] However one may answer the question of how to distinguish between the meaning of a text and the meaning of a text as the reader understands it,

---

70. Green, *Theological Interpretation*, 100; Schorske, *Thinking with History*, 3–4.
71. Thiselton, *Two Horizons*, 11.
72. Palmer, *Hermeneutics*, 224.
73. Westphal, "Philosophical/Theological View," 74.
74. Allen, *Philosophy*, 272.
75. Gadamer, *Truth and Method*, 333, 341; *Philosophical Hermeneutics*, 17.
76. Thiselton, *Two Horizons*, 306.
77. Thiselton, *Two Horizons*, 306; Gadamer, *Truth and Method*, 264.
78. Thiselton, *Two Horizons*, 307.
79. Gadamer, *Truth and Method*, 258; Thiselton, *New Horizons*, 327.

he or she cannot do so without reference to tradition and historical *conditionedness*.[80] The historical nature of the key components in interpretation necessarily expands the definition of hermeneutics.

As influential as Gadamer's idea of the fusion of two horizons has been in some evangelical circles, it has not been without criticism. Bartholomew, while commending Thiselton's shift to focus more upon broader philosophical awareness,[81] provides a helpful corrective to his endorsement of the two horizons concept. Namely, a *third* horizon must be addressed—the horizon of *God and the world as his creation*.[82] Similarly, McCartney and Clayton assert that:

> God's horizon is totally comprehensive of all horizons, which is not to say that all possible meanings of texts are God's meanings, but that the determinate meaning of any text is exhaustively known by him. Further, God is not mutable or bound by time, and so the meaning which he understands of a text is unchanging.[83]

This ultimate horizon, biblically conceived, would necessarily inform how the other two are to be understood not only in terms of *what* they are, but also *how* they are in relation to one another. The implications of God and his role in the process are far-reaching. Unfortunately, this aspect does not receive the attention it deserves in Thiselton's work. He grants the possible model of Wolterstorff concerning divine discourse, but says that this is a *different subject* from hermeneutics. He suggests that the role of the divine author is primarily an issue of *how God inspires Scripture*. Besides affirming the incarnational mystery between the divine and human and avoiding the analogous errors of Docetism and Arianism, there is not much else to glean from such consideration.[84] However, it would seem unnecessarily dismissive and reductionistic to relegate God's role (or horizon) in hermeneutics to acknowledging inspiration and the incarnational analogy. Do not even *these* acknowledgements have implications for hermeneutics? The nature

---

80. Thiselton, *Two Horizons*, 29, 302.

81. However, he is critical of Thiselton's eclecticism and apparent lack of a clear explanation of what *he* understands philosophy to be or how *he* conceives of the relationship between faith, reason, and philosophy (Bartholomew, "Three Horizons," 131–32).

82. Bartholomew, "Three Horizons," 133.

83. McCartney and Clayton, *Let the Reader*, 300. This would complement Vos' notion of "two horizons" which he emphasized in discussing the relationship between biblical theology and hermeneutics—namely, the horizon of the text and the horizon of the larger text (i.e., the epochal unfolding of redemptive history, ultimately found in the Bible as a unified whole) (Lints, "Two Theologies?," 245, 250–51).

84. Thiselton, *Hermeneutics*, 1–34, 185–227, 349–55.

of Scripture as inspired affects how we interpret it. Considerations of God's voice and intent in relation to the horizon of the human author and reader are integral to a proper biblical hermeneutic, not merely supplementary material to consider apart from the main interpretive endeavor. As Zimmerman points out, "the real question is whether philosophical hermeneutics can offer the radical *exteriority* necessary to lift the self beyond its own horizon."[85] This radical exteriority refers to that which *transcends* the two horizons and grounds their very intelligibility and evaluation. For all its awareness of historical complexity, there is an *authority* gap in seeking to distinguish between good and bad prejudice and ultimately between good and bad interpretation via a fusion of the two horizons.[86] As such, the dialogue with the past neither ends nor reaches a state of comprehension, failing to provide a leg to stand on in terms of evaluating divergent interpretations or fusions.

From What it Meant to What it Means

A third factor contributing to the shift concerns the relationship between what a text *meant* and what it *means* to the contemporary reader. Erickson says:

> We are dealing here with what I have chosen to call the problem of getting from there to here: how to move from the message of the Bible in the time it was given to its message for today. In many ways, I think the issue of contemporizing the biblical message is possibly the single most important issue facing evangelical hermeneutics today.[87]

Similarly, Vanhoozer observes that the problem that has dominated scholars' attention in modern biblical studies is "how to overcome the cultural and historical distance that separates present-day readers from the original situation of the authors."[88] Osborne suggests that "the problem of interpretation begins and ends with the presence of the reader."[89] Childs argues that one key issue arising from such consideration is whether the bible can be anything more

---

85. Zimmerman, *Recovering*, 36 (emphasis mine).

86. This has been a constant criticism of Gadamer's work among critics and followers alike (e.g., Hirsch, *Validity*, 250–51; Jeanrond, *Text and Interpretation*, 28, 35–36; Howard, *Three Faces*, 168; Thiselton, *New Horizons*, 315–17, 320; Weinsheimer, *Gadamer's Hermeneutics*, 102).

87. Erickson, *Evangelical Interpretation*, 56; Larkin, *Cultural and Biblical*, 23; Harrington, "Biblical Hermeneutics," 13.

88. Vanhoozer, "Exegesis and Hermeneutics," 53.

89. Osborne, *Hermeneutical Spiral*, 467.

than an expression of a time-conditioned culture—whether any ancient text, for that matter, can have determinate meaning for the present.[90]

These comments from biblical scholars mirror concerns among those in philosophical hermeneutics. Both have come to appreciate the relationship in terms of a *dialogue* between the past and present, between author/text and reader—using the concept of the hermeneutical *circle* or *spiral*. This two-way interaction is preferred over the predominant one-way emphasis of earlier Enlightenment interpretation. Gadamer stresses openness as being essential in the *I-thou* relationship present in this dialogue.[91] In fact, he sums up this major thread in his body of work by stating, "It is the Other who breaks into my ego-centeredness and gives me something to understand. This . . . motif has guided me from the beginning."[92] The interpreter must take caution and be willing to listen to the author/text (other) in the dialogue, without the goal of either horizon winning.[93] For Gadamer, tradition is one main bridge which spans the historical gap,[94] facilitating the fusion of horizons. One implication of this is that meaning is a fluid and ever-evolving entity, as readers from subsequent historical contexts dialogue with the text. Hence, Palmer argues that "meaning is not an objective, eternal idea but something that arises in relationship."[95] Moreover, meaning always transcends the intent of the original author.[96] Consequently, Gadamer can say "the artist who creates something is not the ideal interpreter of it."[97] Meaning cannot be reduced down to merely authorial intent or merely seeking to reproduce that intent in one's interpretation.[98] However, most evangelicals, even if sympathetic to Gadamer's notion of dialogue, have shied away from certain postmodern conclusions based on it. To be fair, even Gadamer and many who follow him still claim

---

90. Childs, "On Reclaiming," 4.

91. Gadamer, *Truth and Method*, 324–25.

92. Gadamer, "Reflections," 46.

93. Gadamer, *Truth and Method*, 379; Thiselton, "Communicative Action," 134; Westphal, *Whose Community?*, 116–17.

94. Gadamer sees this tradition bridge as having a distinctive ontological basis.

95. Palmer, *Hermeneutics*, 227.

96. Gadamer, *Truth and Method*, 264; Westphal, "Philosophical/Theological View," 77.

97. Gadamer, *Truth and Method*, 170.

98. As Westphal observes, Hirsch is unfair in his criticism of Gadamer on these points—he quotes Gadamer, yet leaves out his explicit use of the word, "merely" in his citation ("Philosophical/Theological View," 77n28).

to hold onto a form of hermeneutical stability and deny mere relativism.[99] Yet, the question remains, *how*?

For others, these assertions are unacceptable, as they provide a slippery slope toward rank relativism. According to Hirsch, unchanging *meaning* is to be isolated within the original author's intent, while *significance* is what is in relation to the reader(s) and spans the historical gap.[100] It is not the meaning of a text which actually spans the gap, but rather the significance of that meaning. As Hirsch construes it, the hermeneutical problem ultimately does not include the need to span historical distance, but rather is the search for the verbal meaning intended by the author.[101] Hirsch provides an antithetical alternative to Gadamer's view of application (what Hirsch calls *significance*). According to Gadamer, our understanding of a text is tied to the questions we bring to it, which are never identical to those of the original author. Understanding a text entails seeing how it applies to the situation and questions of the reader. Understanding always involves application.[102]

It would seem that the dilemma facing contemporary evangelical hermeneutics is a choice between two conflicting alternatives. First, in light of the complexity of historical distance and its relation to meaning highlighted in philosophical hermeneutics, evangelicals can follow Gadamer. But in order to do so, important questions must be addressed. For example, how should we conceive of the meaning of a text going beyond its author *biblically*, as opposed to meaning *in general*? Moreover, can interpretation be biblically conceived of as including *both* the element of production and reproduction? If meaning and application are not to be separated, how should we conceive of the relationship between original and modern meaning?

Second, in light of the dangers of relativism implied by Gadamer, evangelicals can follow the way of Hirsch. Yet again, one must address important questions. How should we define *objective* meaning and where is it ultimately grounded? How do we access it accurately if separated from it by historical distance? Moreover, in the case of biblical interpretation, can one understand the meaning of a text if one does not know how to apply it? Does not application presuppose meaning and vice-versa?[103] More importantly,

---

99. Gadamer, *Truth and Method*, 336–37.
100. Hirsch, *Validity*, 8–9; Stein, "Author-Oriented," 460–61.
101. Palmer, *Hermeneutics*, 63.
102. Gadamer, *Truth and Method*, 275, 274–316, 322, 381; Thiselton, *Two Horizons*, 308–9.
103. Frame, *Knowledge of God*, 81–84; Poythress, *God-Centered*, 72–74. Hirsch even seems unable to maintain his own distinction in one of his later writings (Hirsch, "Meaning and Significance," 20).

do the nature of the Bible and its own interpretation of itself match either of the two alternative paths with regard to these issues?

Where is Meaning to be Found?

Fourth, as Vanhoozer points out, there has been an identifiable shift in focus regarding *where* meaning is to be found in interpretation. He describes the shift in terms of the "three ages of criticism." This threefold division parallels the threefold division found in philosophy—metaphysics, epistemology, and ethics.[104] Although Vanhoozer treats these as separate chronological periods (at least in terms of pedagogical expediency), we prefer to treat them as emphases to avoid overgeneralization and to acknowledge the presence of each at various points throughout the history of the church.[105] First, meaning is sought in the intent of the *author* (either human or divine). Second, meaning is sought in the *text*. Third, meaning is sought in the *reader*. Incidentally, there has also been debate regarding which of the three predominately functions to bridge the historical gap mentioned above.[106] In terms of our focus on contemporary hermeneutics, the latter two have received the most attention. However, all three can be generally detected among the key figures present in the discussion. For example, Hirsch emphasizes the human author;[107] Ricoeur seeks meaning in the text; and Gadamer focuses on the reader (and the reader's dialogue with the author/text).[108] It must be noted that neither Gadamer nor Ricoeur deny that an author exists or has relevance, but they do affirm that meaning escapes the limits of the author and that the author cannot provide a determinate object.[109] This shift in emphasis has clearly widened the scope in defining hermeneutics to include more nuanced consideration of both, the text and the reader.

---

104. Vanhoozer, *Is There?*, 25.

105. The fact that different scholars have similarly identified shifts from both directions, a focus on epistemology to ontology (e.g., Ricoeur, *Hermeneutics*, 43–44) and from ontology to epistemology (e.g., Vanhoozer), speaks to their nature, and being perspectives on what constitutes a worldview.

106. Porter and Robinson, *Hermeneutics*, 4.

107. E.g., Hirsch says "there is no magic land of meanings outside human consciousness." Rather, the human author controls meaning (*Validity in Interpretation*, 4).

108. Dockery, *Biblical Interpretation*, 171–75. However, though this is generally true, it does not fully capture the nuanced views of each (e.g., Ricoeur also places an emphasis on the reader) (Ricoeur, *Hermeneutics*, 218–20; Vanhoozer, "Paul Ricoeur," 693; *Biblical Narrative in the Philosophy of Paul Ricoeur*, 286; Laughery, *Living Hermeneutics in Motion*, 149–58).

109. Westphal, *Whose Community?*, 63–66, 77.

It is important to note that for each one of these emphases, deeper questions need to be raised. For instance, what is an *author* or an *intention*? The same question could be asked concerning a *text* and so on. The point is that even the most basic components of written communication, which are often taken for granted, involve deeper presuppositions concerning metaphysics, epistemology, and ethics. Indeed, the question of where meaning is to be found is ultimately a *theological* question, as it relates to the meaning of life and humanity.[110] How one answers these questions depends on what is assumed about the nature of reality, how that reality is known or cannot be known, and whether one has a responsibility in how they understand that reality. In each case, we are confronted with the question of whether there is meaning beyond the human author, text, and human reader. Is there *prior* meaning to be found and understood in a text or is it *dependent* upon the reader to create or supply meaning?

Vanhoozer has argued that the particular *character* of this shift in focus is evident in what he calls the "aesthetic turn." This turn is rooted in Kant's fundamental dualism between the realms of freedom and nature, but more explicitly emerging in the twentieth century.[111] Various movements have been identified with this shift, most notably: New Criticism, structuralism, and post-structuralism. Even Heidegger's own shift between his earlier and later work, it has been argued,[112] exhibits a microcosm of this turn.[113] In biblical hermeneutics, the turn can be detected in some forms of Narrative Theology and literary criticism.[114] In short, a text is seen as essentially cut off from its author in terms of meaning and historical context.[115] This spirit of aestheticism includes "the idea that the realm of art is autonomous and self-sufficient, not susceptible to non-aesthetic standards, rules, or criteria."[116] The practical effect is the concept of an *autonomous* text, which takes on a meaning of its own, apart from its author.[117] However, the shift does not stop with an autonomous text, but has spawned the concept of an autonomous reader. This is seen most clearly in certain

---

110. Vanhoozer, *Is There?*, 30; *First Theology*, 208.

111. Bartholomew labels this general shift as the *postmodern turn* (i.e., a reaction to modernism) ("Post/Late," 25–38).

112. Macquarrie, "Heidegger's Earlier," 3–16; Thiselton, *Two Horizons*, 327–30.

113. Vanhoozer, "A Lamp," 36–37, 43–47.

114. Köstenberger, "Aesthetic Theology," 27–44; Tracy, "Literary Theory," 302; Vanhoozer, "A Lamp," 47–49; *First Theology*, 207–20.

115. Vanhoozer, "A Lamp," 25–26.

116. Vanhoozer, "A Lamp," 26.

117. Frye, *Anatomy of Criticism*.

forms of reader-response hermeneutics.[118] It may be noted that postmodern deconstructionism aims to overthrow meanings rather than to create new ones. However, one may argue that such an agenda assumes a meaning from which it seeks to corroborate through attempts to show how a text undermines possible meanings attached to it.

Vanhoozer's survey of these shifts highlights the *morality* and *goal* of contemporary hermeneutics. Rather than mere neutral, changing interests, he argues that these shifts comprise a series of evasive 'undoings,' which are postmodern reactions to modernity's faith in objective reason and morality. First, there is the undoing of the *author*. This is tied to a suspicion of metaphysics, often exhibited in various forms of non-realism. Characteristic of this undoing is the denial "that language corresponds to some non-linguistic presence."[119] For example, for Saussure and Derrida,[120] there is no thing *signified*, only signs pointing to other signs.[121] Hence, meaning is not signified by linguistic signs in texts,[122] because there is nothing ultimately outside texts (or at least anything able to be known intelligibly).[123] This introduces a *gap* between authorial intent and verbal meaning in which intentionality is not prior to systems of language nor even ascertainable by the *intender*.[124] Perhaps most significant for our purposes is that to whatever degree there is an undoing of the role of the author, *authority* is undone.[125] Even in Gadamer, there is a recognition that the birth of the reader is not the death of the author—only the death of an *absolute* author.[126] This is an especially pertinent point. The very nature of the Bible and its subject matter testifies to its own authority to speak to the contemporary reader as the very word of God, with absolute authority.

The undoing of the *text* and the *reader* are in many ways symptomatic of the undoing of the author and further shows how interconnected each is

---

118. Fish, *Is There a Text in This Class?*

119. Vanhoozer, *Is There?*, 60.

120. For Derrida and other postmodern figures, such as Barthes and Foucault, it is not that the author is categorically irrelevant, but that the author is not the sole producer of meaning in a unilateral fashion (Westphal, *Whose Community?*, 57–58).

121. Grenz, *A Primer*, 115–17; Derrida, *Of Grammatology*, 50.

122. Vanhoozer, *Is There?*, 61.

123. Derrida, *Writing and Difference*, 280. Even if something did exist outside this system of signs, it could not be expressed via those signs. If it did, it would no longer be what it was, being entangled and tainted by the play of linguistic differences (Grenz, *A Primer*, 142).

124. Vanhoozer, *Is There?*, 78.

125. Vanhoozer, *Is There?*, 86.

126. Westphal, *Whose Community?*, 82.

in any theory of interpretation. First, let us consider the text. Thiselton has observed that "the most radical question of all in hermeneutics concerns the nature of texts."[127] Yet, upon deeper consideration, one cannot so easily isolate a theory of a text which does not at the same time imply a theory about the author and reader as well.[128] The idea of an autonomous text is (for all its helpful consideration of structures, metaphor, and textual trajectories) rendered empty and undone if disengaged from purpose and use, which can only be supplied by *persons*. A floating text cannot supply intent, purpose, or use. How can a text *speak*? If it doesn't speak, what can be conveyed by it? The apparent sense of a text turns out to be merely "the sense the words would bear had *we* [the readers] been the author."[129] Moreover, if meaning is found in the text alone, how does one distinguish between the surface and deep grammar of a text? For example, is the question of a mother to a child, "have you finished your homework?" merely an inquiry regarding the surface fact of the situation (i.e., wanting to know so she can know when to plan on eating dinner afterward)? Or is her question actually intended as an *imperative* on a deeper level (i.e., get it done)? This distinction requires the recognition of something being *done* with a text.

The *reader* is also undone. This is true even for those readers seeking to undo authors and texts. After all, isn't undoing a form of doing?[130] Yet, if authorial intent is undone and authors cannot author, then can a reader *act as an agent* if disallowed the similar prerogative of an author? If not, how could this act of the reader be described or understood? Moreover, undoing the author or text does not necessarily liberate the reader in terms of meaning. With no functional author, can we speak *truthfully* about any texts? How would we know if we did or didn't? If the author dies, what is the meaning in a text? Vanhoozer suggests that indeed the author never really disappears, but rather the *reader* simply takes over the role.[131]

These evasive shifts in hermeneutics could be seen as symptomatic of man's sinful desire to preserve his own autonomy and to throw off any notion of an authority over meaning in a text, especially a transcendent one. To borrow a word from Van Til, underneath much of the sophisticated philosophical dress of postmodern hermeneutics lies a sort of *ventriloquism*—to make a text say what the reader wants it to say or not say. For example, Fish states that "the entities that were once seen as competing for the right to constrain

---

127. Thiselton, *New Horizons*, 49.
128. Jeanrond, *Text and Interpretation*, 73.
129. Vanhoozer, *Is There?*, 109; Wolterstorff, *Divine Discourse*, 172.
130. Vanhoozer, *Is There?*, 185.
131. Vanhoozer, *Is There?*, 89–90.

interpretation (text, reader, and author) are now all seen to be the *products* of interpretation."[132] Important questions arise. What authority dictates which direction the interpretive process goes? Are we to establish an interpretation using the given data of the text or is the text already a product of our interpretation? If so, are we to see ourselves as *pre*-interpreters of all of reality?

One last thing must be said with regard to Vanhoozer's assessment. Concerning biblical interpretation, we must ask whether we must choose among the three main autonomy options exhibited in the contemporary discussion. If our response in the face of postmodern relativism is to anchor autonomous control over meaning in the *author* (as many evangelicals have done), we must do so with regard to the *divine author* rather than merely the human author—if we want to avoid the same pitfalls exhibited in autonomous notions of author, text, and reader. We cannot presume to acknowledge a godlike human author nor replace one with a godlike text or reader.[133] Pitfalls persist in each case. By giving due consideration to the *divine* author, we will begin to deal with the legitimate complexities of interpretation highlighted in philosophical hermeneutics and avoid such pitfalls.

Conclusion

All of these factors have contributed to the shift in defining hermeneutics, as it is understood today. This widened scope has simultaneously brought about both rationalistic and irrationalistic tendencies among scholars who seek to address the complexity now opened up for discussion. This shift also raises an important question: how can one offer a general theory of *understanding* while still exercising an appropriate humility which takes into account both, the complexities involved and the limits of the finite mind? Indeed, there is a deeper issue involved which has been already hinted at. It not only affects each one of these factors mentioned above but drives them and their respective influence upon biblical hermeneutics. This will be the subject of the next chapter.

---

132. Fish, *Is There?*, 16–17.
133. Westphal, *Whose Community?*, 60.

Chapter 3: Surveying the Field, Part II

Introduction

AN ISSUE RELATED TO defining hermeneutics is how the relationship between metaphysics and hermeneutics has been understood. Over the years, scholars have had a love-hate relationship with the discipline of metaphysics.[1] Indicative of this tension is Palmer, who states that there is "no particular need to equate hermeneutics with onto-theology, even if there is a markedly onto-theological dimension in hermeneutics."[2] In other words, he sees the need for ontological considerations, but only as a *subset* of a more general concept of hermeneutics.[3] Hence, he disallows onto-theological considerations as a defining factor for hermeneutics in general. In doing so, hermeneutics itself becomes a functional base ontology of sorts.[4] Howard traces the very historical migration of hermeneutics as a discipline, from being a subset of theology to becoming a general meta-theory of its own.[5] There has been an acute awareness of the need for a ground-level, even transcendent, foundation for making sense of the complexities in interpretation. Usually, this has been formulated in ontological terms or in some cases, ironically, *anti*-ontological terms. In what follows, we will attempt to trace this particular thread through some significant figures that have influenced developments in the field. Curiously, evangelical hermeneutics has often failed to articulate a distinct biblical alternative. The question is whether the foundation provided is sufficient, accounting for the pre-conditions of understanding.

---

1. There is a marked lack of consensus in the history of metaphysics (Van Inwagen, *Metaphysics*, 13).

2. Palmer, "On Transcendability," 95.

3. Palmer seeks to define hermeneutics explicitly in a *non*-theological context (*Hermeneutics*, 4).

4. Others, like Van Huyssteen, see biblical hermeneutics functioning within a more general and ultimate *epistemological* context—one more ultimate than the Bible itself (*Essays*, 143–45).

5. Howard, *Three Faces*, 3.

Metaphysics and Hermeneutics

Certainly, metaphysical assumptions have been made, even if not explicitly so, in the earliest discussions of what has now become formally known as philosophical hermeneutics. However, things really started to shift in emphasis with Immanuel Kant. He has been highly influential in that he articulates many of the key elements and tendencies found in those who subsequently sought to describe hermeneutics in relation to metaphysics. Through his *noumenal-phenomenal* scheme, he preserved a notion of metaphysics (i.e., reality in itself—the *noumenal*), while at the same time, claimed it was unknowable in the *phenomenal* realm.[6] There is a reality outside of us and our experience of it, but we cannot know it as it really is in our experience. He positioned the categories of the human mind as necessary, universal, and ahistorical *shapers* of raw reality (*noumena*) into that which can be known in experience. Hence, the only thing known is the shaped reality, not reality-in-itself.[7] This has important implications for hermeneutics. First, by setting forth a dichotomy between human understanding and objective reality, he introduced a gap between the interpreter's understanding of a text and the objective reality behind it. Second, he saw the mind as *active* in imposing order upon what is known. He seeks to bring *a priori* notions (categories of the mind) together with *synthetic judgments* (investigative inquiry). In a sense, the knower is a *creator* of reality (as *we* know it) via the given categories of the mind. Any notion of divine transcendence is subordinated to man's autonomous rationality.[8] Third, he asks the basic presuppositional question which drives much of the hermeneutical discussion today in terms of understanding—*what are the pre-conditions of knowledge?*[9] Fourth, while Kant's ideas are similar to Schleiermacher and Dilthey's notion of the hermeneutical circle with its *a priori* element, he differs in that he suggests it is fixed and ahistorical. To the contrary, many who endorse such a circle or dialogue in contemporary hermeneutics emphasize presuppositions as necessarily historical and changeable.[10]

It is important to point out tendencies in Kant's notion of metaphysics which resurface in different ways among those with a more direct influence on hermeneutics. First, he claims to know that a *noumenal* reality actually exists, but says it cannot be determinatively or conceptually known in any

---

6. Kant, *Prolegomena*, 136; Brown, *Philosophy*, 95; Barth, *Protestant Thought*, 159.
7. Westphal, "Philosophical/Theological," 72; Grenz, *A Primer*, 76–77.
8. Kant, *Critique*, 35; *Prolegomena*, 29.
9. Kant, *Prolegomena*, 117; Brown, *Philosophy*, 94.
10. Westphal, "Philosophical/Theological," 72.

positive sense.[11] Apart from our experience, there is no objective validity—"without sense ... without meaning."[12] This highlights an irrational side in his thinking—inconsistently speaking of knowing something which is unknowable, and without content.[13] Moreover, he posits transcendental categories in the finite mind without clearly explaining why or how they actually correspond to the real world outside us, to language, or even where they come from.[14] Consideration of noumenal concepts, such as *God*, involves regulative, pragmatic concerns, not actual existence.[15] Second, in one sense, his whole system is built upon an ultimate metaphysical scheme, but in another, he suggests that man cannot ultimately know anything about it. He engages in a form of *replacement* metaphysics—he assumes his own set of absolutes in place of traditional philosophical and theological metaphysics:[16] limits of reason and possibility (on the authority of man's reason);[17] the impossibility of divine meaning;[18] the impossibility of divine revelation;[19] and a finite, one-level epistemology.[20] In fact, he asserts that metaphysics must only be considered as a science within this *more ultimate* network of assumptions.[21] One could argue that, rather than making a distinction between Creator and creature, Kant makes a distinction *within* man, in terms of transcendence and experience. He rightly highlights reason's deficiencies but does so in terms of the autonomous ideal of man's reason (rationalism).[22] His conception of the relationship between metaphysics and knowledge is precarious to say the least.

For all of Schleiermacher's influence on author-centered hermeneutics, it is his repositioning of hermeneutics as a discipline which is most significant.

11. Kant, *Critique*, 13, 186–88; *Prolegomena*, 75–76, 116–24.

12. Kant, *Critique*, 182.

13. E.g., Kant, *Critique*, 188–91; Ameriks, "Critique," 272–73, 283; Poythress, *Redeeming Philosophy*, 244.

14. Torrance, *Theological Science*, 92; Ameriks, "Critique," 285.

15. Kant, *Prolegomena*, 130–32; Forster, *Kant and Skepticism*, 34; *Critique*, 372; Ameriks, "Critique," 279.

16. Copleston, *A History*, 432–33; Ameriks, "Critique," 269, 280, 284–85; Van Til, *Sovereignty*, 21; Van Til, *Case for Calvinism*, 113.

17. Kant, *Prolegomena*, 30–31, 78, 91, 93, 117, 129, 135, 138, 141; *Critique*, 15, 18, 37–38.

18. Kant, *Prolegomena*, 94–95, *Critique*, 182; Ameriks, "Critique," 290.

19. Kant, *Prolegomena*, 15, 27, *Critique*, 185; Westphal, "In Defense," 118–41; Forster, *Kant and Skepticism*, 34.

20. Kant, *Prolegomena*, 78–79, 130,

21. Kant, *Prolegomena*, 33–34, 134, 141.

22. Oliphint, *Covenantal Apologetics*, 70.

Ricoeur has observed that one of Schleiermacher's significant contributions was a *de-regionalization* of biblical hermeneutics.[23] He sought a *general* hermeneutic—one which treated the Bible like any other book, regardless of its subject matter.[24] Certainly, there is a sense in which the Bible should be read like any other book in that it is fully human, yet in another sense, it claims full divinity. Hence, it should *not* be read like any other book. Moreover, it makes truth claims which provide a larger framework from which non-inspired texts should be read and understood. As a result, the distinction between general and sacred hermeneutics must be nuanced biblically, rather than as mutually exclusive categories or as merely one and the same category. Commenting on this very point with regard to Schleiermacher, Goldsworthy observes that "the tendency of liberalism is to move the whole concern of the Bible into the common arena . . . as merely a human book to be treated and interpreted like any other book."[25] It is interesting to note that Schleiermacher's theological views mirror this same push for a general, common denominator which provides the ground for particular expressions of religious truth (e.g., Christianity). Namely, he grounds religion in a "feeling of absolute dependence"[26]—which functions as a non-objectifiable and innate aspect to *all* religious experience.[27] In sum, Schleiermacher and Dilthey both endorsed hermeneutics as a general meta-theory of understanding life as given in linguistic expression.[28]

Rather than being metaphysically *neutral*, this move makes a number of important assumptions. One's method assumes truths pertaining to the nature of reality which makes the corresponding method appropriate. For instance, Schleiermacher assumed that appeals to divine authorship cannot settle questions of meaning.[29] Rather, he relied upon the assumed ability of the reader to grasp the author's thoughts and intent as well as or even better than the author himself.[30] Somehow the interpreter must, along with grammatical considerations,[31] project himself or herself into the mind

---

23. Ricoeur, *Hermeneutics*, 44; Schleiermacher, *Hermeneutics*, 28–35, 95–107.

24. Packer, "Infallible Scripture," 355; Dockery, *Biblical Interpretation*, 162.

25. Goldsworthy, *Gospel-Centered*, 126.

26. Schleiermacher, *Christian Faith*, 12–31.

27. Porter and Robinson, *Hermeneutics*, 28.

28. Howard, *Three Faces*, 22; Ricoeur, *Hermeneutics*, 79; Thiselton, *New Horizons*, 318.

29. DeVries, "Schleiermacher," 352.

30. Schleiermacher, *Hermeneutics*, 112; Thiselton, *New Horizons*, 216.

31. Thiselton helpfully points out that Schleiermacher's psychological emphasis was never divorced from grammatical concerns. Rather, both are always present in the hermeneutical endeavor (*New Horizons*, 206, 232).

of the original author through empathy of consciousness. By reducing sacred hermeneutics to general hermeneutics, he assumed the Bible to have a purely human nature, a mere record of human religious experience.[32] This not only produced a radical subjective thrust, it reversed the place of experience in traditional theology. Instead of being the result of doctrinal reflection (and its ontological foundation in God who reveals truth through Scripture), subjective experience became the *source* of doctrine.[33] Since meaning is primarily a matter of an inward, subjective state of mind, the inherent circularity of understanding between the interpreter and the author prevents any final interpretation. In what Schleiermacher and Dilthey call the "hermeneutical circle," there is always an approximation to the truth, but never arriving at it at any given point. Theoretically, this circle is irresolvable in terms of its lack of self-evident, self-contained, and certain knowledge.[34] Hence, we find in Schleiermacher an unstable tension between seeking an almost rationalistic comprehension of the original author's mind behind the text and the realization that no final comprehensive interpretation can be found.[35] Though we may exceed the author's understanding, we still do not have a certain, full understanding. Where then is understanding to be found, if not in the empathy between the interpreter and author? This tension is symptomatic of an assumed view of reality which ultimately undermines the understanding sought after. Goldsworthy sums up this tension in Schleiermacher:

> The problematic feature is that God and Man are seen to share a *common general being*. The real distinction between God and Man is thus muted or even lost. The subject-object relationship will always be a dilemma until it is re-established on the basis of this distinction, of Chalcedon and the incarnation, and is thus grounded in the Trinity.[36]

Schleiermacher reduced the hermeneutical situation down to the human level, and what we know of God is what man subjectively projects via *experience*, which is more ultimate and provides the authority and criteria by

---

32. Goldsworthy, *Gospel-Centered*, 128. This humanistic tendency is clearly evident elsewhere in his writings. For example, he explains that the "attributes which we ascribe to God are to be taken as denoting not something special in God, but only something special in the manner in which the feeling of absolute dependence is to be related to him" (quoted in Brown, *Philosophy*, 111).

33. Hoffecker, "Schleiermacher," 1065; Porter and Robinson, *Hermeneutics*, 27.

34. Grenz, *Primer*, 102–3; Porter and Robinson, *Hermeneutics*, 32.

35. Schleiermacher, *Hermeneutics*, 112; Dilthey, "Development," 259.

36. Goldsworthy, *Gospel-Centered*, 133 (emphasis mine).

which the Bible should be interpreted. He conceives of meaning as grounded not in the comprehension of God but in man. In fact, God has no explanatory comprehension or revealed authority over such things as our notions of objectivity, subjectivity, or experience (even of *him*). At best, God functions merely on the same ontological level as man (i.e., common *being*) in this regard, if not totally irrelevant. Yet, man cannot ultimately comprehend the hermeneutical situation. On the one hand, we find a principle of rational autonomy in man's subjective feelings or intuition, unbound by revelation and intelligible apart from it.[37] On the other hand, we find a principle of irrationality in that there is no ultimate interpretation to be found, only a continual process in the finite realm.

Similarly, Dilthey claimed that there was no transcendental point from which to view human phenomena. Rather, the most fundamental aspect of reality is its *historical* nature. There is *only* historical understanding. His approach assumes only one knowable reality—history, from which no one worldview can be established as ultimate. There is no one objective system of metaphysics to discover. There are only attempts to unify our historical experience.[38] All claims to transcendent realities are mere projections from within experience. For Dilthey, in the words of H. A. Hodges,

> the problem of the relation between God and the world is a reflection of the problem of the relation between the higher and lower worlds within ourselves . . . God is indeed no more than a cipher which serves self-knowledge . . . a projection of inner experience.[39]

His ultimate presupposition for knowledge is demonstrable reality (i.e., experience).[40] Historical consciousness (or history of the mind) replaces metaphysics as traditionally understood.[41] However, he, like Schleiermacher, leaves many questions unanswered. Namely, how can objectivity be achieved in the midst of the relativity of man's finite experience?[42] For both

---

37. In fact, Schleiermacher focused on a *general* act of preunderstanding which is prior to any *specific* act of textual interpretation. In doing so, he precludes the notion of biblical preunderstanding via textual interpretation (Bible) as the framework through which to interpret.

38. Howard, *Three Faces*, 17; Porter and Robinson, *Hermeneutics*, 44; Goldsworthy, *Gospel-Centered*, 133; Thiselton, *Two Horizons*, 235–40; Grenz, *A Primer*, 99–103. This, in itself, is an objective and universal claim, inconsistent with Dilthey's point.

39. Quoted in Thiselton, *Two Horizons*, 239.

40. Gadamer, *Truth and Method*, 196.

41. Gadmer, *Truth and Method*, 203.

42. Gadamer attributed this tension in Dilthey to his Enlightenment assumptions (*Truth and Method*, 203–13).

CHAPTER 3: SURVEYING THE FIELD, PART II

Schleiermacher and Dilthey, God turns out to be a mere figment of man's historical inner life—no more than his own finite existence. This reduction down to one level of historical reality leaves both with rationalistic and irrationalistic tension and incoherence.

Perhaps more overtly than any other figure before him, Heidegger explicitly brought metaphysical concerns into the hermeneutical discussion. Although esoteric and often obscure in style and expression, certain strains of his thought seem clear regarding metaphysics. First, though he is said to have been opposed to metaphysics,[43] he was merely opposing a particular *type* of metaphysics—traditional Western views, exemplified by Greek thought. As Thiselton has observed, the much-discussed distinction between earlier and later Heidegger actually displays significant continuity, with an *increasing emphasis on ontology*, though he perhaps goes about it in a different manner than in his earlier work.[44] In other words, the turn in his thought was not a reversal, but an *intensification* of his earlier ideas.[45] He was opposed to ways in which an understanding of things-in-themselves were sought, apart from experience. Moreover, he opposed traditional distinctions, especially the subject-object distinction,[46] seeking rather to overcome and transcend it.[47] He sought to understand *being* itself—a fundamental ontology, which is *prior* to any theory of knowledge.[48] His key concept of *Dasein* ("being-there" or dwelling-in-the world)[49] refers to the mode of historical human consciousness, but not as an object or as objectifiable.[50] It provides the place and occasion for the disclosure of the being (*Sein*) of beings (i.e., a window to being-in-general).[51] It also implies an ontological circle which involves a

---

43. Grenz, *A Primer*, 108. Heidegger was very much taken with what he deemed the fundamental question of metaphysics—why are there things that are rather than nothing? (Heidegger, *An Introduction*, 1, 83–84, 201).

44. Dreyfus, "Beyond Hermeneutics," 66–83.

45. Thiselton, *Two Horizons*, 328–29.

46. Thiselton, *Two Horizons*, 157–60, 174, 187, 190.

47. Incidentally, this is a characteristic mark in much of contemporary philosophical hermeneutics (e.g., Palmer, *Hermeneutics*, 246; Oxenhandler, "Ontological Criticism," 17–23).

48. Porter and Robinson, *Hermeneutics*, 60.

49. In Heidegger's usage, this term is almost synonymous with *human* being. His notion of *world* is not as an object of man's consideration, but as a priori given with *Dasein* prior to any conceptualization. Hence, both *Dasein* and *world* are involved in one another (Thiselton, *Two Horizons*, 148, 154–55).

50. He equates any objectification with depersonalization (Heidegger, *Being and Time*, 73).

51. Heidegger, *Metaphysics*, 9, 29; Porter and Robinson, *Hermeneutics*, 63–64. This is a key distinction in Heidegger—between being (ontological) and beings (ontic)

knowledge of being inherent in Dasein—man's pre-understanding of being. Interpretation involves knowing something of being *in advance*, prior to the process.[52] In addition, the ultimate meaning of being cannot be grasped without the consideration of time—from the perspective of *Dasein*.[53] The meaning and disclosure of being is prior to all subject-object relations.[54] As such, *Dasein* is characterized more by possibility than actuality.[55] In sum, "hermeneutics is the interpretation of the being of *Dasein* and an event of understanding that cannot be reduced to method, theories of interpretation, or an empathetic projection into another's life."[56] A fundamental ontology "must be sought in the *existential analytic of Dasein*."[57] This analytic is not a method as such, but rather a *way* of being authentic and open to possibility, seeking to let being disclose itself in interpretation. In other words, being is ultimately self-interpreting.[58]

It is important to consider the following observations regarding Heidegger's notion of metaphysics. First, there must be an appropriate *method* of inquiry corresponding the *object* of that inquiry. Due to the nature of *Dasein*, methods concerning objects or things (e.g., scientific method) will not work, for *Dasein* does not have properties, but *possibilities*.[59] *Dasein* is *personal*, not propositional in nature. In short, "thought is dependent on the reality of being which calls it forth."[60] Second, hermeneutics is primarily concerned with the meaning of being through *Dasein*. In his later writings, he emphasizes *language* as having ontological significance, as the "custodian" or "house" of being.[61] Man must let being reveal itself through language by speaking and listening to it.[62] Palmer summarizes that for Heidegger and Gadamer, "language is the 'medium' in which we live, move, and have our being."[63] Yet, *Dasein* (and language) is historically bound in that its essence

---

(Thiselton, *Two Horizons*, 147, 329).

    52. Thiselton, *Two Horizons*, 165–66.

    53. Heidegger, *Being and Time*, 40; Thiselton, *Two Horizons*, 182.

    54. Porter and Robinson, *Hermeneutics*, 70; Thiselton, *Two Horizons*, 148, 188.

    55. Thiselton, *Two Horizons*, 148–49.

    56. Porter and Robinson, *Hermeneutics*, 70.

    57. Quoted in Thiselton, *Two Horizons*, 148 (Heidegger's italics); Heidegger, *Metaphysics*, 175.

    58. De Vries, "Martin Heidegger," 545.

    59. Thiselton, *Two Horizons*, 188.

    60. Gillespie, "Biblical Authority," 197.

    61. Heidegger, *Metaphysics*, 51, 185.

    62. Thiselton, *Two Horizons*, 341.

    63. Palmer, *Hermeneutics*, 9.

CHAPTER 3: SURVEYING THE FIELD, PART II

does not precede its existence. Consequently, man's interpretive stance is always historical and finite. Interpretation is always incomplete.[64] There is no complete interpretation to be found from an independent and objective vantage-point.[65] Heidegger's hermeneutical circle allows him to speak of truth about *Dasein*, as well as truth being "disclosed through Dasein's self-awareness and decision."[66] We only speak about truth as we are *in* it, not searching outside of it.[67]

The key assumption that Heidegger makes in all of this is that being (though distinct in terms of being which is disclosed [*Sein*] and being as *Dasein*)[68] is ultimately *monistic*. Man as *Dasein* participates in and manifests being-in-general. Both are part of the same fabric. Meaning must be in terms of *Dasein* or it has no meaning. Though he seeks transcendence through his concept of *Dasein*, it is incoherent with other aspects of his thought. For example, is truth known in relation to *Dasein* or is all truth really about *Dasein* (i.e., man)?[69] Moreover, how can one presume to know this distinction with any certainty without knowing the whole scheme of things? While *Dasein* is inherently historical, Heidegger argues that man is able to *transcend* chronological time through *temporality*, a mode of openness toward the past, present, and future. As such, *Dasein* is transcendent through projection toward possibility, not as objective actuality.[70] A transcendence which only provides possibility does not provide any certainty. How can one determine any meaningful notion of possibility if there is no actuality which provides a basis for distinguishing it from impossibility, or is possibility just a guise for mere chance? It would seem that Heidegger sees the need for a kind of transcendence, not only in order to avoid sheer irrationalism and arbitrary self-interpretation,[71] but seeks it through distinctions made *within the same level* of being.[72] Another example of incoherent tension is how he describes being as wholly indeterminate yet, at the same time, wholly definite. It is wholly determinate in relation to non-being, but

---

64. Porter and Robinson, *Hermeneutics*, 60–61.

65. Thiselton, *Two Horizons*, 197.

66. Thiselton, *Two Horizons*, 197. Heidegger's *circle* is strikingly ontological in nature (Gadamer, *Truth and Method*, 261; Palmer, *Hermeneutics*, 42).

67. Grenz, *A Primer*, 106.

68. This is the one main distinction in the *same* being (Heidegger, *Metaphysics*, 204–6).

69. Thiselton, *Two Horizons*, 200, 291–92.

70. Porter and Robinson, *Hermeneutics*, 64.

71. Dreyfus, "Beyond Hermeneutics," 73.

72. Heidegger, *Metaphysics*, 93ff.

wholly indeterminate in itself.[73] It would seem that between these poles, Heidegger offers a relative hope to progress in understanding the meaning of one's own being (and being-in-general) through making distinctions within being (e.g., *Dasein*'s orientation toward future possibilities), but without ever reaching full comprehension at any point.[74] Man's real being is always future being.[75] This reduces interpretation down to knowing only our own thoughts concerning ourselves and our own existence. "Insofar as it is in any way understood, being has meaning."[76] That is, understood by *man*. More authentic understanding of being is achieved to the degree that it is oriented toward the possibility of death (i.e., non-being).[77] Not only is the meaning of being sought to be understood from *within* being, it is also necessarily understood in correlation with non-being.[78] Here, we see a rationalistic aim for man to understand being while, at the same time, needing to root its determinacy in the concept of non-being, which is ultimately irrational and indeterminate.[79]

Van Til concludes that existential interpretation (e.g., Heidegger and Bultmann) denies transcendence outside of man, but still sees the need for it.[80] Hence, he looks for it within himself (e.g., in *being*). On the one hand, he must make a universal negative statement about any transcendence outside of himself (rationalism). On the other hand, he seeks a replacement transcendence concerning an ultimate reference point in man's being as authentically free and open toward future possibilities (irrationalism/indeterminism) and participating in being-in-general (transcending the subject-object relationship).[81] However, this transcendence is never absolute, but always on its way home. As we have seen in terms of Heidegger's being/non-being scheme, he seeks to explain man according to both, elements of pure fate (being) and pure chance (non-being).[82] All of this is done

---

73. Heidegger, *Metaphysics*, 78–92.
74. Porter and Robinson, *Hermeneutics*, 66.
75. Van Til, *New Hermeneutic*, 9.
76. Heidegger, *Metaphysics*, 84.
77. Porter and Robinson, *Hermeneutics*, 67.
78. Heidegger, *Metaphysics*, 81.

79. Heidegger, *Metaphysics*, 111ff., 203. In context, he discusses the views of Parmenides and Heraclitus (often discussed by Van Til in his own assessment of unbelieving metaphysics) and observes the unstable interplay between rationalism and irrationalism—which Heidegger sees as the problem with Greek and Western philosophy (*Metaphysics*, 178–79).

80. Van Til, *Theory of Knowledge*, 312.
81. Van Til, *New Hermeneutic*, 9–10, 41.
82. Van Til, *Theory of Knowledge*, 312–13.

not merely from a universal negative, but also from a presupposed negation, concerning the transcendent God of the Bible and any possibility of revelation from outside being-in-general.[83]

Bultmann and the new hermeneutic were significantly influenced by Heidegger's thought. Here, we move closer to predominately *textual* hermeneutics. Bultmann sought to bridge an assumed gap between the mythical thinking of the New Testament and modern man.[84] The goal is not to understand objective historical facts, but rather self-understanding and existential authenticity.[85] Prior to taking up Heidegger's hermeneutical concept of non-objectifying language about man, he adopts "the Neo-Kantian assumption that knowledge which objectifies in accordance with law is a knowledge in which *man* does the shaping and seizes the mastery."[86] He turns to Heidegger for a solution for how to talk about God without objectification. He essentially adopts a similar distinction in terms of being-in-general (ontological) and particular expressions of that being (ontic). Theology and the Bible only speak to the ontic existence—*how* to live an authentic existence, not to the fundamental structure of that existence.[87] In addition, it would seem that he only allows for a *pre*-theological understanding provided by general philosophy, not theology itself.[88] This is one main reason why he can affirm that the sacred character of the Bible does not distinguish it from other texts, for its sacredness is less ultimate than his ontological assumptions about being.[89] Only through language about *Dasein* can one avoid objectification in speaking of God, for in this way, truth is not revealed to man in order to be objectified, but rather being is revealed through man's self-understanding.[90] Perhaps indicative of this restrictive allowance is the tension resulting from his curious notion of a wholly other God who is not known through revelation in terms of this world, but is to be experienced through an event of participation which somehow transcends the limitations of objectifying language and this-worldly description—but only from *within* our existence.[91]

---

83. McCartney and Clayton, *Let the Reader*, 15–16.

84. Thiselton, *Two Horizons*, 218–19.

85. Allen, *Philosophy*, 252; Porter and Robinson, *Hermeneutics*, 232; Thiselton, *Two Horizons*, 232.

86. Thiselton, *Two Horizons*, 226 (emphasis his).

87. Soulen and Soulen, *Biblical Criticism*, 57; Porter and Robinson, *Hermeneutics*, 232.

88. Thiselton, *Two Horizons*, 228.

89. Thiselton, *Two Horizons*, 238.

90. Thiselton, *Two Horizons*, 230, 232.

91. Thiselton, *Two Horizons*, 230.

Again, this begs the question: how can we speak of this *wholly other* at all?[92] Bultmann seems to contradict his notion of the wholly other in his discussion of Paul, who he claims presents a God in relation to humanity—so much so that Paul's theology is at the same time anthropology. "Every assertion about God is simultaneously an assertion about man and vice versa."[93] Again, we have an unknowable, wholly other God, and we have a knowledge of ourselves in participation with being-in-general. Though he proposed his hermeneutic of demythologization with regard to the New Testament, in terms of the interplay between metaphysics and hermeneutics, Bultmann did not go much beyond Heidegger and Kant. He was content to adopt Heidegger's general scheme of being and adapt Christian doctrine accordingly.[94] Even his concept of demythologization contained the notion that the New Testament as myth is true existentially, but not a cosmological, external reality.[95] Indeed, he argued that "to demythologize is not to reject scripture, but . . . the *worldview* of scripture."[96] Instead, he desired a worldview in which real faith is freed from anything expressed in objective terms.[97] With Kant, he retained an ontology characterized by an unstable dualism, with God in one realm and worldly phenomena in the other.[98] Bultmann's hermeneutic allows only for a dialogue of an I-thou relationship, not of the I-it variety.[99] The former, he believes, transcends objectification. After all, Bultmann argued that, at a foundational level, the subject and the object of historical inquiry do not *exist* independently from one another.[100]

The new hermeneutic, influenced more by Heidegger's later thought, saw *all* as interpretation (hence, *hermeneutic* in the singular). This holistic approach necessarily brought epistemological and ontological concerns into the forefront.[101] Also, there is a strong emphasis in biblical interpretation on the word interpreting *us*, not us interpreting the word. This went hand-in-hand with the growing emphasis on how the Bible speaks to the

---

92. Frame, *Knowledge of God*, 14.
93. Bultmann, *Theology*, 191.
94. Porter and Robinson, *Hermeneutics*, 238–39; Thiselton, *Two Horizons*, 232.
95. Soulen and Soulen, *Biblical Criticism*, 45–46.
96. As quoted in Thiselton, *Two Horizons*, 258–59 (emphasis mine); Bultmann, *Jesus Christ*, 35–36.
97. Thiselton, *Two Horizons*, 263.
98. Thiselton, *Two Horizons*, 284–87.
99. This distinction primarily refers to that which is truly personal (existential) and transcends the subject-object relationship (I-thou), and that which is impersonal and objective in the scientific sense (I-it).
100. Bultmann, *History*, 133.
101. Ebeling, *Word and Faith*, 317.

contemporary interpreter. Ontologically, the question asked is not, *what were the facts?* or *how can we explain the facts?* but rather, *what is being mediated through them?*[102] The goal of hermeneutics is to overcome what are seen as breakdowns in language and to overcome the subject-object distinction.[103] Hermeneutics operates on a level prior to analysis involving subject-object reasoning.[104] The focus of hermeneutical inquiry is on the word or language *event*, in which there is an immediate harmony between what is spoken and what is understood, *prior* to any thought process.[105] Fuchs and Ebeling stress that this event, involving the Bible, is a communication and revealing of God's being. To put it another way, language provides the occasion for being as an event.[106] It is not an "understanding *of* language but understanding *through* language."[107] Language is the presupposition and grid for how one sees and understands being. In other words, "language is the horizon of a hermeneutic ontology."[108] When God addresses man, the Bible is not a carrier of conceptual formulations, but a *master*, which "directs us into the language-context of our existence"[109] (i.e., becoming a language event). The being communicated is not conceptual, but a call or pledge to authentic existence.[110] This event gives "voice not to a fragmented set of human concepts, but to undivided 'Being.'"[111]

Various critiques of the new hermeneutic point out flaws rooted in its assumed ontology. First, there is no criterion offered regarding the *correctness* of a given interpretation.[112] As with Heidegger and Bultmann, we are left with being revealing itself in understanding through language without a separation of subject and object. The monistic nature of this being reveals itself especially in man's self-understanding as a participant in it. In such a scheme, there is no outside standard from which to evaluate interpretation—only being becoming itself through the language event. We must just let it be, rather than evaluate it, for that would involve subject-object thinking.

---

102. Ebeling, *Word and Faith*, 295.
103. Ebeling, *Introduction*, 156–57; Krabbendam, "New Hermeneutic," 536.
104. Thiselton, *Two Horizons*, 343.
105. Ebeling, *Word and Faith*, 319; Thiselton, "New Hermeneutic," 84–85.
106. Fuchs, *Studies*, 207.
107. Ebeling, *Word and Faith*, 318 (italics mine).
108. Thiselton, *Two Horizons*, 347.
109. Fuchs, *Studies*, 211.
110. Thiselton, *Two Horizons*, 336, 344–45.
111. Thiselton, "New Hermeneutic," 94.
112. E.g., Thiselton, "New Hermeneutic," 99–101; Packer, "A Response," 567–68.

Second, man, in the language event, participates in the being of God in order to understand (supra-conceptually, that is) the being that is revealed.[113] After all, there is only one level of being acknowledged. Being is understood only through man and his self-understanding. Any theology sought after in this manner essentially reduces to anthropology.[114] Whatever is said about God is essentially self-understanding. For instance, "Jesus is known only as his language addresses *me*."[115]

Third, there is still a persistent aim to root understanding in a general ontology which is somehow prior to and transcends the subject-object relationship and speaks to the present. However, *what* is spoken? If we are not able to articulate any meaningful content or information via language, what are we left with, apart from mere self-expression? Also, while seeking the non-conceptual, non-objectifiable language event, there *is* objectification going on in the very articulation of what is considered the biblical text. Through the historical-critical method and deeming the language of Scripture as metaphysically deficient (in that it does not transcend the level of objectification), proponents of the new hermeneutic still engage in a form of objectification.[116] Once the text is determined through rational, objectifying means, then the playing field is set—on which non-objectifying events take place.[117] These two principles, objectifying and non-objectifying, correspond to the rationalistic-irrationalistic tension. The articulation of the new hermeneutic as a whole is guilty of the very objectification that it seeks to avoid. How does one articulate non-objective speech without objectifying it? Moreover, the language event sought after ceases to be meaningful in terms of communication. Whatever is communicated is a content-less and meaningless blank. This raises the question of whether personal communication can be conceived of without some sense of a subject-object distinction, at least in terms of keeping the other truly distinct from the subject. According to the new hermeneutic, though it seeks a truly personal (I-thou) understanding, it assumes a monistic notion of being with which the interpreting subject shares in order to understand through the language event. In doing so, it would seem that the interpreter actually engages in a functional monologue rather than dialogue.

Fourth, Packer points out that the new hermeneutic cannot adequately explain the relation between the historical text of Scripture and the language

---

113. Gruenler, "A Response," 577–78; Van Til, *New Hermeneutic*, 13–14.
114. Thiselton, "New Hermeneutic," 104–6.
115. Gruenler, "A Response," 578 (emphasis his).
116. Krabbendam, "New Hermeneutic," 552.
117. Krabbendam, "New Hermeneutic," 538–39, 548.

event in terms of meaning. It would seem that the only clear answer given is that it is not the text which is ultimately interpreted, but rather the interpreter, as the text is cut off from the constraints of any objective historical inquiry.[118] A related problem is the tendency of the new hermeneutic to treat the language of Scripture as independent and disengaged from the person who speaks it, whether divine or human, in terms of intentionality.[119] This is another example of assuming a deeper ontology (in this case, *language*) which is more fundamental concerning the text than its author.

Lastly, from a distinctly Christian perspective, it would seem that the new hermeneutic, assumes a Kantian metaphysic:

> God is told to produce the point of synthesis that will keep him out of his own creation, now reinterpreted in terms of the subject-object scheme, and will guarantee man's freedom, now interpreted in terms of the transcendence of the subject-object polarity.[120]

In one sense God is conceived of as wholly other and the only way in which he can reveal himself in this world is to do so without entangling himself in the "sin" of objectification, thus losing himself. Yet, in another sense, he can reveal himself through the language event, but only in a way that reveals the interpreter, not himself as God. Man meets God in his own conscience, not in terms of definite teaching and instruction. In short, man privileges himself with autonomy over both, the objective and subjective aspects of interpretation, over what can and cannot be revealed. Van Til argues that for Fuchs and Ebeling, true objectivity of faith is the *complete correlativity* of the subject and object of faith. The only alternative is each operating in complete isolation from one another. In other words, we are told to choose between exhaustive correlation and utter isolation. Faced with this ontological scheme, the new hermeneutic endorses the former as the only legitimate option in order to avoid destroying the very possibility of knowledge.

We have already introduced some of the main tenets of Gadamer, so our treatment here will be relatively brief. Our focus is more specifically on how he understood ontology in relation to hermeneutics. There are three main aspects of Gadamer's understanding of this relationship.

First, it is clear that Gadamer saw the nature of understanding as primarily ontological. The horizons he speaks of are grounded in being and their fusion is understood as an ontological disclosure of being in

---

118. Packer, "New Hermeneutic," 567.
119. Gruenler, "New Hermeneutic," 830.
120. Krabbendam, "New Hermeneutic," 554.

and through language. Though Heidegger emphasized understanding ontologically, Gadamer develops the ontology of understanding in terms of a dialogue.[121]

Second, Gadamer sets forth his particular view of metaphysics while, at the same time, self-consciously opposing a particular form of metaphysics. Namely, he is opposed to the metaphysics of Descartes and various forms of the modernist-realist school which assumes the standard subject-object model in interpretation.[122] He rejects any metaphysical traces of scientific rationalism and dogmatism stemming from the Enlightenment.[123] However, he does recognize his own affinity with Kant in that we have knowledge only as it is given in space and time. In other words, there is no vantage point outside our experience of the world through language from which that vantage point could itself become an object.[124]

Third, Gadamer's nuanced view of language especially highlights his view concerning the relationship between metaphysics and hermeneutics. Conceptually, he sees language as a universal medium through which one conceives a *world*. One doesn't manipulate language, but rather participates in it.[125] Elsewhere, Gadamer refers to language as universal being, going so far as to suggest that being is coterminous with reason and language, making it the very ground of any hermeneutical activity.[126] Hence, language is the real medium of human *being*, not merely of thought life.[127] Language is the central point where "I" and the world meet and manifest their original *unity*.[128] The nature of this linguistic being is characterized by *finitude*.[129] At the same time, he claims that, in language, the world presents itself, and that our experience of it through language is *absolute* in that it *transcends* all positing of being because it embraces all being-in-itself.[130] Though the world is not itself an object of language (because it is a participatory medium,[131] not manipulated by language as an objective tool), all objects

---

121. Palmer, *Hermeneutics*, 59, 201, 215–17; Thiselton, *Two Horizons*, 296–97.
122. Palmer, *Hermeneutics*, 223–26.
123. Gadamer, *Truth and Method*, 340; *Philosophical Hermeneutics*, 128–29.
124. Gadamer, *Truth and Method*, 410.
125. Gadamer, *Truth and Method*, 350.
126. Gadamer, *Truth and Method*, 341, 434.
127. Gadamer, *Philosophical Hermeneutics*, 68; Osborne, "Genre Criticism," 10.
128. Gadamer, *Philosophical Hermeneutics*, 81; *Truth and Method*, 431–33.
129. Gadamer, *Truth and Method*, 414–16, 433.
130. Gadamer, *Truth and Method*, 408.
131. Elsewhere, Gadamer contrasts "participatory" with "foundation" (i.e., first principles) (Gadamer, "Hermeneutics," 62–64).

CHAPTER 3: SURVEYING THE FIELD, PART II

of knowledge are enclosed within the world horizon of language.[132] From another angle, he asserts, "being that can be understood is language."[133] Interpretation is essentially the hermeneutical relation to being.[134] Perhaps one of the most significant implications of all of this is that language is *prior* to and more ultimate than the hermeneutical situation we find ourselves in when we seek to interpret a text, and prior to "any pre-given system of possibilities of being, with which signs at the disposal of the signifying subject are associated."[135] It would seem that language is prior to *any* philosophical conceptualization. Hence, language, as a general ontology of being, is the necessary presupposition of any hermeneutical activity or conceptualization. Osborne has pointed out that being and the world structure, in Gadamer's view, are also prior to authorial intent.[136]

Before moving on, it is important to highlight a significant emphasis in Gadamer's view of metaphysics which raises important questions. His concept of being is essentially *finite*—a one-level ontology, focused upon man's relationship to the world. Moreover, he says, "to be historically means that knowledge of oneself can never be complete."[137] The disclosure of this finite being through language transcends the two horizons in their fusion, resulting in an emergence of something beyond merely the language of each horizon through their very interaction.[138] This dialectical process leads to the "coming-into-language of the thing itself."[139] This raises important questions. How does meaningful transcendence emerge from finite being disclosed in the fusion of two finite horizons? How can we know that there is meaningful transcendence taking place if we are mired in finitude and lack of objectivity? On the one hand, he states that there is no scientific certainty of truth because man is a finite and prejudiced participant in the dialectical process.[140] On the other hand, he argues that language and understanding provides a universal model of being and knowledge in general, which enables us to define more closely the meaning of the truth involved in

---

132. Gadamer, *Truth and Method*, 408.

133. Gadamer, *Truth and Method*, 432. Interestingly, he argues that this is *not* a metaphysical assertion, because he is speaking not about each instance of being-in-itself, but rather how being-in-*relation* encounters man's understanding (Gadamer, *Philosophical Hermeneutics*, 103).

134. Gadamer, *Truth and Method*, 432.

135. Gadamer, *Truth and Method*, 377, 407.

136. Osborne, "Genre Criticism," 11.

137. Gadamer, *Truth and Method*, 301–2.

138. Thiselton, *Two Horizons*, 296–97, 312–13.

139. Gadamer quoted in Thiselton, *Two Horizons*, 313.

140. Gadamer, *Truth and Method*, 446.

understanding.[141] Yet, it is this very concept of truth which has come under fire for its lack of any positive content or criteria to make sense of or evaluate that which contributes to its emergence.[142] In the end, a one-level concept of being undermines his hope for any transcendence, which will lead to a progressive disclosure and understanding of truth.

Paul Ricoeur, like Gadamer, suggests that language discloses human *being*—in which participation-in or belonging-to precedes our very capacity to conceive of objects as opposed to ourselves as subject.[143] While having a general aversion to systematic theology out of a concern that it ignores the character of the biblical text, he does see hermeneutics as the long route to the promised land of ontology.[144] He states that "hermeneutics is not a reflection on the human sciences, but an explication of the ontological ground upon which these sciences can be constructed."[145] This includes his discourse with the very idea of revelation which occurs on ground more fundamental than any onto-theological articulation.[146] Ricoeur describes his own position as "post-Hegelian Kantianism"—with Kant, he respects the limits of human reason, and with Hegel, he explores reason's many forms, both figurative and conceptual.[147] It is not entirely clear where he is coming from theologically or what he sees as the central message of the Bible. However, the ultimate goal of interpretation is self-interpretation. Texts function autonomously in that they take on a life of their own once they are written. Interpretation is not so much recovering the author's intent but exploring the text's *trajectory* of meaning. In all of this, Ricoeur sees biblical hermeneutics as merely an instance of a more general hermeneutics of self-understanding. More broadly, it would seem to suggest that Christianity is just an instance of a more general and ultimate philosophy and hermeneutic.[148] Hence, Ricoeur's assumed ontology is more ultimate than Scripture and the ontologically-informing message which is conveyed in it. Theology is *before* the text, not transcending it.[149] Also ontologically significant, according to Ricoeur, is that the text is separated from its author

---

141. Gadamer, *Truth and Method*, 445.
142. Thiselton, *New Horizons*, 315–17; Bernstein, *Beyond Objectivism*, 15–52.
143. Ricoeur, *Essays*, 101.
144. Vanhoozer, "Paul Ricoeur," 692; Ricoeur, *Conflict*, 24.
145. Ricoeur, *Hermeneutics*, 55.
146. Ricoeur, *Essays*, 96.
147. Vanhoozer, *Biblical Narrative*, 7, 17; "Paul Ricoeur," 694.
148. Ricoeur, *Essays*, 104; Vanhoozer, *Biblical Narrative*, 276, 277, 282, 285; Laughery, *Living Hermeneutics*, 155.
149. Bayer, "Theology," 499–500.

and becomes autonomous in terms of meaning.[150] The Bible and other poetic texts reveal the "transcendent" in that they project worlds which open possible ways of being in the world (not merely the self-expression of the author)—which, if appropriated, can transform the world of the reader.[151] Transcendent, here, merely means finite *possibility*. Elsewhere, Ricoeur says that "a text is a *finite* space of interpretations."[152] In sum, his notion of ontology and hermeneutics is reminiscent of both Heidegger and Gadamer in that he seeks to preserve a notion of transcendence, yet it is ultimately undermined by a metaphysical finitude.

Ricoeur has positively contributed to the growing awareness of the literary dimension of texts and how it contributes to a more nuanced appreciation for the fullness of meaning. He also provides somewhat of a corrective to Heidegger and Gadamer's ontological bent, which tended to circumvent the actual text.[153] However, the lack of ontological transcendence from which to objectively conceive of a text and its meaning do not alleviate the anchor-less subjectivity he seeks to avoid. For example, his concept of a text having a surplus of meaning ("plurivocal"), which is not ascertained by scientific exegesis but through imagination and practical wisdom, is problematic.[154] Where does the surplus of meaning come from and what is its foundation for intelligibility? Does it originate internally or externally to the text?[155] Even if a text is *about something*, how can one achieve meaningful objectivity about this "something" when there is a surplus of meaning without a clear means of evaluation concerning compatibility with such projected probabilities coming out of the text? He seems to suggest "logical probabilities" and "textual intention" as criteria to be used in evaluating the validity of interpretive possibilities, but where does he locate his authority which defines these criteria—if they come from outside the text, not from the author?[156] Laughery sees no absolute certainty or uncertainty of meaning in Ricoeur's thought.[157] Likewise, Palmer says that Ricoeur holds to no ultimate standards for exegesis and only sees separate and opposing theories concerning the rules of interpretation.[158] It would seem that he sees the

---

150. Vanhoozer, *Is There?*, 107, 214, 215; Gillespie, "Biblical Authority," 201–2.
151. Vanhoozer, "Paul Ricoeur," 693; Paul Ricoeur, *Interpretation Theory*, 92.
152. Ricoeur, "World of Text," 496 (emphasis mine).
153. Laughery, *Living Hermeneutics*, 152–53.
154. Stiver, "Paul Ricoeur," 866.
155. Porter and Robinson, *Hermeneutics*, 121.
156. Porter and Robinson, *Hermeneutics*, 125–27.
157. Laughery, *Living Hermeneutics*, 150.
158. Palmer, *Hermeneutics*, 43–44.

need for ontological consideration in hermeneutics, but disengages it from the author, embeds it into the text, assuming an ambiguous ontological finitude along the way. We are left with persistent questions regarding issues of transcendence, criteria, and objectivity. Meaning is always *approaching*, but it lacks ultimate proof and coherence.[159]

The last main figure[160] we will look at, before moving on to those in the broad evangelical camp, is Derrida, who in many ways is even more elusive than Heidegger. Whereas, for Heidegger, metaphysics became something he could speak less definitely about over time, Derrida seeks to erase the notion altogether.[161] However, he does frequently discuss the role of metaphysics in Western thought. His treatment is largely negative, yet has a significant bearing on his view of hermeneutics. Though his views have had significant implications for hermeneutics, Derrida himself would not call them *hermeneutical* per se, because that would imply there is meaning to be recovered through it.[162] He denounced what he called "logocentrism"—a term encompassing philosophical preoccupation with language (especially written) as the carrier of meaning. This is connected to what he calls the "metaphysics of presence"—the assumption that there is at the foundation of language, a presence, being, or essence which we can come to know.[163] Going beyond structuralism's assertion that there is no *necessary* connection between words and what they signify, Derrida argues that language does *not* refer to objective reality.[164] Rather, meaning is the product of the interpreter's free play with signs (or words) merely pointing to other signs. Hence, meaning is always deferred, incomplete, and uncertain, without grounding.[165] There is no access to "a stable, self-authenticating knowledge."[166] There is

159. Ricoeur, *Essays*, 152–53.

160. Though not considered here, Wittgenstein, for all of his creative contributions, does not progress ontologically beyond his predecessors. His emphasis on language and its relation to human existence and use suggests a one-level, finite reality. Like Kant, any reference beyond this is inexpressible and unknowable (Thiselton, *Two Horizons*, 357–438 [378–79]).

161. Thiselton, *New Horizons*, 106–10.

162. Carson, *Gagging of God*, 73n52.

163. Grenz, *A Primer*, 141.

164. Carson, *Gagging of God*, 72–73.

165. Porter and Robinson, *Hermeneutics*, 203, 205. Postmodernity also emphasizes the contextual character of knowledge, yet when it comes to hermeneutics, there is an inconsistency revealing a marked agenda. For instance, decontextualizing often takes place when considering particular biblical passages (e.g., Derrida, "Des Tours," 3–34), but contextualizing when considering the Bible in the context of extra-biblical writings (e.g., Aichele, Miscall, and Walsh, "An Elephant," 403).

166. Norris as quoted in Bartholomew, "Post/Late Modernity," 30.

no transcendental signified or signifier.[167] He is opposed to notions of God's being and created beings. In particular, he rejects the *theological* nature of metaphysics.[168] Yet, a distinct recognition of something wholly other still seems to pervade his work.[169] Though metaphysical assumptions cannot be entirely avoided, neither are they to be rightly accepted, for "there is no metaphysical concept in and for itself."[170] He seeks to show how such assumptions break down, involving a subversion of dogmatic binary descriptions and oppositions (always one correct truth and always a false one), showing that it is impossible to draw a clear line between reality and representations of it.[171] Almost by default, Derrida and many postmodern thinkers absolutize language as the most fundamental aspect of reality, yet a language without ground or meaning beyond itself.[172]

We see in Derrida a self-conscious attempt to deny metaphysical realities in connection with a text in opposition to those who would define meaning in a rationalistic or univocal way (focused on the author, text, or reader)—what he sees as characteristic of traditional Western metaphysics.[173] However, he uncritically makes ontological assumptions of his own along the way. In doing so, he engages in a form of *replacement* metaphysics.[174] Derrida admits that one cannot critique metaphysics without metaphysical categories.[175] First, he rationalistically asserts his own form of irrationalism. This has been the unavoidable critique of Derrida and others who suggest that the ultimate meaning of texts is that they don't have ultimate meaning. Second, though suggesting that language is absolute, he claims an autonomous omniscience for himself (as absolute?) in declaring this to be the case, making a universal negative truth claim. Third, he assumes an otherness which cannot be known or reduced (e.g., through a fusion of horizons). Again, this is an assumption about the nature of reality and communication. He seems to emphasize otherness while also suggesting a common ground of sorts as the context for further deconstruction.[176] Fourth, he assumes that there is no

---

167. Derrida, *Of Grammatology*, 49; Osborne, *Hermeneutical Spiral*, 482.

168. Ingraffia, "Ontotheology," 286; Bartholomew, "Babel and Derrida," 311, 322.

169. Porter and Robinson, *Hermeneutics*, 193, 195; Osborne, *Hermeneutical Spiral*, 483.

170. Derrida, "Signature Event Context," 329.

171. Porter and Robinson, *Hermeneutics*, 199; Grenz, *A Primer*, 148.

172. Bartholomew, "Post /Late Modernity," 30–31.

173. Goldsworthy, *Gospel-Centered*, 164.

174. This is similar to Lyotard's penchant for metanarrative replacement under the guise of being opposed to the very idea of it (Edgar, "No News," 374, 378–79).

175. Derrida, *Of Grammatology*, 19.

176. Porter and Robinson, *Hermeneutics*, 208.

intelligible interpretation accessible for the gap that he claims exists between the sign and the thing signified. If that is so, why believe such a gap even exists? Moreover, does a difference between the sign and the thing signified demand an unintelligible gap which has no real connection at all and if so, why? Fifth, he seems to include biblical metaphysics in the "metaphysics of presence" as he calls it, not recognizing the significant differences that exist between the stream of Western philosophy in general and what is found in Scripture regarding metaphysics. Lastly, in assuming the ultimate context of reality as language, he precludes any consideration or possibility of a revelatory text which could inform the nature and function of language. The reader's worldview is ultimate in the interpretation of a text, regardless of the worldview of its author or previous readers. Essentially, the motive here is primarily a pragmatic one.[177] He takes Gadamer to task for his inconsistencies and pushes his ideas to their logical end.[178] However, Derrida does not escape inconsistencies of his own, especially in the area of metaphysics. He assumes something to be deconstructed, telling us what is *not* rather than what *is*. His emphasis on ambiguity and possibility under the guise of being open to the *other* may be merely an unwillingness to listen to the other.

Summary

It may be expedient to summarize some of the main points of continuity among the thinkers discussed. Three particular observations demand our attention. First, the love-hate relationship with metaphysics is evidenced in hating a particular *form* of traditional metaphysics (i.e., Greek-influenced Enlightenment rationalism), but loving in the sense of making unavoidable metaphysical assumptions, regardless of the level of confidence in establishing a formal ontology. Second, a general finite ontology is assumed which is *prior* to any text under consideration. This is significant when it comes to biblical interpretation. It precludes the very possibility of any *biblical* ontology. Third, a need for transcendence is recognized (e.g., to get beyond the subject-object distinction), but undermined by merely locating it in the *same* stream of ontology in general—be it history, being, language, or some other concept. A one-level reality does not provide meaningful understanding because there is no transcendent reference point from which to make

---

177. Greene labels this as an "ontological gap" by which the postmodernist is cut off from the past so that the only way to conceive of the past is through current ideological and epistemological preferences—an enterprise which is necessarily anachronistic (Greene, "In Arms," 235).

178. Porter and Robinson, *Hermeneutics*, 207.

sense of particulars. Frame sums up the dilemma concerning the subject-object distinction in terms of transcendence and immanence:

> Non-Christian philosophers have been utterly unsuccessful at maintaining a workable balance here. It seems either that the world is something utterly alien to the self, so alien that it can hardly be known or spoken of ("transcendence"), or that it is identical to the self, so that there is no world to speak of, only self ("immanence"). Some, in desperation, seek a special kind of knowledge that allegedly 'transcends the subject-object distinction,' but they are unable to state coherently what that knowledge is or how it is to be obtained. Their claim is essentially a claim to know the unknowable, to achieve, by a mystical leap, access to the transcendence that is unknowable by ordinary means.[179]

This highlights the unstable mix of rational and irrational elements present in the figures surveyed above.

Metaphysics and Evangelical Hermeneutics

Have evangelicals faired any better? How have they conceived of the relationship between metaphysics and hermeneutics? Sontag bluntly states that "biblical study needs . . . a metaphysical inquiry."[180] If evangelicals are to engage with the shifting definition of hermeneutics, this is certainly true. With regard to biblical exegesis, Bartholomew rightly asserts that "there is always a philosophical subtext . . . Notions of ontology, epistemology and anthropology inevitably shape biblical interpretation. The only question is *how* they shape interpretation."[181] How does the *Bible* speak to these philosophical categories? Notwithstanding the earlier comment from Noll regarding the predominant lack of self-conscious ontological awareness, evangelical hermeneutics has largely operated with an *assumed* ontology. The following is a brief sample of how some have engaged with metaphysics, whether self-consciously or not.

Hirsch's work still has widespread appeal among many evangelicals concerned with anchoring meaning in human authorial intent.[182] However, there is little attention paid to certain ontological assumptions which are

---

179. Frame, *Knowledge of God*, 70.
180. Sontag, "Metaphysics," 189.
181. Bartholomew, "Uncharted Waters," 24.
182. E.g., Kunjummen, "Single Intent," 81–110; Kaiser, *Exegetical Theology*, 33–34; "Meaning of Meaning," 42–45; "Legitimate Hermeneutics," 111–41; Fair, "Disciplines," 34–35; White, *What is Truth?*, 193–96; Virkler, *Hermeneutics*, 23–24, 158.

uncritically adopted in the process. By his own admission, Hirsch not only treats the Bible like any other text (i.e., without consideration for the role of the divine author), but seeks definite, objective meaning in the human author, yet on the basis of ultimate uncertainty and probability.[183] This notion is often seen in evangelical hermeneutics. For instance, after affirming Hirsch's distinction between meaning and significance, Flatt discusses the role of presuppositions in biblical interpretation and offers a set of assumptions he finds to be fit for the task. Among these is "a sound attitude of objectivity"—i.e., good mental health and the equally ambiguous idea that one "should not make any exegetical conclusions with more certitude than are supported by his knowledge."[184] One should also assume the *possibility* of God's existence.[185] Inconsistently, in seeking objectivity, Flatt ends up proposing a hermeneutic of uncertainty which undermines clear biblical affirmations to the contrary. As Palmer has pointed out (in addition to the probability issue), Hirsch's approach tends toward a "scientific reductionism," including assumptions about the nature of things involved in his pursuit of validity (e.g., nature of meaning, language, validity, and understanding), not to mention his problematic notion of timeless objectivity in meaning as rooted in an *historical* author and understood by an *historical* reader.[186] Insightfully and a bit ironically, Palmer points out that Hirsch treats hermeneutics as a general theory of interpretation based on Aristotelian presuppositions which end up being just as *dangerous* to theology as those theories Hirsch opposes in his book.[187] To be fair, Hirsch and his followers often do not discuss their metaphysical assumptions. However, questions should be raised concerning them in interpretation.

Thomas and others have emphasized a strict grammatical-historical method which downplays the consideration of philosophical categories. First, Thomas explicitly argues for withholding the analogy of faith until the exegetical task is finished. This inevitably raises the question, if deeper assumptions are being made about reality, what is being presupposed, if not a doctrinally-informed ontology? What is being assumed in even making the interpretive move to suspend the analogy of faith in the first place? While not overtly arguing a particular ontology, Thomas betrays certain curious assumptions. For instance, he states that "neutral objectivity originates with the Creator of all things and is available through the

---

183. Hirsch, *Validity*, ix, 14–19, 164, 173, 223.
184. Flatt, "Function of Presuppositions," 60–61.
185. Flatt, "Function of Presuppositions," 69.
186. Palmer, Review, 243–34.
187. Palmer, Review, 245–46.

illumination of the Holy Spirit."[188] Are we to understand that God himself is *neutral* with respect to interpretative possibilities? In the same context, he suggests that a "Kantian dialecticism may be necessary in other realms," but the interpretation of divine revelation demands a correspondence of reality between the objective and subjective realms.[189] Is this consistent? In arguing for a stringent single-sense meaning of a text, he says "meaning is static and locked up in the past."[190] He claims that all that is needed for biblical hermeneutics is grammar, history, and derived common sense.[191] Each of these statements must be evaluated in terms of larger philosophical assumptions to avoid unbiblical notions.

Some have focused, with varying degrees of strictness, on the historical-critical method.[192] Sparks' practical realism epistemology seems to assume an unstable mixture of modernist and postmodernist elements—an epistemology which seeks a certainty based on human probability and pragmatic concerns. While God does not err, his relation to interpreters of Scripture is one of *adequacy* not inerrancy (either in revealing from his side or interpreting from ours).[193] On the more conservative side of the spectrum, Blomberg argues for a combination of complementary approaches, but prefers the foundational *priority* of the historical method.[194] Moreover, he endorses a "critical realism" which would seem to imply the priority of historical verification methods which are more functionally ultimate than the truths revealed in Scripture in terms of authority.[195] What if history is rooted in God, who transcends and is distinct from it? For without divine ontological and epistemological grounding, the best historical methods prove only probabilities. Blomberg claims to have shorn his method of its anti-supernaturalism,[196] but the question remains as to what exactly it has been replaced with.

Others, from a more distinctly philosophical perspective, have acknowledged the need for ontological grounding. According to one writer, the function of the text is to link the *real* author and *real* reader in terms of

---

188. Thomas, *Evangelical Hermeneutics*, 53.
189. Thomas, *Evangelical Hermeneutics*, 54–55.
190. Thomas, *Evangelical Hermeneutics*, 143.
191. Thomas, *Evangelical Hermeneutics*, 155.
192. For a more balanced endorsement see: Harrisville, *Pandora's Box*.
193. Sparks, *God's Word*, 53–55.
194. Blomberg, "Historical-Critical," 28, 41.
195. Klein, Blomberg, and Hubbard, *Introduction*, 162–63, 167; Blomberg, *Historical Reliability*, 35.
196. Blomberg, "Historical-Critical," 46.

the *real* world in which they find themselves.[197] However, the question is how "real" is defined and according to what authority. Some, like Corduan, suggest adding a generic theistic worldview as a deeper dimension in order to ground hermeneutics and transcend the historical—one which does not necessarily take into account the "entire set of Christian beliefs" or inspiration.[198] This general approach, hesitant to affirm that there is a distinctly Christian ontology to be found in Scripture, is not uncommon. For example, Hasker cites Alfred Whitehead in favor of his point that Christianity is a religion of salvation, not a metaphysical system. In his opinion, the search for a definitive Christian metaphysic has failed.[199] Johnson seeks to provide ontological grounding via what he calls the "Transcendental Thomist" school of Wilhem Coreth. He argues that a comprehensive horizon must ground all the particulars involved in the hermeneutical situation, which he concludes is the "world." "Hermeneutics transcends itself insofar as the openness to being is the transcendental ground of all understanding of the world, history, and language."[200] Being-in-general (or "totality of being") is that which transcends the particulars, making understanding possible. Others see an approximation of this grounding in an eclectic blend of various ontological and epistemological perspectives. For example, Porter and Robinson conclude their work on hermeneutics by recommending that we not rely on opposing absolute categories (e.g., foundationalism or anti-foundationalism), but rather we must combine aspects of different approaches into a sort of hybrid which will overcome false mutual exclusivism.[201] However, one must ask whether there are deeper, more systemic flaws which pervade and transgress such "absolute" categorical boundaries. If so, any combination, no matter how eclectic and multi-faceted, will only complicate matters. Yarbrough rightly observes that many of the major contemporary forms of hermeneutical approaches assume human autonomy and a denial of the special relevance of inspired revelation. Any synthesis will presuppose a certain view of God.[202] Westphal seems to suggest *adding* a consideration of special hermeneutics to Gadamer's general (de-regionalized) hermeneutics, "without presupposing any particular theory of inspiration."[203] In other words, he assumes compatibility between the

197. Lategan, "Reference," 75.
198. Corduan, "Philosophical Presuppositions," 509–11.
199. Hasker, *Metaphysics*, 20, 23, 119–22.
200. Johnson, "Philosophical Presuppositions," 530.
201. Porter and Robinson, *Hermeneutics*, 302–3.
202. Yarbrough, "Variation," 451–52.
203. Westphal, "Philosophical/Theological," 86.

two.[204] He emphasizes the finitude of the reader to such a degree that error in interpretation is linked with it. His ultimate grounding which guards against sheer relativism is the community of readers, which inevitably leads to a probable and pragmatic interpretation.[205] It appears that all we are left with is fallen interpretations of the voice of God.

Those who generally see postmodern developments as helpful to the church often remain entangled in similar metaphysical issues that we identified in secular philosophy. David Tracy sees hermeneutics (including theology) taking place in a merely horizontal dialogue, with understanding rooted in *human* thought and existence according to secular standards of knowledge.[206] Even if the conversation is extended across disciplines and societies, it is still finite and more consumed with demythologizing modernist assumptions than it is with providing its own solutions.[207] Grenz, in his reaction to what he calls evangelical "propositionalism," has endorsed a norm for theology which includes Scripture *and* tradition and culture, providing an indirect commentary on metaphysics in terms of authority.[208] McKnight introduces a dichotomy between "absolute" and "relational" meaning, as well as an emphasis on the impossibility of objective *and* historical truth.[209] Perhaps, more directly problematic is his insistence that God must be defined *not* in relation to himself, but rather "in terms of dynamic relationship—*just as* self and world."[210] Raschke, like Bultmann, pits knowing *about* God against interacting with him personally, introducing a problematic dichotomy. "The Bible is the supreme text for the 'overcoming' of metaphysics and of ontotheology."[211] In other words, personal interaction trumps metaphysics, which he sees as inherently impersonal and propositional. Emphasizing the role of narrative, Roth argues for what he calls "story ontology" (reality as story) in order to account for the plurality evident in history and to avoid the impersonal ontological abstractions of older points of view. However, this story ontology is more ultimate than even the triune God and his relationship to the world.[212]

204. Westphal, *Whose Community?*, 120.
205. Shannon, "His Community," 421–22, 424.
206. Carson, *Gagging of God*, 80; Tracy, *Blessed Rage*.
207. E.g., Moore, *Literary Criticism*, 173–78.
208. Carson, *Gagging of God*, 481; Kurka, "Before 'Foundationalism,'" 145–65.
209. Mcknight, *Post-Modern Use*, 22–23, 59.
210. Mcknight, *Post-Modern*, 266 (emphasis mine).
211. Raschke, *Next Reformation*, 139.
212. Roth, "Theological Fantasy," 258–68.

Perhaps more directly than others who have been receptive to postmodern developments, Smith seeks to deal with the relationship between hermeneutics and metaphysics. He insightfully treats interpretation as a not a postlapsarian phenomenon, but as a good creational task prior to the fall.[213] Though rightly seeking to avoid equating finitude with fallenness, he ends up saying that it is never a sin to misinterpret because it is a finitude issue—each interpretive judgment is a kind of uncertain leap of faith (similar to Derrida and Kierkegaard).[214] God's role in interpretation is apparently dismissed from Smith's treatment as an example of seeking an improper immediacy (i.e., God's perfect interpretation). He takes issue with Lints, who argues that Scripture itself is God's immediate pre-interpretation given to man in mediate form.[215] Smith claims that there is no available metanarrative or God's eye view of things. Rather, invoking Heidegger's concept of *Dasein*, he argues that every interpretation is *of this world*.[216] While he seeks to interpret according to the nature of what is being interpreted, with subjectivity and plurality of finite interpretive possibilities, his object is no greater than this world. This poses a problem when dealing with a book which claims divine authorship.[217]

Francke emphasizes aspects of postmodernity's critique of modern foundationalism in terms of hermeneutics of suspicion and finitude in search of a reforming approach to interpretation, yet still keeps with Reformed tradition.[218] However, in doing so, he ends up caught in a dialogue between the gospel and culture in which the dialogue informs *both*, and provides the normative witness for the hermeneutical trajectories of confessional doctrine.[219] One is left wondering what role the author (especially God) has in the process. Besides oversimplifying matters, Francke has surreptitiously introduced his own metanarrative—namely, the collapse of metanarratives, claiming an even more ultimate and *transcendent* point of view.[220] His stance seems to deny the standard locus of authority in the Reformed tradition, and also paint

---

213. Smith, *Fall of Interpretation*, 21–23, 148.

214. Smith, *Fall of Interpretation*, 156–58. Curiously, he conceives of *finitude*, not in relation to God as an infinite being, but rather in terms of human situatedness and difference (i.e., on a horizontal level).

215. Incidentally, Smith also takes issue with the Chicago statement on hermeneutics (article XIX) regarding this point (*Fall of Interpretation*, 54–56); Lints, *Fabric of Theology*, 264, 269, 279.

216. Smith, *Fall of Interpretation*, 170–71.

217. For a critique of Smith's ideas, see Poirier, "Why," 175–84.

218. Francke, "Reforming Theology," 1–12.

219. Francke, "Reforming Theology," 19–20, 24–25.

220. Trueman, "Ain't Necessarily So," 315.

the conservative Reformed epistemological tradition in rationalistic colors.[221] He projects a sense of ontological agnosticism which demands elaboration especially in light of his strong assertions.

Recent Developments in Evangelical Hermeneutics

Two recent developments in evangelical hermeneutics have provided a helpful corrective to the current landscape, especially as it relates to metaphysics. By "recent developments," we certainly do not mean the genesis of such trends, but rather their increasing influence in recent decades. We will simply provide a brief overview of each and their relevance for the subject at hand.

Speech-Act Theory

First, *speech-act theory* (SAT) has provided linguistic categories which bring the author back into focus in terms of meaning and what is being *done* through texts. Its initial proponents, Austin and Searle, identified three kinds of linguistic acts: locutions (saying words), illocutions (what we do with what we say—e.g., issue a command), and perlocutions (what we bring about by saying something—e.g., obedience to a command).[222] These categories highlight the speaker or author as the one *doing* things with words. Austin and Searle see meaning as grounded in the speech-act, rather than merely in the word or sentence. It is this very aspect of *doing* which is often neglected and opposed by those who would ground meaning in something other than the author.[223] Actually, each of the three main linguistic acts corresponds to the three main elements involved in hermeneutics: author, text, and reader.[224] Hence, each is recognized without the process being reduced down to any one element.

Many evangelical scholars have adopted versions of basic speech act theory,[225] often to rescue the role of the author in the midst of postmodern influences.[226] Out of an apologetic concern to affirm that God indeed *speaks*,

---

221. Francke, "Reforming Theology," 10–12.
222. See Austin, *How to*; Searle, *Speech Acts*; *Expression*.
223. Vanhoozer, *Is There?*, 209.
224. Goldsworthy, *Gospel-Centered*, 215.
225. Others have combined SAT and Relevance theory, emphasizing that any speech act is an utterance with a *context* (e.g., Brown, *Scripture*, 35–38).
226. Blue, "Meaning, Intention," 162–63; Briggs, *Words in Action*; Watson, *Text, Church*.

Wolterstorff endorses SAT as a way to do justice to both the human and divine elements of Scripture.[227] However, he succumbs to a two-level hermeneutic, bordering on a division of the human and divine, in which methodological assumptions respective to each seem different and incompatible with one another.[228] Though he believes certain safeguards exist, he admits ultimate uncertainty concerning *what* God actually said or did not say.[229]

Thiselton, like Wolterstorff, prefers "authorial discourse" over "authorial intention" in order to avoid the intentional fallacy.[230] However, he is more nuanced in his use of SAT for biblical interpretation, often articulating it alongside insights from Gadamer and Wittgenstein. In general, SAT highlights that it is not merely information that is communicated in Scripture, but there is also a *performative* force.[231] While arguing for a spectrum of illocutionary acts (from weak to strong), he sees *promise* as a key illocution.[232] Ontologically, things are not quite as explicit. He at least endorses a hermeneutic which theologically steers clear of what he sees as the trappings of modernism and postmodernism (i.e., neither foundationalist nor anti-foundationalist), while also doing justice to the historical horizons involved. He also endorses a concept of "proper basicality" in epistemology as expounded by Wolterstorff and Plantinga.[233] However, his work tends toward a *this*-world emphasis, leaving many metaphysical questions unanswered.

Timothy Ward provides a helpful corrective to this tendency in his attempt to describe the nature of the relationship between God and Scripture using SAT. He argues that God is present personally and semantically in Scripture.[234] In particular, it is the triune God who uses the Bible to *perform* actions (Heb 4:12).[235] "In philosophical terms, there is an ontological relationship between God and his words. It seems that God's actions, including his verbal actions, are a kind of extension of him."[236] In God's verbal actions, we encounter God *himself* in action.[237] He also highlights the fact that

---

227. Wolterstorff, "Promise of Speech," 73–90; "Importance of Hermeneutics," 25–47; *Divine Discourse*.

228. Childs, "Speech Act Theory," 387–88; Barker, "Divine Illocutions," 1–14.

229. Childs, "Speech Act Theory," 387.

230. Thiselton, "Speech-Act Theory," 97–110.

231. Thiselton, *First Epistle*, 52; *Two Horizons*, 437.

232. Thiselton, "Communicative Action," 223, 231–38.

233. Thiselton, "Communicative Action," 212–13.

234. Ward, *Words of Life*, 65–66.

235. Ward, *Words of Life*, 12, 49.

236. Ward, *Words of Life*, 31.

237. Ward, *Words of Life*, 95.

God's speech-acts are *covenantal* in nature, having important interpersonal implications. For instance, to separate a person (e.g., God) from his words is an attack on that person. What one does with the *words* of the speaker, one does to the *speaker*.[238] Ward also suggests that the goal in preaching is to reenact the *original* speech-act that the Holy Spirit performed in the original authoring of the text.[239]

Vanhoozer has probably done the most in recent years to incorporate SAT into a theological hermeneutic. First, he slightly modifies the standard speech-act categories by adding a fourth type of act—*interlocutionary*. The interlocutionary dimension recognizes that "language is the means of social interaction through messages."[240] Hence, human agents are not wholly determined by language, but rather use it to communicate, responsibly or not. This highlights the *covenantal* nature of communicative actions, involving both propositional and interpersonal elements. This speaks to the tendency of some to see the two in an either/or dichotomy. Second, *triune* communication seen in Scripture reveals the ultimate paradigm for the nature of human communication,[241] bringing the doctrine of the Trinity into the hermeneutical discussion. Third, he sees interpretation and understanding as involving the recognition of authorial intentions and illocutionary acts. The Spirit is active in the process, not producing new illocutions, but illuminating ones *already* in text.[242] This approach avoids pitting personal communication against the use of verbal propositions (i.e., *people* do things with propositions).[243] Fourth, he stresses the *canonical* level of speech-acts. What *God* is doing in Scripture is seen most clearly in the canonical context. The Bible, as a whole, is also a communicative act of God. This multifaceted act is centered upon Christ, his primary illocutionary act, and the bringing about union with Christ by the Holy Spirit (perlocution).[244] Vanhoozer does justice to the three main elements in communication through his brand of Trinitarian SAT: author, text, and reader—without reducing hermeneutical concerns only to one.

Though many have acknowledged the positive influence of speech-act theory, some have pointed out weaknesses pertaining to its use in

---

238. Ward, *Words of Life*, 36, 60, 63.

239. Ward, *Words of Life*, 162.

240. Vanhoozer, *Is There?*, 219.

241. Vanhoozer, *Is There?*, 456.

242. Vanhoozer, *Drama of Doctrine*, 67.

243. Vanhoozer, "A Person?," 56.

244. Vanhoozer, *Drama of Doctrine*, 16, 68, 193; *First Theology*, 203. Some see speech-act theory as a better tool in appreciating divine authorship and meaning than *sensus plenior* (e.g., Barker, "Speech Act Theory," 227–39).

hermeneutics. I will briefly list three which pertain to the issue of metaphysics. First, in an interesting exchange with Searle, Derrida insightfully points out that there is no determinative foundation for establishing the intent and context of a speech-act of an author.[245] Searle denies one must choose between certainty and Derrida's relativism. Vanhoozer, citing Thiselton, concludes that "our knowledge of text acts may not be founded on *metaphysical* certainties, but that does not mean that it has no basis at all."[246] Again, we see a problematic defense of determinative meaning. Derrida rightly recognizes that there must be a certain ground of meaning somewhere if we are to assert meaning (with any level of determination) anywhere. Otherwise, relativism inevitably creeps in and chips away at *any* certainty. Vanhoozer's conclusion raises questions about the possibility of metaphysical grounding of our knowledge of the Bible. Is there such grounding to be found? If so, where?

Second, Poythress points out certain limitations of SAT. One danger is *de-contextualizing* a text due to the selective attention to human acts and their complexity (let alone that of the divine author). The very move to start with atomistic propositions is a de-contextualizing move. The context of a speech-act includes not only the complexity of the speaker, but also of the environment in which they speak, involving history and ultimately God who rules it. Larger blocks of discourse only complicate matters further in terms of classification. Strictly applying SAT can prove to be reductionistic and lead to allowing its categories to become the basis on which metaphysics is built.[247] Perhaps more problematic is the ideal of complete knowledge lurking in Searle's work. Often, the human speaker is invested with God-like transcendence and control over language use and meaning. The speech-act interpreter assumes such control and clarity on behalf of the author in seeking to understand a text.[248] In sum, its reductionistic tendencies and failure to capture the complexities of human personhood, let alone God, fail to provide a transcendental ground for what it seeks to understand. We need something more for there to be "a transcendent adjudication of truth."[249]

Third, many evangelical adherents of SAT also assume Hirsch's distinction between meaning and significance,[250] Plantinga's epistemology,[251]

---

245. Vanhoozer, *Is There?*, 211.

246. Vanhoozer, *Is There?*, 211 (italics mine).

247. Poythress, "Canon and Speech," 338–39, 345–46, 349–52; Poythress, *Redeeming Philosophy*, 255.

248. Poythress, "Canon and Speech," 348.

249. Poythress, "Canon and Speech," 353–54.

250. E.g., Vanhoozer argues that meaning corresponds to illocution and significance to perlocution (*Is There?*, 261).

251. E.g., Wolterstorff, Thiselton, and Vanhoozer.

and a form of "critical realism."[252] Space does not permit a discussion of these influences. However, the question should be raised as to how they inform the use of SAT in terms of metaphysical presuppositions. Can these assumptions be allowed to stand? For example, Vanhoozer defaults to Hirsch's secular view of meaning, rooted in the human author and distinct from significance, leaving us with the feeling that stable and controlled meaning can be found in the human author *apart* from considering the divine author.[253] It seems that important theological foundations are left in the background and their implications left unexplored.

Theological Interpretation

Second, *theological interpretation of Scripture* (TIS) has been receiving more attention in recent years. Due to emphasis on divine authorship, there is overlap among proponents of SAT and TIS. Daniel Treier argues that Christians have always been engaged in hermeneutics theologically—that is, the Bible was read as the authoritative word of God. To interpret Scripture is to encounter *God*.[254] Vanhoozer defines TIS as reading for the theological significance for the community of the faithful as opposed to merely imposing a theological system or general hermeneutic on the text or any reductionistic preoccupation with the world behind, of, or in front of the text.[255] While there is no one standard definition or method,[256] certain core values are evident.[257] It has a governing interest in *God*—to hear his word and be changed by it. This, of course, assumes that God speaks in and through the biblical text. Vanhoozer explains:

> God must not be an afterthought in biblical interpretation. God is not simply a function of a certain community's interpretive interest; instead, God is prior to both the community and the biblical texts themselves. A properly theological criticism will

252. Vanhoozer, *Is There?*, 299–303, 322–23.

253. Poythress, Review of Vanhoozer, 128.

254. Treier, *Theological Interpretation*, 12–13; Zimmerman, *Recovering*. Though beyond the aim of this present chapter, many proponents acknowledge the influence of Karl Barth in shaping contemporary expressions of theological interpretation, though not without critical consideration (Treier, *Theological Interpretation*, 14–20; Burnett, *Theological Exegesis*; Wood, *Barth's Theology*; Vanhoozer, "A Person?," 26–59; Provence, "Sovereign Subject," 241–62; Madueme, "Theological Interpretation," 143–56; Torrance, *Karl Barth*, 116).

255. Vanhoozer, "Introduction," 19–20.

256. Moberly, "What is?," 162–63.

257. Hays, "Reading the Bible," 5–21.

therefore seek to do justice to the priority of God. One way to do so is to guard against idols: images of God manufactured by interpretive communities.[258]

The nature of God and his relation to the world lies behind what TIS seeks to recover—the Bible's own governing purpose.[259] Non-Trinitarian hermeneutical approaches tend to give priority to historical knowledge as an omniscient determiner of theological truth.[260] TIS seeks to interpret according to the *intent* and *content* of Scripture.[261] The key is to avoid what Leithart describes as detaching the message from the medium, which in effect, muzzles the message itself.[262] This tendency is often seen in seeking to understand the words of the text through a lens foreign to its message. Rather, the Bible should be read according to the *rule of faith* (i.e., doctrinal summary of the Bible's story and God as triune).[263] This rule of faith dovetails with Scripture being analogous with itself and "cannot be forced to correspond in analogy to some extra-biblical subject matter, norm, criterion, motif, or interpretation of reality."[264] TIS recognizes that we must utilize certain theological presuppositions from the message of Scripture in order to interpret it. Moreover, the interpreter is in dialogue with the text so that not only are presuppositions conformed to Scripture, but there is also a holistic and restorative transformation that progressively takes place in the interpreter by the Holy Spirit. Another core value is discerning the human and divine discourse in *canonical* context.[265] In particular, attention is paid to the *final form* of the canonical text.[266] In addition, with its attention on the divine author, TIS focuses on how Scripture is *not* like other human writings.[267] Lastly, there is an emphasis on following the way of *biblical wisdom* (vs. human wisdom).[268] This leads to a more holistic approach—one which takes into account ontology, epistemology, *and* ethics.

---

258. Vanhoozer, "Introduction," 22.

259. Vanhoozer, "Exegesis and Hermeneutics," 63.

260. Donfried, "Alien Hermeneutics," 20–21.

261. Vanhoozer, "Introduction," 22; Green, "Scripture and Theology," 19.

262. Leithart, *Deep Exegesis*, 34.

263. Treier, *Theological Interpretation*, 57–70; Green, "Practicing Gospel," 394, 397.

264. Preus, "Unity," 684.

265. Vanhoozer, "Imprisoned or Free?," 71; Thompson, "Scripture, Christian Canon," 253–72.

266. Vanhoozer, "Introduction," 23.

267. Watson, "Authors, Readers," 119.

268. Treier, *Virtue*.

The main appeal of TIS is threefold. First, it seeks to provide a biblical corrective to hermeneutical methods foreign to the message of Scripture (e.g., a general, more ultimate theory of textual meaning)—modern *and* postmodern varieties. This avoids adding theological concerns to non-theological grounds.[269] Indeed, this is contrary to viewing the facts of Scripture as distinct from theology, as if they were theologically uninformed.[270] Second, it highlights the nature of God and his relation to the world, including the rule of faith as guiding presuppositions for interpretation. Webster argues that this calls for a distinctly Christian hermeneutical *ontology*, which answers many of the questions raised, filling the gaps present in philosophical hermeneutics.[271] The right interpretation involves looking through the right *lens*—one provided by Scripture.[272] The hermeneutical situation is not unformed or undefined, but rather contingent upon God's assessment. Hence, man cannot transcend it in order to make sense of it. Rather, he must contingently participate in light of God's transcendence and interpretation of it.[273] Third, it appreciates the role of the reader in interpretation and how the Bible speaks today. Green says this involves asking whether the reader is ready to be the "model reader" the biblical author implies in a given text.[274] In other words, will the reader respond in his interpretation in a way consistent with the message and intent of the author in the text? In addition, communal aspects of the reader's role are given more attention in terms of interpretation taking place in an historical believing community. Jenson captures this distinctive in stark fashion: "The question, after all, is not whether churchly reading of Scripture is justified; the question is, what could possibly justify any other?"[275]

Like SAT, TIS is not without its critics, both inside and outside the movement.[276] Some, like Thiselton, perhaps do not disagree in principle, but dismiss some expressions of the approach as too simplistic, generalized, and dogmatic.[277] Others have objected to what is implied by the movement and

---

269. Fowl, "Further Thoughts," 125–26; Webster, "Hermeneutics," 317; Watson, *Open Text*, 6.

270. Moberly, "What is?," 165.

271. Webster, "Hermeneutics," 316.

272. Green, *Theology, Hermeneutics*, 17.

273. Webster, "Hermeneutics," 322–23, 326.

274. Green, *Theological Interpretation*, 42; "Modernity, History," 317, 327–29; Lints, *Fabric of Theology*, 293.

275. Jenson, "Scripture's Authority," 29.

276. For a balanced critique, see Carson, "Theological Interpretation," 187–207; Köstenberger, "Of Professors," 3–18.

277. E.g., Thiselton, *Hermeneutics of Doctrine*, 121–22; *Review*, 588–89. However,

its problematic label—namely, that other hermeneutical approaches cannot be equally *theological* in nature.[278] Ironically, critics fault TIS for its built-in assumptions while uncritically making their own in their very critiques. For example, Poirier assumes Scripture is merely a religious testimony about God's activity (not divine revelation), and that this has no real bearing on what should be considered "theological" interpretation. Later, he assumes a dichotomy between theological truth being text-mediated and event-mediated.[279] He argues that all interpretation in the interest of theology should be labeled as "theological."[280] This assumes that there is nothing more ultimate or authoritative than man's own theological interpretation of the Bible.

Those more receptive to the overall program of TIS see the need for further refinement. For some, this refinement comes in the form of seeing a methodological spectrum of TIS, and exercising caution with the use of the *rule of faith*, especially as a guide or heuristic to better understand a text.[281] Poythress, while commending Watson for his canonical awareness and his emphasis on God as the Creator, faults him for arguing his position according to the rules of the academy rather than Scripture. Consequently, he fails to do justice to the Bible's own authority to interpret all of life. As such, Watson is left without an ultimate standard for his claims.[282] According to Bowald, further refinement involves the doctrine of God and the role of divine agency in hermeneutics, as opposed to merely giving attention to the human level. In part, this is due to that fact that we interpret from a worldview, involving ontological presuppositions.[283] Too often, Bowald argues, biblical hermeneutics displays deistic tendencies in construing the meaning of Scripture primarily as "a by-product of *human* agency, as an expression of its created capacities and conditions."[284] Rather, we should read the Bible "against a thicker theological horizon of divine agency or we do not read it at all."[285] He insists that we must frame the problem of herme-

---

some would see Thiselton's stated influences as uncomfortably eclectic and ambiguous in terms of his theological and philosophical commitments (e.g., Thiselton, *Hermeneutics of Doctrine*, xxi; *Two Horizons*, 354; Thiselton, "Authority and Hermeneutics," 134–40).

278. Poirier, "Theological Interpretation," 106–18.
279. Poirier, "Theological Interpretation," 116–17.
280. Poirier, "Theological Interpretation," 109.
281. Trimm, "Evangelicals, Theology," 315–29.
282. Poythress, Review, 475–77.
283. Bowald, "Rendering Mute," 367–72, 380–81.
284. Bowald, "Rendering Mute," 372 (emphasis his). He traces this back to Kant's ontological influence in hermeneutics.
285. Bowald, "Rendering Mute," 373.

neutics not in terms of the tension between the reader and text or reader and human author, but rather ontologically, focused on divine agency.[286] Bowald and Webster both point out the absence of an *ontology* of Scripture in the contemporary literature. The biblical text and the reader are both shaped by divine acts, and human interpretive acts should be ordered by these acts and correspond to them.[287]

Conclusion

Vanhoozer observes that "the great lesson of twentieth-century hermeneutics is that understanding is a matter not strictly of epistemology but, more fundamentally, of ontology: human being."[288] The earlier part of our survey evoked an uneasy sense of entrapment. First, there seems to be a general confusion regarding the nature of metaphysics and its role in hermeneutics. As scholars have grappled with these issues through the various shifts in the contemporary landscape, we see a back and forth monotony—from rationalistic attempts to pin down meaning to an almost irrational mysticism in hopes of transcending the essential historical elements involved. In the latter, attempts are made to avoid the Enlightenment ideal of knowledge, while at the same time, projecting that *same* ideal, albeit under the guise of *degrees* of objectivity[289] and subjectivity in limited perspectives where supposedly one will find solid ground on which to stand.[290] In the words of Walhout, "much contemporary thinking about philosophical hermeneutics can be characterized as a debate over the issue of relativism."[291] Yet, even among postmodern thinkers on the farthest end of the spectrum, there is an assumed objectivity from which conclusions are drawn, which undermines their own subjective tenets.[292] The same could be said for those on the modernist end of the spectrum. In seeking the Enlightenment ideal, essential aspects of that ideal have been abandoned, such as certainty in favor of probable consensus. We have also seen that prominent evangelical scholars are not immune to this tension. How are we to escape such a

---

286. Bowald, "Rendering Mute," 381.
287. Merrick, "Giving God," 301.
288. Vanhoozer, "Imprisoned or Free?," 54.
289. E.g., Marshall, "Evangelicals and Hermeneutics," 25.
290. Carson points out that deconstructionists appeal to indefensible antitheses—either absolute knowledge or complete relativism (*Gagging of God*, 107, 129; Juhl, "Playing with Texts," 61).
291. Walhout, "Narrative Hermeneutics," 91.
292. Carson, "Recent Developments," 41.

vicious cycle in hermeneutics which both, modern and postmodern scholars have succumbed to? How can we evaluate what constitutes a good or bad interpretation amidst such instability? From a Christian perspective, one could see each attempt which emphasizes one aspect of interpretation to the exclusion of another as a *counterfeit* of the biblical worldview, including ontology. To round out Vanhoozer's observation above, it is necessary to add that human *being* must be defined in relation to God, the Creator. Ward sums it up well:

> If God is not taken into account as the ultimate solid ground on which all meaning rests, and as the basis on which our language can be said reliably to bear meaning, then we do indeed end up staring into the abyss in which meaning is forever undecidable.[293]

Disregard for the divine author eschews proper metaphysical consideration in hermeneutics.

Recent developments, like SAT and TIS, have been helpful correctives, highlighting the need to attend to the divine author's role in interpretation. In doing so, certain aspects of the nature of God have been brought into the discussion. However, each approach is not without need for further development and refinement in terms of biblically-informed ontological and epistemological presuppositions.

Throughout our survey, it has become evident that certain questions demand attention in light of recent shifts and focus. How does ontology shape biblical interpretation? How does one avoid the pitfalls of both modernism and postmodernism? How do we best re-examine ontological foundations on a distinctly Christian basis?[294] What is the "relationship between a strictly theological hermeneutic for biblical interpretation, and issues of general hermeneutics and philosophy"?[295] Getting at this need for a Christian framework, Erickson calls for the development of a "meta-hermeneutics" to provide a proper theoretical basis for discussion.[296] We need a Christian hermeneutic which can not only help diagnose counterfeit methods, but also comes from the Bible itself—God's interpretation on *his* terms.[297]

Van Til has addressed many of these questions in a stimulating and fruitful way. In his search to establish a strictly Christian apologetic, he

---

293. Ward, *Words of Life*, 64–65.
294. Bartholomew, "Uncharted Waters," 2, 24; "Post/Late Modernity," 33.
295. Bartholomew, "Introduction," in *Renewing Biblical Interpretation*, xxx.
296. Erickson, *Evangelical Interpretation*, 124.
297. Poythress, "Philosophical Roots," 170.

addressed many of the same philosophical questions receiving significant attention in hermeneutics. *How* did he address them? In the next chapter, we will begin examining the root of his thinking on these matters.

Part II: **Van Til's Doctrine of God**

Chapter 4: Creator-Creature Distinction

Introduction

As we have seen in the previous two chapters, contemporary hermeneutics has exhibited two main trends: defining hermeneutics more holistically, with an explicit awareness of the ontological and epistemological assumptions involved, *and* searching for a general theory of understanding to ground interpretation. However, there has been significant confusion and disagreement over the nature of such assumptions and how they actually relate to interpretation.

We have looked at two recent developments in evangelical hermeneutics which have provided some helpful contributions to the discussion—namely, SAT and TIS. Most importantly, each in its own way has directed attention to *God's role* as the ultimate author of Scripture and the need for an explicitly *theological* account of understanding.[1]

One key aspect of Van Til's thought was his unwavering insistence upon bringing all aspects of human thought under the authority of the self-interpreting God of the Bible. This includes providing *biblical* definitions to philosophical categories and critiquing unbiblical notions. Methodologically, he argued by presupposition—to identify what ontological and epistemological principles control one's method.[2] He opposed any generalized philosophical system which claimed to be more ultimate than the one found in the Bible. One's system and method must match its content.[3] A Christian system and method should match the content and intent of Scripture. At the core of his program and critique was the nature of God and his relation to creation as revealed in the Bible.[4] He states that "our concept of God has specific implications for every branch of human knowledge."[5] Furthermore, "unless God is back of everything, you cannot

---

1. Thompson, *Clear and Present*, 132–33.
2. Van Til, *Christian Apologetics*, 128.
3. Van Til, "My Credo," 15.
4. Roberts, "Van Til," 75; Van Til, *Defense of Faith*, 30.
5. Van Til, *Christian Epistemology*, xiv.

find meaning in anything."[6] Perhaps, one could locate his emphases in the current stream of concerns found in both SAT and TIS. However, neither provides exactly the same type of articulation found in Van Til's works. The type of creative expression found in Van Til is different, largely due to the context in which he engaged, requiring unique summaries of the biblical message in order to meet the challenges of his day. In that sense, Van Til's thought could be considered a corrective complement and contribution to the evangelical cause in both movements.

The Creator-Creature Distinction

As hinted at in our brief survey of Van Til's macro-hermeneutical statements in chapter 1, his doctrine of God is the primary principle of explanation for everything else.[7] One of the main ways in which he asserts this principle is in terms of the *Creator-creature distinction*.[8] It is "the most fundamental distinction of orthodox theology . . . a distinction that is presupposed in all its other differentiations. Upon it rests the whole construction of the direct revelation of God in history."[9] Elsewhere, he states that "the Christian doctrine of god implies a definite conception of the relation of God to the created universe."[10] This is opposed to unbiblical notions, such as a distinction made between a self-existent temporal world and a self-existent timeless world of ideas or any other proposed distinction merely *within* creation.[11] To the contrary, the Creator-creature distinction revealed in Scripture necessarily provides a two-level metaphysic which should inform all our thinking and interpretive efforts from start to finish.[12] Indeed, it is this distinction which sets the Christian worldview apart.[13] Responding to Pinnock, Van Til says, "I agree with you that Scripture should speak for itself. In fact, I want it to tell us what God is, what the world is, and what we as men are, not *after* but *before* we start speaking of metaphysics, epistemology, and ethics."[14] "The Christian concept of hermeneutics is based first of all

6. Van Til, *Why I Believe*, 3.
7. Roberts, "Van Til," 80; Van Til, *Christian Apologetics*, 97.
8. Halsey, *Such a Time*, 20, 24.
9. Van Til, *New Modernism*, 7.
10. Van Til, *Defense of Faith*, 32.
11. Van Til, *New Modernism*, 7.
12. Van Til, *Christian Apologetics*, 30; *Doctrine of Scripture*, 16; *Defense of Faith*, 229; *Systematic Theology*, 265.
13. Bavinck, *Reformed Dogmatics*, 2:407.
14. Geehan, *Jerusalem*, 426.

upon the creation idea, that is, upon the conviction that there are not merely one but two levels of existence, and that man must be interpreted in terms of God."[15] The Bible nowhere speaks of a general concept of *being* to which this distinction can be subsequently added.[16] Rather, it is the given context for all *creaturely* thinking.[17] According to Van Til, all non-Christian thought can be summed up as *monistic* at some level, seeing all reality as equal in nature, even if not in degree (e.g., scale of being).[18] We saw this monistic trend among many key figures surveyed in the last chapter—a tendency to conceive of a one-level metaphysic-in-general, while also seeking to achieve a kind of transcendent or god-like vantage point from which to establish interpretation. In this pursuit,

> The distinction between the approach of the "ancient" mind and the "modern" mind is not fundamental. The "objectivism" of the ancient mind is only gradationally distinct from the "subjectivism" of the modern mind. There is no true transcendence in Platonism, Aristotelianism, or Stoicism, any more than there is in modern existentialism and dialecticism.[19]

The main distinction which sets off the Christian metaphysic from the non-Christian variety is the Creator-creature distinction. Van Til's emphasis on this distinction is pervasive and discussed in a number of contexts. In the following discussion, we will look at *seven* such contexts and consider some implications for hermeneutics.

Facts, Possibility, and Interpretation

First, this distinction informs his discussions of *fact, possibility,* and *interpretation*. Van Til argues that all too often in apologetic dialogues, these concepts are treated uncritically in terms of the Creator-creature distinction.[20] Van Til maintained that the meaning of any fact (and its relation to all other facts) was determined by God as their Creator and pre-interpreter, according to his own self-knowledge and its place in his

---

15. Van Til, *Psychology*, 53; "Introduction," 9.
16. Van Til, *Intellectual Challenge*, 10; *Reformed Pastor*, 91, 141, 144.
17. Van Til, *Christian Epistemology*, 1.
18. Van Til, *Christian Apologetics*, 30–31, 37–38; *Systematic Theology*, 56, 118, 291, 353; Frame, *Van Til*, 74.
19. Van Til, *Systematic Theology*, 202; *New Hermeneutic*, 23.
20. Van Til, *Systematic Theology*, 25.

all-encompassing plan.[21] Hence, they are not only dependent upon God for their existence and meaning,[22] they are also inherently *contextual* in nature (known in-relation). In other words, states of affairs include not merely things, but also their properties and relation to *other* things.[23] Created facts are governed by created laws and, as objects of knowledge, are so fashioned by God as to come into fruitful contact with the mind of man as a knowing subject.[24] In sum, all facts are *theistic*-facts.[25] However, creation is in no way necessary to the being of God, who freely relates to it in terms of his plan, creation, and providence.[26] God himself is the most basic Fact from which all created facts are determined and defined—with the Fact-facts distinction paralleling the Creator-creature distinction. Moreover, all created facts are revelational of God.[27] Even man, as a created fact, can have no pre-understanding of himself apart from or prior to the revelation of God.[28] Man cannot reason apart from an atmosphere of revelation—his created mind and capacity to reason (as with the rest of his being) is itself an aspect of general revelation.[29]

Unbelieving thought and methodology tend to assume the uncreated nature of facts in the universe (i.e., *brute* or uninterpreted facts),[30] treating them as essentially indeterminate.[31] According to Van Til, without the counsel of God as the ultimate principle of *individuation*,[32] man is left to appeal to an individuation of chance.[33] In terms of metaphysics, "unless we begin with the Creator-creature distinction, participation in non-being is

---

21. Van Til, *Christian Apologetics*, 128, 194; *Christian Epistemology*, 1–2; *Theory of Knowledge*, 35–36; *Theistic-Evidences*, 51, 54; Rushdoony, *Biblical Philosophy*, 40.

22. Van Til, *Reformed Pastor*, 5–6; *Theistic-Evidences*, 52, 64–65.

23. Frame, *Knowledge of God*, 99–100.

24. Van Til, *Systematic Theology*, 122–23.

25. Van Til, "Antitheses," 16.

26. Van Til, *Systematic Theology*, 393; *Defense of Faith*, 32, 46, 50, 53, 228, 233–34; Van Til, "Bavinck," 60.

27. Van Til, *Systematic Theology*, 40; *Apologetics*, 79, 150; "Nature and Scripture," 274–75, 280.

28. Van Til, *New Hermeneutic*, 25; "Nature and Scripture," 273; *Theory of Knowledge*, 348.

29. Van Til, *Systematic Theology*, 119, 122, 129; *Theory of Knowledge*, 15; *Christian Epistemology*, 123–24.

30. Shannon, "Christianity and Evidentialism," 323–53.

31. Van Til, *Common Grace*, 2; *Christian Epistemology*, 117–25.

32. I.e., facts intelligible according to a pattern or by way of contrast.

33. Van Til, *Defense of Faith*, 295.

CHAPTER 4: CREATOR-CREATURE DISTINCTION

the only principle of individuation there is."[34] To the contrary, one must speak not merely of facts in general (akin to a being-in-general), but rather of one's *philosophy* of fact in light of the above truths. This is what Van Til sought to expose in apologetics.[35]

Following close upon his view of facts is his understanding of possibility and interpretation. Any assertion about reality involves assumptions about the nature of that reality and possibility.[36] God alone, as Creator, determines what is possible and impossible in relation to facts. *He* is the source of possibility, not man's reason.[37] "The very words *possibility* and *probability* have no meaning unless the God of Christianity actually exists"[38]—for Scripture tells us there is no other God but the one who determines meaning. Antithetical to this are notions of an ultimate abstract and absolute possibility. Such a concept is ultimately rooted in indeterminate chance, for it does not take God's revelation as ultimate, but rather posits an unknown mystery encompassing *both* man and God—both *subject* to possibility rather than possibility being subject to God.[39] Van Til concludes that:

> a "possibility" that is above God is the same thing as chance. A God surrounded by chance cannot speak with authority. He would be speaking into a vacuum. His voice could not be heard. And if God were surrounded by chance, then human beings would be too. They would live in a vacuum, unable to hear either their own voices or those of others. Thus the whole of history, including all of its facts, would be without meaning.[40]

Treating God as merely one fact among many surrounded by bare possibility is a negation of the self-attesting God of Scripture—*the* Fact who determines all things. To assume neutrality toward facts as created and determined by God is to assume the universe is ultimately open to *both* God and man. Such neutrality assumes God's pre-interpreted system of facts is non-existent.[41] For example, to ask *whether* such a God exists and

---

34. Van Til, *Reformed Pastor*, 221.

35. It may be noted that recent work in the area of historiography has also recognized the importance of these concerns (e.g., Provan et al., *Biblical History*, 56–102).

36. Van Til, *New Modernism*, 66.

37. Van Til, *Defense of Faith*, 293; *Systematic Theology*, 396; *Doctrine of Scripture*, 131; *Theistic-Ethics*, 35.

38. Van Til, *Christian Apologetics*, 39 (emphasis his).

39. Van Til, *Systematic Theology*, 197–98, 201; *Is God Dead?*, 35–37; *Christianity and Idealism*, 8.

40. Van Til, *Defense of Faith*, 327.

41. Van Til, *Christianity and Idealism*, 9.

whether what he says about reality through Scripture is true, presupposes such a concept of possibility.[42] In expounding Paul's argument in Romans 1, Van Til highlights that God does not *probably* exist, nor is there any fault in objective revelation in the created order in expressing this—no one can escape confronting it at every point.[43] The non-Christian view of possibility involves a suppression of the Creator-creature distinction (Rom 1:18–25). This distinction is so real and clear that there is no excuse for denying it and condemnation is just (Rom 1:20). So, to ask *whether* this God exists denies the God of Scripture. Van Til also connects possibility with special revelation in a similar fashion:

> True Protestantism starts from the fact or actuality of the book [Bible]. The meaning of the word *possibility* is first determined by God who has spoken to sinners through *the* book. That, and only that, is possible which the God of the Bible determines. The 'possibility of the book' is no better than the idea of the 'possibility of *a* book.'[44]

Hence, an unbiblical notion of possibility with regard to the Bible is a negation of it and the very possibility of an authoritative, self-attesting divine revelation.[45] In essence, the non-Christian sees man "as the ultimate judge of what can and cannot be."[46] However, determination and certainty is only found in the Creator revealed in Scripture.[47]

One may object to such circular reasoning. However, when considering the issue of ultimate authority, it is unavoidable.[48] Has the absolute Creator revealed truth or is it up to man to decide such truth? This gets at the very heart of Van Til's transcendental approach. "The only argument for an absolute God that holds water is a transcendental argument . . . a truly transcendental God and a transcendental method go hand in hand."[49] An argument which does not presuppose what God has said in his word to be true, reasons as if it were untrue and uncertain. Reasoning

---

42. Van Til, *Theory of Knowledge*, 263.
43. Van Til, *Intellectual Challenge*, 5.
44. Van Til, *Intellectual Challenge*, 20 (emphasis his).
45. Van Til, *Theory of Knowledge*, 31.
46. Van Til, *Doctrine of Scripture*, 13.
47. Van Til, *Systematic Theology*, 103.
48. Rushdoony, *By What Standard?*, 139–40; Bahnsen, *Van Til's Apologetic*, 284–85, 523–25; Frame, *Van Til*, 299–309; *Knowledge of God*, 130–33. For helpful study of Van Til's view on the place of evidence in relation to ultimate commitments, see Notaro, *Van Til*.
49. Van Til, *Christian Epistemology*, 11.

in a circular or spiral fashion[50] is the only biblical option open to the finite creature. "Unless we are larger than God we cannot reason about him any other way, than by a transcendental or circular argument."[51] This kind of circularity is not fallacious because it is cogent in terms of the Christian worldview. God's absolute coherence in his comprehensive knowledge of facts is the basis for man's reasoning about them. Van Til explicitly connects this issue with metaphysics:

> our reasoning cannot fairly be called circular reasoning,[52] because we are not reasoning about and seeking to explain facts by assuming the existence and meaning of certain other facts on the *same level of being* with the facts we are investigating, and then explaining these facts in turn by the facts with which we began. We are presupposing God, not merely another fact of the universe.[53]

When it comes to special revelation, "the kind of God that speaks in Scripture can only speak on his own authority."[54] If God's word must be verified by some other criteria in order to be his word, then that criterion is more ultimate than God and hence, inconsistent with his nature revealed in Scripture.[55] In short, we *must* reason as such if we are to interpret reality and the Bible consistent with the content of revelation involving the Creator-creature distinction.[56] This issue is important not only for Van Til, but also for philosophical hermeneutics.[57]

In addition to what has already been said about the interpretation of facts, a few pertinent points can be made related to contemporary hermeneutical concerns. First, it is impossible for man to make a statement about any fact "without doing so in terms of an all-inclusive view of reality."[58]

---

50. Van Til prefers "spiral" in emphasizing that we grow in our understanding of the facts (of creation and Scripture) in this process, analogously approximating God's understanding of them with his help (Frame, *Van Til*, 306–7).

51. Van Til, *Christian Epistemology*, 12.

52. That is, in a fallacious sense.

53. Van Til, *Christian Epistemology*, 201–2 (emphasis mine).

54. Van Til, "Nature and Scripture," 265.

55. This would include the inner-circularity of God's triune nature (Van Til, *Christian Epistemology*, 202). In discussing the issue of canon and authority, Ridderbos argues in a similar fashion (Ridderbos, *Redemptive History*, 33–38).

56. Elsewhere, Van Til boldly asserts that "Christianity does not need to take shelter under the roof of a scientific method independent of itself. It rather offers itself as a roof to methods that would be scientific" (*Theistic-Evidences*, 52).

57. Poythress, "Biblical Studies," 134.

58. Van Til, *Case for Calvinism*, 115.

We have seen that ontological assumptions are inevitable in hermeneutics, even when seeking to avoid them. This is especially made clear in light of Van Til's treatment of the Creator-creature distinction. In order for man to engage in hermeneutics in terms of its holistic nature, he must not *decontextualize* himself nor treat his own reason as uncreated. Moreover, he must not *re-contextualize* himself in a different metaphysical context considered more ultimate. Rather, "the great presupposition of all his efforts at interpreting himself and the world about him is the fact that he and the world are first interpreted by God in Christ as revealed in Scripture."[59] Man cannot interpret himself rightly, as if in a vacuum, based on his own autonomy—as if able to determine the nature of things.[60]

Second, any theory of interpretation that does not assume facts to be created and pre-interpreted by their Creator assumes the existence of *brute* facts and treats God on the same ontological level as man, reducing him to "at most a co-interpreter, with man, of brute fact." Without God creating the universe, facts would be ultimately unrelated.[61] Subjectively, at least, we would never know for sure *if* or *how* they were related. Not only are brute facts mute facts, but as uninterpreted, they are *uninterpretable*.[62] Facts and their interpretation cannot be separated. "It is impossible to discuss any particular fact except in relation to some principle of interpretation." Put another way, we cannot distinguish between facts as something we experience and arguments about the source of those facts.[63] Only the God of Christianity can provide: source, interpretation, and determinate meaning.[64]

On this basis, Van Til was opposed to what he called the "block-house method" in apologetics.[65] In short, this method seeks to prove Christianity in a piecemeal fashion, building story by story. Often, one seeks first to prove a generic theism, and then secondly, to establish that this theism is of the Christian sort.[66] Van Til argues that this type of method undermines the Creator-creature distinction in that it assumes the existence of a being-in-general to which one may subsequently add certain ontological characteristics of the *Christian* God, such as Creator and triunity. What has actually been proven with a generic theism which bears no particular resemblance to

---

59. Van Til, *Barthianism*, 432.
60. Van Til, *Great Debate*, 221.
61. Van Til, *Theistic-Evidences*, 80–81.
62. Van Til, *God of Hope*, 308.
63. Van Til, *Psychology*, 155.
64. Van Til, *Theistic-Evidences*, i.
65. E.g., Van Til on Warfield (*Theory of Knowledge*, 229–54).
66. Van Til, *Christian Apologetics*, 148–49.

CHAPTER 4: CREATOR-CREATURE DISTINCTION

the God of Scripture? By not making the Creator-creature distinction basic at the outset of all prediction, foreign material is introduced which distorts other doctrines of the Christian system of truth. It treats the facts of creation and redemption as brute facts, encouraging a philosophy of fact which *already* denies the Creator-creature distinction before it is even introduced.[67] *That* God exists is involved in *what* God exists, from the start.[68]

One could argue that there are forms of contemporary biblical hermeneutics which could be labeled as hermeneutical block-house methods—not self-consciously beginning with the presuppositions of the Creator-creature distinction and special revelation but seeking to add them later in the process. For example, Dempster argues that Brevard Childs' canonical approach, though not without significant merit, inconsistently utilizes the historical-critical method *uncritically*, then seeks to add to this historical "depth dimension" a canonical role which cannot be explained by such a dimension.[69] In short, Childs seeks to cross Lessing's ditch with a canonical hermeneutic constructed upon unstable assumptions exhibiting a reason-faith dichotomy.[70] The issue is *not* that Childs' method is ahistorical, but rather that he deals with history uncritically and inconsistently in light of his canonical concerns.[71] What is needed is an approach which does not drive a wedge between the historical and the canonical or between general and special revelation.[72] The issue of hermeneutical authority again surfaces in Childs' work—*whose intent has ultimate authority*, the author (or authors) or the canonical shapers (i.e., canonical intention)?[73]

Third, Van Til discusses the relationship between history, revelation, and interpretation in ways which seek to maintain the Creator-creature distinction. Due to this distinction, man must be interpreted in terms of his Creator and then interpret history in light of God's pre-interpretation of it found in Scripture.[74] In any philosophy of history, men seek to bring facts into a pattern or framework.[75] However, even historical description of the facts involves explanation and patternization (i.e., the *what* and the

67. Van Til, *Defense of Faith*, 136, 310–12.
68. Van Til, *Defense of Faith*, 128.
69. Dempster, "Canon," 322–23; Barr, *Holy Scripture*, 133; Davies, *Whose Bible?*, 31.
70. Dempster, "Canon," 321, 324.
71. E.g., his inconsistent conclusions regarding the historical audience of Isaiah 40–66 (Childs, *Introduction*, 323–27).
72. Dempster, "Canon," 324–25.
73. Vanhoozer, *Drama of Doctrine*, 217–18.
74. Van Til, *Psychology*, 53; *Apologetics*, 21, 53–54.
75. Van Til, *Paul at Athens*, 11–13.

that involved in one another). Hence, the difference between Christian and non-Christian philosophies of history involves more than merely an explanation of the facts. It also involves their very idea of what counts as a fact to begin with. Van Til cites Eddington's "ichthyologist" analogy in support of this point. The ichthyologist surveys his catch of fish and concludes that fish are what his net can catch (i.e., of a certain size, shape, and so on), and conversely, what his net cannot catch are not fish. The only fish are those that can be caught by the net. The description fits the pattern. In other words, a non-Christian philosophy of history includes not only the view that facts must be utterly pliable in order to fit a pattern of their own making (i.e., catchable fish), but also the impossibility of falsification due to their patternization, which determined the nature of what those facts can be to begin with.[76] Van Til reminds us that "the facts of history cannot be disentangled from the principles of interpretation by which they can be presented to us as *history*, that is, as a coherent and connected series or order of events."[77]

Hermeneutically, this exhibits itself in how the role of the interpreter is conceived of in terms of shaping meaning. A Christian hermeneutic, while recognizing the role of the interpreter in the process, opposes any concept of shaping which assumes the completely open, pliable, or uncreated nature of the facts being interpreted.[78] "According to any consistently Christian position, God, and God only, has ultimate definitory power."[79] Consequently, to follow the facts where they lead is to follow them in relation to God. However, there has been a general tendency in Western thought to resist using theological categories to understand history.[80] This anti-metaphysical tendency, in order to make room for man-made objectivity and subjectivity in those who do not recognize or seek to be consistent with a two-level metaphysic based on the Creator-creature distinction, contradicts the Christian worldview and its corresponding philosophy of history.

Inerrant Autographa

In terms of revelation and interpretation, Van Til also discusses the importance of the inerrant *autographa* in the context of the Creator-creature

---

76. Van Til, *Common Grace*, 3–4; *Theistic-Evidences*, 140.
77. Van Til, "Introduction," 5–6 (emphasis his).
78. Van Til, *Defense of Faith*, 342–43.
79. Van Til, *Common Grace*, 5.
80. Rae, "Creation and Promise," 268.

distinction. Arguing against the misguided notion that one can have a general trust in Scripture without infallible inspiration,[81] he says:

> But we have seen that man needs absolutely authoritative interpretation. Hence, if the *autographa* were not infallibly inspired, it would mean that at some point human interpretation would stand above divine interpretation. It would mean that man were, after all, not certain that the facts and the interpretations given to the facts in Scripture are true.[82]

This statement shows that Van Til saw Scripture not merely as a collection of brute facts, but God's interpretation of them according to his counsel and plan of redemption, centered on Christ. Furthermore, he ties together the issues of infallibility and authority in terms of the *autographa*. Restating things from a different angle, the Creator-creature distinction demands an infallible *autographa* in order to maintain the absolute authority of the Creator over the creature and a certain interpretation of the facts. Assuming man's metaphysical freedom undermines the possibility for God's absolute authoritative revelation to man. Such a denial of the Creator-creature distinction leads to claiming revelation to be unclear, with no *finished* facts in history, hence, no *finished* revelation,[83] and—in light of Van Til's view of special revelation as God's interpretation of reality—no *finished* interpretation.[84] Consequently, one's rule of faith becomes indistinguishable from canon. Unbelieving thought seeks to bury the idea of divinely authoritative revelation by means of a being-in-general, based on a monistic assumption not found in Scripture.[85] Often, this being-in-general is conceived of as *history* itself. However, according to Scripture, history is not the master category for interpretation, but rather, due to the Creator-creature distinction, *God* is—through his word—revealed *in* history. This is the proper lens through which we are to make sense of the world.[86] It is "folly for a creature of time to try out the interpretation of God in the test tube of time."[87]

---

81. In context, his concept of infallibility includes inerrancy.

82. Van Til, *Systematic Theology*, 251.

83. Van Til, *Reformed Pastor*, 91–92. Incidentally, Childs roots his "canonical" concept in the community and with regard to the OT, ultimately in the fourth century church, which subjects his approach to a similar critique (Kruger, *Canon Revisited*, 52–59).

84. Van Til, *Reformed Pastor*, 189–90; *New Modernism*, 287.

85. Van Til, *Reformed Pastor*, 152.

86. Wright, "Inhabiting Story," 497.

87. Van Til, *Christian Epistemology*, 22.

Analogy

The Creator-creature distinction is the root from which Van Til formulates his concept of *analogy*. Man is a created analogue of God. By this, he means that there are two levels of existence and two levels of knowledge, with man being dependent on and derivative of God.[88] By *analogy*, Van Til seeks to understand how two levels of being and knowledge are related.[89] In terms of knowledge, God is the original and "has an absolute, self-contained system within himself . . . what comes to pass in history happens in accordance with that system." Man cannot have a replica or exact reproduction of that system.[90] Rather, man's system should be "self-consciously analogical."[91] Elsewhere, he describes this as "thinking God's thoughts after himself."[92] Man must form his finite system by seeking to think God's thoughts after himself in submission to God's authority, according to what he has revealed. "For this reason all of man's interpretations in any field are subject to the Scriptures given him."[93] However, this does not mean that our knowledge is doomed to uncertainty or that knowledge does not require absolutely certain foundations.[94] "Man does not need to know exhaustively in order to know truly and certainly."[95] At a fundamental level, man's interpretation of nature and Scripture must "be a re-interpretation of what is already fully interpreted by God."[96] God's certainty is the very essence of true knowledge.[97] Van Til, speaking of the ethics of knowledge according to the Christian worldview, describes this type of dependent re-interpretation as "receptively *reconstructive*" as opposed to non-Christian ethical knowledge, which is "creaturely *constructive*." The main difference is that the former is in creaturely submission to the Creator, while the latter seeks epistemological and ethical independence, without reference to God.[98]

What are some hermeneutical implications of this? First, metaphysically speaking, there are two levels of interpreters—Creator and creature.

---

88. Van Til, *Systematic Theology*, 33; *Defense of Faith*, 62–63.

89. Weaver, "Man," 324.

90. This is opposed to univocal thinking, where there is an epistemological *identity* at any given point of correspondence (Van Til, *Defense of Faith*, 71).

91. Van Til, *Theory of Knowledge*, 16.

92. Van Til, "Nature and Scripture," 278; *Theory of Knowledge*, 16.

93. Van Til, *Theory of Knowledge*, 16; *Apologetics*, 77.

94. E.g., Evans, "Tradition, Biblical Interpretation," 331.

95. Van Til, "Nature and Scripture," 277–78.

96. Van Til, "Nature and Scripture," 278, *Scripture*, 8; *Sovereignty of Grace*, 61–62.

97. Van Til, *Psychology*, 142–43.

98. Van Til, *Defense of Faith*, 72–73, 76; *Systematic Theology*, 213.

If man does not think God's thoughts after himself, God merely becomes a collaborator with whom we think thoughts that have never been thought by God or man.[99] Second, if man refuses to interpret as an analogue of God, there is a tendency to set up a contrast between reason and faith in terms of revelation. Hence, man's attitude toward one type of revelation (general) is set in opposition to another type (special).[100] This is a false antithesis according to Scripture. Third, man must interpret the Bible actively and creatively but only re-constructively *according to* the pre-interpretation *already* there in the text, in its context (including canonical context). As a creature, man cannot engage in the creation of meaning. An example of such an attempt is Peter Enns, who denies an objective message in the Bible and concludes that "we are all free to put the pieces together as we think best."[101] To the contrary, creaturely hermeneutics can only seek a re-creative summary of what is already there. The key issue is not whether interpretive creativity or subjective elements are involved, but whether they are of the rebellious sort or not. To put it in contemporary hermeneutical terms, man must re-interpret Scripture in dialogue with God as the ultimate authority.

Van Til was careful to distinguish his doctrine of analogy from that of Rome and what he saw as its Greek philosophical influences.[102] He seeks to avoid any trace of an Aristotelian analogy of being which "envelops God and man in a common reality."[103] This notion, found in Aristotle and Neoplatonism, having influence on Aquinas (though inconsistently so), saw being on a scale or continuum, with God's being at the top and non-being at the bottom. The higher on the scale, the more unity there is between essence and existence (i.e., nature governing actions and experience).[104] Weaver has succinctly highlighted three main differences between Aquinas and Van Til on "analogy." First, whereas Aquinas presupposed partial autonomy of human reason, Van Til argued that all human knowledge was dependent upon divine revelation. Second, Aquinas believed all knowledge begins in sense experience apart from revelation, while Van Til said that sense experience functioned only in the context of revelation. Third, whereas Aquinas' concept was rooted in a common scale of being with *analogy* being a middle ground between univocal and equivocal predication, Van Til's was based on two

---

99. Van Til, *Defense of Faith*, 70–71.

100. Van Til, *Christian Apologetics*, 73.

101. Enns, *Bible Tells Me*, 86.

102. E.g., Van Til, *Systematic Theology*, 34, 38–39, 47, 52–53, 326, 333; *Defense of Faith*, 177, 187. This is contrary to claims of critics (Clark, "Bible as Truth," 166; Reymond, *Justification*, 104).

103. Van Til, *Defense of Faith*, 343; *Case for Calvinism*, 58, 100.

104. Frame, *Van Til*, 90–91.

distinct levels of being. Rather than seeing *analogy* dealing primarily with names or words applied to subjects, Van Til saw it as applying to the overall process of human thought—in both being and knowledge.[105]

Frame points out a further nuance in Van Til's concept of analogy. Our thinking is reflective of God's thought in two senses: all human thought reflects God, but in another sense, only *obedient* thought does. This is indicative of how theologians have spoken of man in the image of God in broad (structural) and narrow (functional) senses.[106] In the former, man remains in the image of God after the fall, but in the latter, man ceases to function properly in the image of God. This nuance highlights the ethical component of epistemology related to analogy.

Another way in which Van Til speaks of analogy is in terms of the *archetypal-ectypal* distinction found in the Reformed tradition.[107] Although he references this distinction (though not always in those exact terms) in the context of epistemology and the incomprehensibility of God, it is closely related to his doctrine of analogy.[108] Discussing the attributes of God, Van Til uses it to emphasize God as the original and man as derivative, both metaphysically and epistemologically. Only on this foundation can we safely apply the way of eminence and negation. An abstract notion of either way, without this distinction in place, ends in conceiving of a finite god—either as an expanded creature (eminence) or as an abstract blank, without positive or knowable qualities (negation). In the former, one ends in subjectivity, while in the latter, one ends in an empty, bare concept. Van Til argues that sinful man conveniently employs both ways in order to avoid thinking of himself as a creature, but rather as the original. However, "our attempts to say something about God then have back of them the original fact that God has said something about himself."[109] Hermeneutically, our interpretations of reality in general and Scripture in particular have God's revealed interpretation in back of both.

At this point, a word may be said about *accommodation* and *anthropomorphism*. Both are closely related, with the latter being a narrower subset of the former. Due to the Creator-creature distinction, "any knowledge that we have of God is the result of divine accommodation."[110] Poythress points

---

105. Weaver, "Man," 326–27.

106. Frame, *Knowledge of God*, 36.

107. Van Til, *Defense of Faith*, 62n25; Van Asselt, "Fundamental Meaning," 319–36; Muller, *Prolegomena*, 225–38; Bavinck, *Reformed Dogmatics*, 2:107–10.

108. Clark, "Janus," 157–60.

109. Van Til, *Systematic Theology*, 324.

110. Horton, "Consistently Reformed," 137; Tinker, "John Calvin's Concept," 325–58.

out that accommodation is really an expression of the Creator-creature distinction for understanding the nature of revelation. If we make a distinction between what God knows and what man knows, we infer that God's communication to man will take into account that we are creatures. This steers us away from making creaturely knowledge the standard into which God must fit.[111] Van Til observes that "every non-Christian philosophy and science seeks therefore to envelop God in his creation."[112] An important implication follows. If general and special revelation are both divine accommodations to the creature, there is *for man* no "unaccommodated" viewpoint (e.g., human reason) from which to judge Scripture or sift through its anthropomorphisms in order to decide whether it is revelation from God or not.[113] Rather, God, as the archetype of communication in himself among the persons of the Trinity, *is* the unaccommodated vantage point. In light of these truths and in close relation to reasoning analogically, Van Til argues that "we must speak of God anthropomorphically."[114] There is no other way to speak of God as Creator. In affirming accommodation, he is not promoting an agnostic attitude toward the knowledge of God but rather a greater confidence.[115] This is because God is in control as Creator and has so fashioned his creatures that he is able to communicate exactly what he intends without hindrance, and they are able to apprehend it without inherent *metaphysical* deficiencies.

Antecedent Being

Van Til also emphasizes the Creator-creature distinction in terms of God's antecedent being and the corresponding relation to man. This is especially evident in his writings on the theology of Karl Barth. It must be said from the outset that much has been written about Van Til's critique of Barth's theology, both positively[116] and negatively.[117] In fact, in his earlier work on Barth, Van Til admits that "he is deeply aware of the fact that to discuss a system of theology

---

111. Poythress, "Rethinking Accommodation," 145.
112. Van Til, *Doctrine of Scripture*, 126.
113. Poythress, "Rethinking Accommodation," 153–54.
114. Van Til, *Systematic Theology*, 326; *Common Grace*, 73; *Theory of Knowledge*, 37.
115. Frame, *Van Til*, 93–94.
116. E.g., Rushdoony, *By What Standard?*, 135–48; Frame, *Van Til*, 353–69.
117. E.g.,Torrance, Review, 144–49; Berkouwer, *Triumph of Grace*, 387–90; Richardson, *Reading Karl Barth*, 70–71; Ortlund, "Wholly Other," 35–52. Others have had more mixed reviews of Van Til's critique (e.g., Henry, *Fifty Years*, 96; Vanhoozer, "A Person?," 26–59).

in relation to its deepest philosophical bases is a hazardous undertaking."[118] It is beyond the scope of this chapter to discuss the nuances of this debate. However, whether one agrees with Van Til's assessment of Barth, it nonetheless exhibits his own concerns regarding the doctrine of God. We will merely highlight a few important emphases in Van Til's work on Barth which flesh out his own concerns regarding the Creator-creature distinction.

Van Til's general critique is that Barth's *wholly other-wholly revealed* scheme suggests unbiblical notions of transcendence and immanence. He claims that in such a scheme, God ironically ceases to be considered as an *antecedent* being when the two are brought together (e.g., Christ event).[119] This leads Van Til to emphasize certain truths related to the Creator-creature distinction which he believes are compromised. God has comprehensive self-knowledge and is self-contained (i.e., sufficient unto himself),[120] with his activities *ad intra* and his activities *ad extra* remaining distinct. Van Til was careful to preserve God as *a se*—as self-existent, self-sufficient, and self-contained, and who does not limit himself in order to relate to man.[121] Moreover, God "is self-contained rationality." This means that his infinite rationality is coterminous with his infinite being,[122] not dependent on anything outside himself, nor subject to any mystery within himself or subordinate to a more ultimate mystery from without.[123] Implied in this is the idea that *fact* and *interpretation* are coterminous in God, apart from the world.[124] God has absolute self-consciousness and is the only self-explanatory being.[125]

---

118. Van Til, *New Modernism*, viii.

119. For a similar critique, see: Ovey, "A Private Love?," 220.

120. Van Til, *New Modernism*, 364, 370, 373–74, 387. Sometimes Van Til refers to God as "self-contained fullness," by which he means to guard against univocal thinking in terms of the way of negation (no positive qualities) or the way of eminence (merely extrapolating a larger universe) (Frame, *Van Til*, 54–56; Van Til, *Systematic Theology*, 332–33).

121. Van Til, *Systematic Theology*, 27, 58, 117, 197, 267, 324, 327, 369, 373, 376, 385, 393, 397; *Defense of Faith*, 33, 75, 83, 228, 277, 296, 327, 335, 401; *Theory of Knowledge*, 12, 16, 44, 202; *Christian Epistemology*, 16, 32, 100, 118.

122. Van Til, *New Modernism*, 362; *Systematic Theology*, 201, 230, 364, 371–72; *Defense of Faith*, 59–61; *Christian Epistemology*, 102; *Apologetics*, 26. Van Til claimed Barth did not see being and rationality as coterminous, but only as "limiting concepts" (i.e., not actual) of each other in God (*New Modernism*, 215, 218, 230).

123. Van Til, *Christian Apologetics*, 25, 28; *Barthianism*, 490.

124. Van Til, *Systematic Theology*, 30; *Defense of Faith*, 31–32; "Introduction," 5–6, 19.

125. Van Til, *Systematic Theology*, 341; *Theory of Knowledge*, 15, 19, 56.

Van Til argued that Barth's scheme undermined these truths by creating an unstable dualism between God and creation which needs to be *overcome*,[126] as opposed to a created relation to be embraced. Horton concludes that for Barth, "grace does not so much restore nature as replace it."[127] The only way to overcome such a dualism is through participation, wherein God wholly reveals himself to man and man participates in God through identification in Christ. Hence, this notion of transcendence carries with it a corresponding immanence (wholly revealed).[128] Yet, there remains an inconsistency between such conceptions of transcendence and immanence. It would seem that a wholly other and wholly revealed scheme would contain irrationalistic and rationalistic elements, respectively.[129] For example, "If God is 'wholly other,' then how can we know or say that he is 'wholly other'?"[130] Barth, without direct special revelation given by God through an infallible and inerrant word in history,[131] is left with an ambiguous revelation in Christ (which is from time to time and "strictly future" for us),[132] and an equally ambiguous participation in him. How would we know if and when this revelation occurs without revealed parameters? As one of Van Til's mentors put it, "without God's acts the words would be empty, without his words the acts would be blind."[133] Van Til argued that Barth's concept of participation and identification is inconsistent with God as an antecedent being. The wholly other cannot speak to man until wholly identical or wholly revealed to man.[134] God and man end up in a correlated relationship with each other for either to be themselves.

While some have faulted Van Til for overlooking Barth's own emphasis on the antecedence of God,[135] few have sufficiently answered his critique of Barth's twofold view of history, in terms of *Geschichte* and

---

126. Barth, *Church Dogmatics*, III.3, 351–52, 366–68; Berkouwer, *Triumph of Grace*, 69–88.

127. Horton, "A Stoney Jar," 354.

128. Van Til, *New Modernism*, 367–68; *Barthianism*, 307.

129. E.g., Barth, *Church Dogmatics*, I/1, 201; Frame, *Van Til*, 364.

130. Frame, *Knowledge of God*, 13–15.

131. Barth, *Church Dogmatics*, I.1, 126; I.2, 507–33; II.1, 88; Fackre, "Revelation," 10; Beale, *Erosion*, 281–83.

132. Barth, *Church Dogmatics*, I.1, 16, 111, 124, 258.

133. Vos, "Idea of Biblical Theology," 10.

134. Van Til, *Barthianism*, 428.

135. E.g., Ortlund, "Wholly Other," 39–43; Molnar, *Divine Freedom*, 315. Van Til would counter that such affirmations in Barth are heuristic and limiting, rather than constitutive (i.e., actual) (*Barthianism*, 106–7; Frame, *Van Til*, 362n33).

Historie.¹³⁶ At best, these concepts are confusing, especially in how they relate to one another.¹³⁷ At worst, unorthodox implications follow. In short, *Geschichte* encompasses a number of concepts: God, divine revelation, redemptive acts, and reality in Christ. These are significant events for faith which illumine ordinary history yet are distinct from it. *Historie*, on the other hand, refers to ordinary calendar time-space history. The latter is subject to historical investigation and critique, while the former is not.¹³⁸ This inaccessibility is primarily due to God's sovereign freedom being at stake.¹³⁹ Divine revelation takes place in *Historie*, but does not leave lasting or reliable information concerning what actually took place, nor does it make historical claims. Though there is debate as to whether the events of *Geschichte* actually take place in *Historie* and on what level, to Van Til, the most problematic implication is that there is no ultimate transition from wrath to grace in our ordinary time-space history.¹⁴⁰

Much could be said of Barth's histories, but one particular point which Van Til makes is especially pertinent to the Creator-creature distinction. It would seem that for Barth, the fundamental relation between God and man is ultimately in terms of *Geschichte*, not the Creator-creature distinction, traditionally understood.¹⁴¹ This is problematic in that it seems to give priority to Christ's initial creative and universal work, to the neglect of his re-creative, particular work in redemption.¹⁴² Grace becomes the ground and essence of

---

136. This is curiously absent from Ortlund's assessment of Van Til, considering its prominence in both of his major works on Barth. Van Til faulted Berkouwer's assessment of Barth for neglecting his view of history (*Sovereignty of Grace*, 89). Cassidy's recent work identifies three *times* in Barth: God's time, our time, and God's time for us (Cassidy, *God's Time*, 4). Using Cassidy's categories, Van Til's reference to a two-fold scheme is focused on the distinction between God's time for us and our time.

137. E.g., Barth, *Church Dogmatics*, I.2, 58; Bartholomew, *Biblical Hermeneutics*, 359. Horton suggests that using the NT categories of "this age" and "the age to come" would help to avoid the unbiblical dualism found in Barth ("Stoney Jar," 350).

138. Frame suggests that Barth's main concern was to insulate revelation from autonomous historical investigation represented by the liberalism he was combatting. However, if this is the case, why not attack autonomous historical scholarship rather than introduce two histories? (*Word of God*, 30–31).

139. Barth, *Church Dogmatics*, I.1, 16. This suggests that God's freedom in redemption would be somehow compromised if expressed in our space-time history. Rather than human sin being the reason for this inaccessibility, the problem is God's nature being incompatible with history (general revelation).

140. Berkouwer, *Triumph of Grace*, 255–58; Van Til, *Barthianism*, 111.

141. Barth, *Church Dogmatics*, II.1, 10, 31–32, 53, 61–62, 367–68, 622–23; II.2, 94–99, 180–81; III.2, 55, 133, 135, 155; 464–65, 552; III.3, 429–30; Van Til, *New Modernism*, 152, 158; *Barthianism*, 21–22, 74, 99, 314, 416, 447; Cassidy, *God's Time*, 58.

142. Barth, *Church Dogmatics*, IV.1, 54–66, 90, 103. Van Til faulted Barth for his

CHAPTER 4: CREATOR-CREATURE DISTINCTION

the original ontological relation between God and man, and reconciliation does not follow creation in our time-space history.[143]

James J. Cassidy's recent study of Barth's view of eternity and time provides a balanced alternative to Van Til's work on Barth, which is much more polemic and antagonistic. While more appreciative of Barth's contributions as a whole, Cassidy raises some of the *same* concerns seen in Van Til's work. Namely, he questions the ontological dualism between God and creation expressed in Barth's depiction of "God's time" and "our time," and how he proposes to overcome this dualism theologically. Moreover, can Barth's Christology avoid charges of Eutychianism, merging created time and eternity in an unbiblical form of participation?[144]

There are many hermeneutical implications from the above discussion. First, Barth's scheme seemingly creates a dualism between God and creation which provides a more ultimate interpretive grid than what is revealed in Scripture.[145] Moreover, Van Til argues that Barth ends up with a monistic ontology using *one* scale of being, with indeterminism (wholly other) at one end of the scale and determinism (wholly revealed) at the other end.[146] Second, his stress on God's revelation as a *continued future* act (from time to time) implies that there is no *finished* revelation (not unlike issues related to inerrancy cited above).[147] This is opposed to Van Til's assertion that the Bible is the *finished* interpretation of Christ's work of redemption in history.[148] Third, in light of his twofold concept of history, Barth does not identify the Bible with revelation. Certainly, the Word of God (Christ) is distinct from the written word, but the latter is God's directly inspired, corresponding witness to the Word. Hence, they are distinct but not separate, nor in opposition to one another.[149] After all, Jesus explicitly appeals to and

---

latent universalism related to a universal participation in *Geschichte* (*Barthianism*, 8, 15, 17, 28–29).

143. Van Til, *Barthianism*, 453, 454, 485; Cassidy, *God's Time*, 100.

144. Cassidy, *God's Time*, 171–73.

145. Van Til, *New Modernism*, 216–17; *Barthianism*, 145, 232.

146. Van Til, *Barthianism*, 429. Barth would deny this to be the case, but his notions of transcendence and immanence seem to imply this notion.

147. Van Til, *New Modernism*, 156; *Scripture*, 36. Barth sees the written word as ever newly *becoming* the word of God—otherwise, it would lose its divine content and validity (Torrance, *Karl Barth*, 97–98). As such, the biblical canon remains open to revision, at least in principle (Johnson, "Karl Barth," 164). While his intent in his notion of "becoming" is debatable, Scripture attests to itself in different terms.

148. Van Til, *Barthianism*, 326; *Psychology*, 149.

149. Also, the written word is God's personal, verbal communication to us. The created medium is not divine, but its message and origin are divine (Frame, *Word of God*, 67–68).

assumes the written word as no less from God in his own teaching.[150] Van Til argues that we must begin from the Bible as identical with revelation when interpreting any fact of the world.[151] A Christian philosophy only works on the foundation of the redemptive history revealed in Scripture. Though distinct, there is no biblical justification for a *disjunction* between Christ and the written word in terms of revelation, authority, and interpretation.[152] The revelation of the Word (Christ) is divinely interpreted by the revealed written word. In the words of Warfield, "at the basis of Christianity [lies] not only a series of great redemptive facts, but also an authoritative interpretation of those facts."[153] Fourth, while rightly intending to interpret the Bible according to its message, Barth ends up distorting that message by conceiving of a revelation history incongruent with it.[154] This is one reason why Barth's theological interpretation differs from that of Van Til. Other differences could be added, such as not recognizing the Bible's own inner-hermeneutic as direct revelation.[155] It would seem that Barth was right to emphasize subject matter in hermeneutics over against attempts to get behind the text, but wrongly saw the Bible's subject matter as Jesus Christ experienced in an event divorced from a divinely inspired text. This leaves his subject matter without clear content and his theological hermeneutic without bearings. Lastly, Barth seems to remove the distinction between God's revelation and man's acceptance of it.[156] The recipient becomes part of special revelation itself, confusing the traditional distinction between inspiration and illumination.[157] Revelation is redefined as *experience*, not finished instruction, leading to issues involving authority, not unlike more reader-response approaches in hermeneutics.[158] God *with* man in *Geschichte* is the ultimate shared reference point of interpretation rather

---

150. It is worth noting that "we have no Christ except the one whom the apostles have given to us" via the written word (Warfield, *Revelation and Inspiration*, 187).

151. Van Til, *Barthianism*, 118, 138. This is opposed to Barth seeing the Bible as a mere witness away from itself to the truth of Christ (Torrance, *Karl Barth*, 111–12, 115–16).

152. Van Til, *Barthianism*, 172–73.

153. Warfield, *Shorter Writings*, 238.

154. Van Til, *Barthianism*, 136–37; *Sovereignty of Grace*, 61.

155. Provence, "Sovereign Subject," 241–60.

156. Van Til, *New Modernism*, 375; *Barthianism*, 488–90; *Reformed Pastor*, 93.

157. Barth, *Church Dogmatics*, I.1, 123–24.

158. Van Til, *Barthianism*, 249–50; Bromiley, "Authority of Scripture," 290–92. Barth saw Scripture as having only a fallible, occasional, and functional authority (Johnson, "Karl Barth," 164; Fackre, "Revelation," 20–21).

than the antecedent God.¹⁵⁹ Whether or not one agrees with his assessment of Barth, Van Til affirms significant truths regarding the Creator-creature distinction with implications for hermeneutics.

Recently, Oliphint has highlighted another implication of the Creator-creature distinction for hermeneutics related to the above discussion. Citing Muller in support,¹⁶⁰ he argues for an *ontological* priority in interpretation based on the fundamental *aseity* of God. This ontological priority means that rather than interpreting texts in isolation (with the danger of imposing an extra-biblical conception of God on a given text), the unity of Scripture must be taken into account because God is immutable and independent of his creation. The unity of Scripture is dependent on the nature of God. Hence, the unity of Scripture must be given priority in interpretation. By being created in the image of God, man has an inherent understanding that God exists as independent from his creation (Rom 1:18ff.). An understanding of God *as God*, apart from and prior to creation, informs our "ontological conception," which functions as our guide in handling other texts which speak of God (or anything else for that matter). This is merely another way of affirming the Reformed principle of Scripture interpreting Scripture, letting clearer passages interpret the less clear (e.g., WCF 1.9).¹⁶¹ We could say that as a creature, man cannot interpret Scripture as uncreated and God as not independent without undermining the ontological priority of the text.

The Person of Christ

The Creator-creature distinction is prominent in his discussion of the person of Christ. Taking his cue from Chalcedon, Van Til affirms that the eternal Son, the second person of the ontological Trinity assumed a fully human nature in the incarnation, yet did not lose his full deity in any way.¹⁶² Only non-Christian notions of the divine-human relationship involve God having to limit himself.¹⁶³ The eternal Son took on full humanity, without being absorbed by it.¹⁶⁴ He did not become a human person, nor did he mingle the two natures and become a third entity. Rather, "in Christ, the divine and the human natures are so related as to be 'two natures, without confusion, without change,

---

159. Van Til, *Barthianism*, 405.
160. Muller, *The Triunity of God*, 451–52.
161. Oliphint, *God with Us*, 26–29.
162. Van Til, *Defense of Faith*, 37.
163. Van Til, *Theistic-Ethics*, 37.
164. Van Til, *Great Debate*, 109.

without division, without separation.'"[165] One implication is that "even in the incarnation Christ could not commingle the eternal and the temporal. The eternal must always remain independent of and prior to the temporal."[166] All heresies related to the doctrine of the Trinity "may be reduced to the one great heresy of mixing the eternal with the temporal."[167] Van Til's main concern was to keep God and man in a proper relation to one another, without confusion. In creation and no less, re-creation, the Creator remains distinct from the creature, expressed uniquely in the incarnation.[168]

Van Til repeatedly measures his critique of others according to the Chalcedonian formulation to evaluate whether justice is done to the Creator-creature distinction. For example, as opposed to one level of being with two aspects, eternal and temporal, in which the temporal is merely a particular expression of the eternal (e.g., Platonism), Van Til points to Chalcedon as showing the close union between the two in Christ, yet *without intermixture*. Against Bowne, he argues that the divine does not merge into the human person of Christ, which would involve the eternal merging in the temporal.[169] It is important to note that exactly *how* the eternal and temporal are combined without intermixture is only exhaustively known by God.[170] In combating forms of dialecticism that would correlate notions of being and non-being, Van Til again points to Chalcedon to affirm the distinction between deity and humanity.[171] In his critique of Barth, he opposed any notion that God, in Christ, is free to submit himself to the limitations of the creature in *Geschichte*, with man participating in it.[172] Furthermore, he argues that Barth's stress on the identity between Christ, the revelation event in *Geschichte*, and man's participation removes the restrictions of Chalcedon. This is what Van Til calls *actualizing* the incarnation. This involves interpreting the two natures of Christ "in terms of the one act that takes place within both" wherein the immutability of the divine nature and the "immutability" of the human nature are compromised in the Christ-event.[173] Van Til also stresses that man was and always will be a creature,

165. Van Til, *Defense of Faith*, 37–38.
166. Van Til, *Defense of Faith*, 38.
167. Van Til, *Systematic Theology*, 358.
168. Van Til, *Systematic Theology*, 359–60.
169. Van Til, *Christian Epistemology*, 180; *God of Hope*, 290–91.
170. Van Til, *Christian Epistemology*, 31.
171. Van Til, *Theory of Knowledge*, 316–20.
172. Van Til, *Barthianism*, 44.
173. Van Til, *Barthianism*, 96–97, 269, 315. By *immutability* of the human nature, he means not being able to become uncreated or some created being outside the bounds of being "human."

even in redemption. We must not confuse ethical rebellion with ontology.[174] Hence, in the incarnation and work of redemption, the distinction between the Creator and creature remains unchanged.[175] Re-creation follows and restores creation, it does not establish it.

Some may fault Van Til for over-emphasizing the distinction between the two natures of Christ, seemingly at the expense of their union, which was also affirmed at Chalcedon and reinforced at Constantinople II (hypostatic union). Van Til does argue against Barth using the term "separation" to describe the relation between the two natures,[176] but elsewhere he uses the more traditional language of "distinct."[177] Granted, his argument suffers from inconsistent terminology. He often emphasized the distinction between the natures for his apologetic purposes. However, upon closer examination, his discussion of Chalcedon clearly denounces the error of Nestorianism, which he sees as both an assault on the Trinity and as confusing the eternal with the temporal (resembling a form of deism in which the divine is separated from the human).[178] However, he also affirms the union of the two natures in the one person of the Son.[179] Indeed, he even stresses the indivisible and inseparable relation between the two natures to avoid any notion that it is not a real union.[180]

One key hermeneutical implication is that we cannot allow temporality to limit our consideration of the divine author in all of his self-contained fullness. Historical and temporal concerns are prominent in contemporary hermeneutics. Rather than taking away from human authorial intentions, consideration of the divine establishes them in their Spirit-inspired intent.[181] The only way consideration of either the human or divine author becomes problematic is if both are seen on the same level of being or participation, in which justice done to one necessarily takes away from the other and one attempts to merge the two in a way that neither remain themselves.

---

174. Van Til, *Sovereignty*, 8.
175. Van Til, *Systematic Theology*, 209, 212.
176. Van Til, *Barthianism*, 315.
177. Van Til, *Barthianism*, 463.
178. Van Til, *Systematic Theology*, 358–60.
179. Van Til, *Defense of Faith*, 37.
180. Van Til, *Christian Apologetics*, 47.
181. Poythress, "Dispensing," 481–99.

Sovereignty and Election

Another context where Van Til emphasizes the Creator-creature distinction is in terms of sovereignty and election. In discussing the issue of divine sovereignty and human responsibility, he points out that both hyper-Calvinists and Arminians fall into similar errors. The former compromises responsibility to maintain sovereignty, while the latter do the reverse. Van Til sees the two extremes as stemming from one common denominator. Frame summarizes as follows:

> Unwittingly, both hyper-Calvinists and Arminians at this point see God and man on a *common scale of being*, so that anything ascribed to God must be taken from man, and vice versa . . . There are two distinct levels of reality: that of the Creator and that of the creature. There are also two distinct levels of causality: divine causality and causation from within the world . . . thus, it is Van Til's "two-circle metaphysics," his *distinction between Creator and creature*, that enables him to have a strong doctrine of divine sovereignty together with a strong doctrine of human freedom.[182]

Rather than divine sovereignty and human freedom on one balanced scale, wherein affirming one side necessarily takes away from the other side, Van Til asserts two levels of being in which exercising the nature of one does not limit the other. He argues that the absolute will of God is very presupposition of the will of man:

> Looked at in this way, that which to many seems at first glance to be the greatest hindrance to moral responsibility, namely the conception of an absolutely sovereign God, becomes the very foundation of its possibility.[183]

This insistence on consciously presupposing two levels of being with the issue of sovereignty and responsibility could also be applied to interpretation. For example, consider the role of creativity in interpretation. In terms of one level of being, one may conclude that any human creativity used in interpretation would necessarily detract from or at least modify the objective creativity of God's revelation. This may lead to avoiding all creativity by seeking to isolate the meaning of a text in a way that ignores complexity, reducing the fullness of meaning down to what is deemed scientific or controlled. However, if a two-level ontology is assumed, human creativity,

---

182. Frame, *Van Til*, 81–82 (emphasis mine).
183. Van Til, *Defense of Faith*, 84–85.

though never absolute, would reflect the absolute creativity of God. It is *necessary* for finite creatures to creatively summarize the complex truth revealed in Scripture in order to grow in understanding it according to its nature. The Bible would still function as the ultimate authority—this would not inhibit creativity but enhance it. The only creativity prohibited would be of the rebellious sort. Complexity is only a problem for hermeneutics if a one-level ontology is assumed, resulting in a search for ultimate certainty and objectivity in the human mind. However, with a two-level ontology, we can embrace complexity without reductionism.

This brings us to the issue of election. Van Til again stresses the importance of the Creator-creature distinction in seeking to avoid mixing the eternal with the temporal in soteriology:

> Even if we say that in the case of any one individual sinner the question of salvation is in the last analysis dependent upon man rather than God, that is if we say that man can of himself accept or reject the gospel as he pleases, we have made the eternal God dependent upon man. We have then, in effect, denied the incommunicable attributes of God. If we refuse to mix the eternal and the temporal at the point of creation and at the point of the incarnation, we must also refuse to mix them at the point of salvation.[184]

In conceiving of election and reprobation in these terms, he guards against thinking of man as exercising his created will as if in a void, without relation to or dependence upon the all-embracing will and counsel of God.[185] God is the source of ultimate causation for both election and reprobation, notwithstanding the presence of secondary causes. However, while God's decree is behind both election and reprobation (with "equal ultimacy"), it is *not* behind them in the same manner.[186] Van Til seeks to articulate the doctrine of election in such a way as to affirm God's pre-interpretation of all things, including reprobation, before the foundation of the world.[187] While he acknowledges great mystery here for man, it is no mystery to God.

---

184. Van Til, *Defense of Faith*, 40.
185. Van Til, *Theory of Knowledge*, 195; *Apologetics*, 36.
186. Frame, *Van Til*, 87; Van Til, *Theology*, 90.
187. Frame, *Van Til*, 88.

Rebellion against the Creator-Creature Distinction: The Fall

Perhaps one of Van Til's most innovative contributions is his diagnosis of unbelieving thought patterns in terms of the biblical account of the fall. He often uses the fall narrative as *the* case study and origin of rebellious epistemology. Prior to the fall, man was to know and interpret reality with God as the final reference point in all predication. God gave a sure command with a determined outcome. However, Satan suggested to Adam and Eve that what God said was not determinative of reality and that they could make that determination themselves, apart from God. Through mere observation and future prediction, based on the powers of their own logic, they could legislate what was possible or impossible, moral or immoral.[188] Presented with God's word and Satan's antithetical word, they were tempted to decide which was true—as ultimate judge. This assumes that God (and his word) is merely one fact among many to be evaluated, rather than *the* Fact which determines all others. However, in assuming the role of neutral judge and the fallibility of God, they already decided *against* God.[189] "This . . . was a denial of God's absoluteness epistemologically. *Thus neutrality was based upon negation. Neutrality is negation.*"[190] In short, Satan tempted them to think and act autonomously.

When man sinned, he sought to interpret reality without reference to God. The revelatory character of every fact, even his own consciousness, was denied. Man assumed an *uncreated* stance from which interpretation would be original, not derivative.[191] Rather than thinking according to God's sure revelation, man searches for ideals *in general*, in terms of knowledge and morality. "Man made for himself a false ideal of knowledge, the ideal of absolute inderivative comprehension. This he could never have done if he had continued to recognize that he was a creature."[192] When man saw that he could not obtain comprehensive, knowledge of all things, he blamed his own finitude. Hence, he confused the ontological and ethical aspects of reality—a common trait among non-Christian philosophies.[193]

Van Til helpfully summarizes the epistemological effects of the fall in terms of a *rationalistic-irrationalistic dialectic*:

---

188. Van Til, *Christian Apologetics*, 33–34; *Theory of Knowledge*, 42–44, 47.
189. Van Til, "My Credo," 6; *Reformed Pastor*, 139.
190. Van Til, *Christian Epistemology*, 21 (emphasis his).
191. Van Til, *Christian Apologetics*, 79–80; *Barthianism*, 324.
192. Van Til, *Christian Apologetics*, 42–43.
193. Van Til, *Christian Apologetics*, 43. He points out that a denial of ethical rebellion of the fall always denies a proper Creator-creature relationship (*Systematic Theology*, 76).

CHAPTER 4: CREATOR-CREATURE DISTINCTION

> The root of both irrationalism and rationalism is the idea of the ultimacy of man. If this root is not taken out, it will do little good to trim off some of the wildest offshoots of irrationalism with the help of rationalism, or to trim off some of the wildest offshoots of rationalism with the help of irrationalism.[194]

The solution is not found in striking a balance between the two. Rather, the unstable combination of *both* stems from a faulty starting point. There is no essential difference between *what* the rationalist and irrationalist are defending. They only differ in *how* they defend it. Both are interested in suppressing the fact of their own creaturehood and have become friends against their common foe—Christianity.[195] In rejecting God's revelation, man *irrationalistically* assumes that no rational scheme could explain or control reality.[196] This included the idea of uncreated, uninterpreted brute facts and an uncontrolled environment of chance (i.e., pure contingency).[197] Hence, God is reduced by man to the same level as man, with both seeking the truth in an ultimate environment of unknown mystery and chance.[198] In essence, the Creator-creature distinction is discarded in favor of God and man as both of one being surrounded by a factual space over which *no one* has control.[199] Unbelieving thought exhibits epistemological irrationalism correlated with a metaphysic of chance.[200] On the other hand, man also *rationalistically* assumes no need to obtain information from any outside source other than his own mind in order to know and judge reality. In effect, man made a universal negative judgment—assuming to know all things, knowing for certain that no absolute truth can be found anywhere and what God said could not be true.[201]

Ironically, man "has to be both in order to be either"[202] and seeks to combine elements of both, in order to preserve his own autonomy—unifying experience through a principle of coherence rooted in his own mind.[203] For example, he irrationally claims that all things are possible, but

---

194. Van Til, *Intellectual Challenge*, 19.
195. Van Til, *Intellectual Challenge*, 17–19.
196. Van Til, *Christian Apologetics*, 154.
197. Van Til, *Doctrine of Scripture*, 13.
198. Van Til, *Theory of Knowledge*, 47–48; *Reformed Pastor*, 150; "Creation," 51.
199. Van Til, *Barthianism*, 231–33.
200. Frame, *Van Til*, 233. Van Til suggests for the unbeliever that "only if reality as a whole is wholly contingent is man wholly free" (*Sovereignty of Grace*, 11).
201. Van Til, *Christian Apologetics*, 154–55; *Reformed Pastor*, 145.
202. Van Til, *Intellectual Challenge*, 17.
203. Van Til, *Great Debate*, 214.

rationalistically, that no one knows. He rationalistically claims, through universal negative propositions, that some things are not possible, but irrationalistically, that no one knows all things. Van Til explains:

> About chance no manner of assertion can be made. In its very idea it is the irrational. And how are rational assertions to be made about the irrational? If they are to be made, then it must be because the irrational is itself wholly reduced to the rational ... he must assert on the one hand that all reality is nonstructurable in nature, and on the other hand that he himself has virtually structured all of it. Thus all predication is, in the nature of the case, self-contradictory.[204]

The bottom line is that once man assumes ultimacy, he must either know everything or he cannot know anything.[205] This creates insurmountable tension and an unstable mix of both notions, ending in self-contradiction. For example, seeking to know all things, man is frustrated by the limits of human language and driven to conclude that the reality is a mirage.[206] Moreover, through a denial of the Creator-creature distinction, man ceases to know the limits of his own reason, ending in futility.[207] "The proper limits of human thought cannot be ascertained unless one first takes one's stand upon the position of revelation."[208] The history of philosophy could be seen as a grappling with the limits of human reason—even the escape from *creaturely* reason since the fall. This is not a neutral pursuit, but one in which the idea of pure factuality and chance are employed to "guarantee that no true authority, such as that of God as the Creator and Judge of men, will ever confront man."[209] To the contrary:

> the biblical position is not like that of rationalism or like that of irrationalism. Nor is it like any combination of these two. It is based on the presupposition that man knows truly though not comprehensively because God does know all things in terms of his self-contained being and has revealed himself to man.[210]

---

204. Van Til, *Defense of Faith*, 148; *New Hermeneutic*, 101–7.
205. Van Til, *Christian Apologetics*, 156.
206. Van Til, *Sovereignty*, 47, 50.
207. Rom 1:18–32; Wright, *Mission of God*, 164.
208. Van Til, *Reformed Pastor*, 150.
209. Van Til, *Defense of Faith*, 147. Elsewhere, he states that "not being creatures of God, they could not have sinned against such a one" ("My Credo," 7).
210. Van Til, *Barthianism*, 433.

Though there are wide-ranging hermeneutical implications concerning this dialectic as a diagnostic tool, we will consider a few of the more salient ones. First, in evaluating hermeneutical philosophy from a Christian perspective, one must ask, what ultimate reference point is being presupposed? Is it the creature or Creator?[211] If the former, without succumbing to a superficial simplicity or over-generalization,[212] it would be expedient to ask where inconsistencies exist in such methods, in terms of an unstable mixture of both rationalism and irrationalism. Rather than seeing the different approaches in philosophical hermeneutics as merely a battle between modern and postmodern schools, it would be more consistent and helpful to address the deeper issues of autonomy and monistic metaphysics in both.

Second, in discussing the fall and its effects on the history of philosophy, Van Til argues that certain *gaps* are introduced through this dialectic not present prior to the fall. One is the gap between truth and reality (e.g., there are facts but no fully known system of reality to make sense of those facts). Another is the gap between fact and the mind (e.g., between what is outside and inside the mind). Irrationally, man assumed that truth was found *apart* from a rationally controlled scheme of reality given by God. Rationalistically, man sought to provide unity rooted in his own mind—a system based on comprehensive knowledge. However, this only functions as a limiting notion due to it being an ultimate context of irrational mystery. Both gaps are symptomatic of an essentially *atomistic* approach. All non-Christian philosophies virtually deny the unity of truth. This introduces a certain dualism which cannot adequately be resolved while still holding onto the ultimacy of the human mind.[213] Regarding biblical interpretation, unbelieving thought tends toward *decontextualizing* the Bible from its revealed contextual system of truth concerning God and his relation to man as a creature, and then seeks to *re-contextualize* its parts back together again from the ultimacy of the human mind. Inevitably, this re-contextualizing distorts the message of Scripture.[214]

Conclusion

The Creator-creature distinction is paramount in Van Til's theology proper, expressed in a number of different contexts and connected to other

---

211. Van Til, *Theory of Knowledge*, 49, 51.

212. E.g., things are complicated by the fact that the unbeliever knows the truth in some sense and suppresses it in another (Rom 1:18–20).

213. Van Til, *Christian Apologetics*, 153–57.

214. Van Til, *Systematic Theology*, 63–66; Frame, *Knowledge of God*, 53.

important emphases. In addition, it is the basis for evaluating various forms of non-Christian philosophy, which deny this distinction. Since the fall, man has conceived of his own mind as autonomous and ultimate, resulting in an unstable and inconsistent mixture of rationalistic and irrationalistic elements and insurmountable gaps in epistemology. Such things as comprehensive knowledge, history, and language only become problematic if man seeks to understand them *in himself*, seeking to go beyond his creaturely limits. Finitude is only problematic if one is seeking to think other than as a creature.

This is a helpful approach for evaluating contemporary biblical hermeneutics from a Christian worldview, and to avoid methodology which undermines its message. "If God is not made first in human interpretation, then he is not God at all."[215] Doing justice to the Creator-creature distinction is the first step in making God first in interpretation. In the next chapter, we will address another important emphasis in Van Til's doctrine of God with implications for contemporary hermeneutics.

---

215. Van Til, *Barthianism*, 262.

Chapter 5: Incomprehensibility

Introduction

WHILE THE CREATOR-CREATURE DISTINCTION is most prominently expressed in Van Til's doctrine of God, it is *incomprehensibility* for which he is notoriously known in reformed circles. If the Creator-creature distinction is seen as his most pervasive category for theology proper, incomprehensibility can be seen as an important subset of that distinction. In what follows, we will first consider his debate with Gordon Clark over God's incomprehensibility and his further elaborations. Next, we will look at how Van Til discusses incomprehensibility in relation to the concepts of *paradox* and *mystery*. Lastly, we will consider hermeneutical implications related to the divine and human authors of Scripture in terms of incomprehensibility and meaning.

The Clark Debate

Incomprehensibility was at the center of Van Til's feud with Gordon Clark. Clark was a Christian philosopher who sought ordination in the Orthodox Presbyterian Church (OPC). During the examination process, Clark's views regarding epistemology were questioned by some as to their consistency with Reformed theology. The debate revolved around the relationship between God's knowledge and man's knowledge. Our concern here is not with the politics and procedure of their dispute in the OPC (1944-1948), but rather with the theological and philosophical elements expressed therein. After addressing the substance of the debate, we will suggest two potential remedies overlooked *within* its very documents[1] and one remedy not mentioned but found in the writings of *both* Clark and Van Til. In these remedies, we will get a clearer picture of Van Til's view of incomprehensibility.

---

1. Orthodox Presbyterian Church, "Minutes of Twelfth"; "Minutes of Thirteenth"; "Minutes of Fifteenth." The initial complaint against Clark can be found in "Minutes of Twelfth," 5-30. For other contextual factors and discussion related to the debate, see: Hakkenburg, "Battle," 329-50; Klooster, *Incomprehensibility of God*.

Van Til's doctrine of the incomprehensibility of God was represented in the complaint against Clark,[2] yet more nuanced in his own writings on the subject. Because God is on another level of being as Creator, man cannot have the same identical knowledge, but only derivative knowledge.[3] Therefore, there must not merely be a quantitative, but also a *qualitative* difference between God's knowledge and man's knowledge. A mere quantitative difference implies a difference in degree rather than in kind, which would transgress the Creator-creature distinction and the majesty of God.[4] The complaint objected to Clark's view that:

> any knowledge that man possesses of any item must coincide with God's knowledge of the same item in order to be true knowledge, thus failing to distinguish with respect to content between the Creator's knowledge of any thing and creaturely knowledge of the same thing.[5]

In short, Clark was charged with not rising above a mere quantitative distinction in terms of content. The emphasis on the Van Til side was clearly on avoiding unbiblical rationalism.

While the dialogue suffered from terminological confusion, Clark "argued that Van Til's notion of 'qualitative difference' . . . with no coincidence 'at any single point' leads to irrationalism and to not only an analogy of the truth," but something other than the truth.[6] Clark was adamant that there cannot be two levels of truth (one for God and one for man), with neither being the *same* truth for the other. While he believed that God knows an infinite number of propositions, including all proper relations between them, this was not qualitatively different in terms of the meaning regarding any one proposition known by God and man.[7] For Clark, the emphasis was clearly on avoiding any form of unbiblical irrationalism.

Those who followed Clark continued to press the point that Van Til's notion of incomprehensibility led to skepticism and put a true knowledge of God in jeopardy. Hoeksema argued that "if what God has revealed to us has a different meaning for him than for us, God is not only incomprehensible, but also unknowable." He suggested that the real crux of the debate was not

---

2. It is important to note that the debate was carried out in an indirect manner. Van Til agreed to and signed the complaint against Clark, but probably did not author it, nor did he directly examine Clark. His engagement is found in his own writings.

3. Van Til, *Systematic Theology*, 33.

4. Orthodox Presbyterian Church, "Minutes of Twelfth," 9–10.

5. Orthodox Presbyterian Church, "Minutes of Twelfth," 30.

6. Hunt, "An Introduction," 68–69.

7. Orthodox Presbyterian Church, "Minutes of Fifteenth," 22; Clark, *Logic*, 129.

incomprehensibility, but whether revelation is intelligible to man.[8] Nash, though not uncritical of Clark's later ideas, concludes that there must be points of *identical* coincidence for there to be true knowledge.[9] Moreover, he claims that Van Til rejects that anyone can know something about the mind of God without it being the product of special revelation.[10] Reymond explicitly endorses what he calls Clark's "Christian rationalism," seeing this as a "wholesome corrective" to Van Til.[11] However, his critique is somewhat perplexing, considering that elsewhere he explicitly endorses Van Til's two-level ontology and epistemology based on the Creator-creature distinction.[12] Yet, he contends that God is able to impart knowledge to man *univocally*, and that man must think God's thoughts *univocally* after him (i.e., true knowledge is univocal knowledge).[13] He sees Van Til's doctrine of analogy as problematic—as an unstable blend of univocity and equivocity. To him, Van Til had not sufficiently stated the clear nature of the qualitative difference between divine and human knowledge.[14] He suggests that, according to Van Til, God is still as incomprehensible after his revelation as he was prior to it, leading to an unbiblical skepticism.[15]

Latent Remedies and Further Nuances

The impasse created by the use of poorly defined terminology unfortunately obscured two latent remedies embedded in the OPC documents themselves which could have not only provided clarity, but also could have highlighted helpful nuances in Van Til's writings on incomprehensibility.[16] Indeed, one pitfall was that Clark emphasized the identity of the *object* known by God and man, whereas the Van Til side emphasized difference in the *subjective knowing* between God and man. Hence, neither side adequately distinguished between *knowing* and the *thing known*.[17]

---

8. Hoeksema, *Clark-Van Til*, 12.
9. Nash, "Gordon Clark's Theory," 173–74; *Mind of Man*, 90, 101.
10. Nash, *Mind of Man*, 100.
11. Reymond, *Justification*, 109; *Systematic Theology*, 109.
12. Reymond, *Justification*, 42–43; *Systematic Theology*, 97–98.
13. Reymond, *Justification*, 44–45, 101–4.
14. Reymond, *Systematic Theology*, 102–3n19; *Justification*, 100, 104.
15. Reymond, *Justification*, 100–1.
16. Hunt, "An Introduction," 82–89.
17. *Minutes of Twelfth*, 9–15, 29–30; *Minutes of Fifteenth*, 22.

God's Simplicity

The first latent remedy is *God's simplicity*, which was affirmed by both sides. Van Til often stressed that God's being is coterminous with his knowledge (as well as his attributes).[18] Consequently, God's knowledge has divine attributes. Indicative of divine simplicity with respect to God's knowledge is his statement that "God's thought with respect to anything is as a unit . . . in God's mind, any bit of information that he gives to man is set in the fullness of his one supreme act of self-affirmation."[19] Clark also clearly affirmed divine simplicity,[20] even with respect to knowledge. For example, the committee appointed to examine the debate acknowledged his belief that "God's knowledge of any truth is not divorced from his knowledge of all truth" (as opposed to imperfect man), seeing in his position an acknowledgment of an essential distinction between God and man.[21] The committee goes on to conclude that Clark, considering the evidence he provided, would not deny a qualitative difference, in spite of both parties failing to make important distinctions in their argumentation.[22] In fact, the complaint even acknowledged that Clark recognized a difference in *mode*—God's knowledge is intuitive, whereas man's is discursive and dependent. However, it goes on to dismiss this point as not the issue of the debate, which in their mind concerned *contents* of knowledge related to incomprehensibility.[23] This was clearly a confusing and short-sighted conclusion. Elsewhere, Clark explicitly recognized a qualitative difference in this distinction as a necessary implication of divine simplicity.[24]

The committee also indicated that it was unfortunate that the complaint against Clark merely focused on an epistemological comparison between God and man, rather than emphasizing a qualitative difference against the backdrop of God's being and attributes.[25] Going one step further, the committee concluded that any definition of incomprehensibility should be deemed inadequate if it is not considered in relation to God's

---

18. Van Til, *Systematic Theology*, 201, 364, 371–72.
19. Van Til, *Systematic Theology*, 270.
20. Clark, *Logic*, 120–23; *Trinity*, 76–79.
21. Orthodox Presbyterian Church, "Minutes of Thirteenth," 50.
22. Orthodox Presbyterian Church, "Minutes of Thirteenth," 73.
23. Orthodox Presbyterian Church, "Minutes of Twelfth," 15. Perhaps Clark's emphasis on *object* and *mode* as opposed to subjective experience kept the view he *did* have implicit, about how God and man experienced knowledge differently (Frame, *Van Til*, 105).
24. Clark, "Bible as Truth," 163.
25. Orthodox Presbyterian Church, "Minutes of Thirteenth," 50.

being and perfections. They called this a "fundamental datum of theological thinking."[26] A later committee appointed by the 1947 General Assembly found that the "content of divine psychology is indivisible . . . knowledge in this sense is an attribute of God in which man cannot participate."[27] Clearly both sides mistakenly left this out of their consideration in terms of emphasis. Yet, if explored, both parties may have found common ground rather than talking past each other.

How might the consideration of divine simplicity have helped in the debate? Confusing terminology, such as "content," "mode," and "subjective knowledge" could have been more clearly understood in terms of divine attributes.[28] This would have done justice to Van Til's concerns regarding the Creator-creature distinction, as well as Clark's concept of "mode" without battle over the ambiguous "no point of coincidence."[29] Moreover, attention to divine simplicity could have highlighted the important relationship between epistemology and ontology for incomprehensibility.[30] While it is not clear to what extent Clark presupposed this relationship during the debate, his later writings indicate that he saw epistemology as *prior* to metaphysics, and did not speak of them in terms of a mutually dependent relationship.[31] To the contrary, Van Til often emphasized the relation between the two as involved in one another.[32]

God's Self-Knowledge

The second latent remedy affirmed by both sides is God's exhaustive self-knowledge. The Van Til side clearly saw a relationship between God's self-knowledge and incomprehensibility.[33] In stating its case, the complaint emphasized that God knows himself and all things and that this knowledge remains a mystery to the finite mind.[34] Any true knowledge for man must be analogical to God's knowledge of himself and all things.[35] The committee recognized that the complainants defined incomprehensibility in terms

26. Orthodox Presbyterian Church, "Minutes of Thirteenth," 76.
27. Orthodox Presbyterian Church, "Minutes of Fifteenth," 92.
28. Frame, *Van Til*, 106–7.
29. Hunt, "An Introduction," 84.
30. Orthodox Presbyterian Church, "Minutes of Fifteenth," 11, 14, 89–90.
31. Clark, *Trinity*, 80; Bahnsen, *Van Til*, 668–70.
32. E.g., Van Til, *Theistic-Ethics*, 34; *Defense of Faith*, 55, 70–71; *Apologetics*, 31–32.
33. E.g., Van Til, *Theory of Knowledge*, 150–51.
34. Orthodox Presbyterian Church, "Minutes of Twelfth," 9.
35. Orthodox Presbyterian Church, "Minutes of Twelfth," 13–14.

of God's self-knowledge, and that he can only be known "to the extent that he voluntarily reveals himself."[36]

Clark did not explicitly affirm God's self-knowledge in articulating incomprehensibility. However, he did affirm that God has infinite knowledge of his own being and that he cannot exhaustively reveal this knowledge to man. It is in this sense that man can never comprehend God. Though he describes this self-knowledge in terms of knowing an infinite number of propositions, finite man cannot know "a single attribute of him who knows himself and all things exhaustively 'at a glance.'"[37] Elsewhere, Clark states that "God is eternally omniscient" and that he is the "source of his own knowledge."[38] Even when arguing against Van Til for the identity of content between the knowledge of God and man, he recognizes that God knows all truth and "unless we know something that God knows, our ideas are untrue."[39] This implies that man must know truth with reference to God's knowledge, even if man cannot actually obtain this knowledge in full. However, Clark distanced himself from Van Til's emphasis on defining incomprehensibility in terms of God's self-knowledge, claiming such reason is circular (i.e., seeking to define God's incomprehensibility by his own comprehension of himself) and something to be avoided in matters of logic.[40]

The committee saw essential agreement between both sides regarding God's self-knowledge. Moreover, it specifically mentioned that God's self-knowledge could have provided a solution to the terminological difficulty which hampered the proceedings.[41] Because the object and content of God's knowledge are identical, man's knowledge is necessarily indirect and an "analogue of the truth rather than the object, the truth itself."[42] Hence, there is a qualitative difference present, not in any way destructive of true knowledge, but established by God, making knowledge possible.[43] The committee concluded that the key difference between God's knowledge and man's knowledge is not the *object* of that knowledge, but in the *apprehension* of it.[44] This difference in apprehension is *ontological* in

---

36. Orthodox Presbyterian Church, "Minutes of Thirteenth," 43.
37. Orthodox Presbyterian Church, "Minutes of Thirteenth," 43–45.
38. Clark, *Logic*, 118.
39. Clark, *Logic*, 129.
40. Clark, *Trinity*, 89.
41. Orthodox Presbyterian Church, "Minutes of Thirteenth," 76.
42. Orthodox Presbyterian Church, "Minutes of Thirteenth," 49.
43. Orthodox Presbyterian Church, "Minutes of Thirteenth," 49–50.
44. Orthodox Presbyterian Church, "Minutes of Fifteenth," 13. Clark failed to make the important distinction between *comprehension* and *apprehension* in the debate (e.g., *Minutes of Fifteenth*, 19–20, 93).

nature, rooted in the Creator-creature distinction, not merely a difference in quantitative degree.[45] This is contrary to Clark's assertion that what is not revealed is incomprehensible, implying that what God does reveal *is* comprehensible.[46] The committee summed up its report, following Berkhof: "our knowledge of God is on the one hand ectypal and analogical, but on the other hand also true and accurate, since it is a copy of the archetypal knowledge which God has of himself."[47]

Reference Point for Knowledge

This second remedy also highlights other important themes in Van Til regarding incomprehensibility in terms of God's knowledge. First, he often speaks of God's knowledge of himself as the *ultimate reference point* for man's knowledge. As we saw in chapter 4, the non-Christian dilemma is that man must know everything, or he knows nothing. However, this dilemma is removed by the Christian doctrine of incomprehensibility. Van Til explains:

> It is true that there must be comprehensive knowledge somewhere if there is to be any true knowledge anywhere, but this comprehensive knowledge need not and cannot be in us; it must be in God.[48]

This is another way of affirming that God is the *principium essendi* of knowledge. Citing Bavinck, Van Til argues that without God's self-conscious self-existence, man could not know anything.[49] Our knowledge must be dependent on God's self-contained knowledge, which is not correlated (i.e., co-dependent) with anything in creation. God has comprehensive knowledge of all things, not only because he created and controls all things, but *also* because he knows them in reference to his comprehensive self-knowledge. "God knows his own being to its very depths in one eternal act of knowledge."[50] God's incomprehensibility to man is rooted in the fact that God is exhaustively comprehensible to himself.[51] As the final reference point for all knowledge and interpretation, God must know all

---

45. Orthodox Presbyterian Church, "Minutes of Fifteenth," 13–14.
46. Orthodox Presbyterian Church, "Minutes of Fifteenth," 19, 31.
47. Orthodox Presbyterian Church, "Minutes of Fifteenth," 36; Berkhof, *Systematic Theology*, 35.
48. Van Til, *Defense of Faith*, 65.
49. Van Til, *Systematic Theology*, 29, 268.
50. Van Til, *Christian Apologetics*, 25.
51. Van Til, *Christian Apologetics*, 76.

things in relation to himself, which he must know exhaustively, to know truly and certainly.[52] By implication, "true human knowledge corresponds to the knowledge which God has of himself and the world."[53] However, as Van Til explains:

> It is impossible for man to know himself or any of the objects of the universe about him exhaustively as it is impossible for man to know God exhaustively. For man must know himself or anything else in the created universe in relation to the self-contained God. Unless he can know God exhaustively, he cannot know anything else exhaustively.[54]

This does not mean that any created thing is infinite (as God is), making comprehension impossible, but an object of knowledge can only be interpreted rightly if it is brought into relation with *both* the human mind and God's mind.[55]

Alluding to the "point of coincidence" language in the Clark debate, Van Til expresses another important nuance to his doctrine of incomprehensibility. However, before we proceed, we must reiterate its foundation. Without God's revelation, God is inapprehensible and unknowable to man. However, God has revealed himself in creation and through man's very constitution and capacities, and there is not one aspect of creation which does not display something of God's nature.[56] This is the very basis and presupposition upon which man is able to apprehend God or make any predication concerning him. By being in the image of God and by virtue of living in God's world, man knows something about *everything*, but does not know anything exhaustively, whether it be God *or* his creation.[57] This fact will help to avoid two particular errors. First, it keeps one "from making the false distinction between content of God's knowledge as being incomprehensible bit by bit, and the mode of God's knowledge as always incomprehensible."[58] In other words, the difference in mode is not dependent on component parts of knowledge, but rather on the nature of God as self-contained. Second, it keeps one from seeking the false ideal of exhaustive knowledge in the human mind and reducing facts to a system of timeless logic. Such a pursuit

---

52. Van Til, *Theory of Knowledge*, 36, 56–57; *Apologetics*, 27–28; *Psychology*, 142.
53. Van Til, *Christian Epistemology*, 1.
54. Van Til, *Systematic Theology*, 269; *Defense of Faith*, 67.
55. Van Til, *Defense of Faith*, 67.
56. Calvin, *Institutes*, 1.1–5.
57. Van Til, *Systematic Theology*, 268–70.
58. Van Til, *Systematic Theology*, 272.

is self-defeating, for there is no *a priori* resting place, for the human mind is part of moving history and time-bound.

This is where we come to Van Til's further commentary on the "point of coincidence" issue raised in the debate with Clark. In principle, God's knowledge and man's knowledge "coincide at *every* point in the sense that always and everywhere man confronts that which is already known or interpreted by God. *The point of reference cannot but be the same for man as for God.*"[59] However, on the other hand, divine and human knowledge *do not* coincide at any point in that human knowledge is always dependent upon prior divine knowledge (including God's self-knowledge). It is important to note that they coincide in such a way as to preclude any antirealism or ultimate skepticism, because anything the human mind could know is *already* known by God.[60] Moreover, "If there *could* be an identity of content, there *would* be and always has been an identity of content."[61] In other words, identity of content would necessitate an ontological identity of mind, transgressing the Creator-creature distinction. Identity is only properly understood in terms of the object of knowledge and analogy, not in terms of mode. In short, if the Creator-creature distinction is assumed, there is no point of coincidence in one sense, and coincidence at every point in another sense. This nuance avoids the either-or dilemma posed in the debate.

We may now briefly summarize Van Til's emphasis on God as the reference point for knowledge in light of the Clark debate. God reveals himself by eternally knowing himself. "Man has no approach to the knowledge of the nature of God—on which truth is admittedly dependent—except on the self-conscious activity of God as expressed in revelation."[62] Hence, there is identity of reference point—God's self-contained, self-referential knowledge. Van Til claims that the Clark controversy has shown that "any attempt that aims at identity of content between the mind of man and the mind of God overreaches itself and ends in skepticism."[63] Rather than Van Til's position ending in skepticism, it is Clark's insistence on identity of content, with its tendency to obscure the Creator-creature distinction, that ends in skepticism.

In light of the above discussion, a word may be said in response to the objections of Clark and his followers mentioned earlier.[64] First, Hoeksema

---

59. Van Til, *Systematic Theology*, 270 (emphasis his).
60. Anderson, "Frequently Encountered."
61. Van Til, *Systematic Theology*, 271 (emphasis his).
62. Van Til, *Systematic Theology*, 281.
63. Van Til, *Systematic Theology*, 281.
64. Hunt, "An Introduction," 89.

charges Van Til with bringing the very intelligibility of God's revelation into question, if it is not comprehensible in a univocal way to man. However, God's revelation is ultimately intelligible to himself in relation to his eternal, exhaustive self-knowledge. Therefore, it is *never* unintelligible, but rather both incomprehensible and apprehensible to man. Second, Nash argues that without identical coincidence in terms of object and nature, there is no true knowledge for man. However, in light of Van Til's refinements, the foundational point of coincidence is properly found in God's knowledge as a reference point for both God and man, not in the nature or mode of knowing which is rooted in the ontology of the human knower. We can say that both God and man can know the same object (e.g., a rose), but this object is what it is based on God's pre-interpretation of it (related to his divine self-knowledge) prior to it being an object of man's knowledge. Third, both Clark and Reymond take Van Til to task over not precisely defining *incomprehensibility* in terms of qualitative difference.[65] Yet, to what degree are we to define incomprehensibility without undermining it? What standard of precision is sufficient? Perhaps more importantly, what ontological assumptions underlie such questions?

Coherence and Correspondence

Another important nuance in Van Til's doctrine of incomprehensibility is in terms of epistemological coherence and correspondence. In setting out his terminology, he calls his position a "correspondence theory of truth" (which is actually opposed to what is often understood by the label).[66] Simply put, something is true if it corresponds to a fact in reality, as opposed to something being true if it merely coheres with other propositions. The main difference concerns the primary relation as to the conditions of a truth. Van Til distinguishes his position from an either-or approach concerning correspondence and coherence theories of truth in the tradition of Kant and Hegel, seeking to understand matters from a consistently Christian worldview. The struggle between realists and subjective idealists often ignores God as a foundational reference point. To the contrary,

> If all our thoughts about the facts of the universe are in correspondence with God's ideas of these facts, there will naturally be

---

65. Clark, *Trinity*, 84–85; Reymond, *Justification*, 100.
66. Van Til, *Christian Epistemology*, 2–3.

coherence in our thinking because there is complete coherence in God's thinking.[67]

A Christian epistemology will take into account true elements of both in relation to God, without reducing things down to either one (with man's reason as the ultimate reference point). First, there is perfect coherence in the mind of God and in his plan prior to anything outside of himself to which his knowledge might correspond.[68] Second, man's thinking must begin with correspondence to God's thoughts if there is to be any creaturely coherence, for it is rooted in the coherence of God.[69] In this sense, correspondence between God and man is necessarily more fundamental than correspondence between man and any other created thing. Though our coherence will never be as comprehensive or inclusive as God's, because it is based upon God's coherence and analogous to it, it will still be true knowledge.[70] However, if coherence is sought ultimately in the mind of man, with God merely treated as a fact to cohere with other facts in our experience, then God becomes a subset of man's coherence and no longer distinct from creation. If there is to be any true correspondence and coherence for human thought, it must be in relation to God's mind.

How does this intersect with *incomprehensibility*? How one conceives of it depends on whether one sees correspondence or coherence as rooted in God or man. If they are seen in relation to God, creaturely correspondence and coherence depends on God's *comprehensive* coherence. While God is incomprehensible to man, God is not incomprehensible to himself.[71] Hence, he can reveal truth in part with certainty. However, if correspondence and coherence are seen as rooted in the mind of man, then what is incomprehensible to man is also incomprehensible to God. In terms of Van Til's argument, either coherence is most complete in God or in man from which the correspondence of the other follows suit. If in the former, then man begins with correspondence in order to achieve analogous coherence. If in the latter, God must correspond with man's coherence in order to achieve his own coherence. This second notion wrongly correlates the Creator with his creation.

---

67. Van Til, *Christian Epistemology*, 2.
68. Van Til, *Defense of Faith*, 64.
69. Van Til, *Christian Epistemology*, 3; *Systematic Theology*, 375.
70. Van Til, *Christian Epistemology*, 200.
71. Van Til, *Systematic Theology*, 29–30.

The Incarnation

A third remedy *not* included in the debate documents is the doctrine of the incarnation.[72] Neither Clark nor Van Til made the explicit connection between incomprehensibility and the incarnation during the debate. However, both would have endorsed the Chalcedonian statement regarding the natures of Christ. As we have seen, Van Til particularly emphasized this doctrine as a model for the Creator-creature distinction. Perhaps the problematic phrase, "no point of coincidence," could have been placed in the context of the incarnation, rightly nuancing the emphasis on discontinuity in knowledge between God and man without separation, producing a more balanced account. For example, thinking in Chalcedonian categories may have helped to steer clear of accusations of nominalism regarding Van Til's view, since both would have been opposed to a corresponding Nestorian Christology. On the other hand, it may have helped to avoid accusations of univocity regarding Clark's view, since both would have been opposed to a corresponding Eutychianism. This would have also helped the complaint to present the idea of analogous knowledge in more explicitly *theological* rather than philosophical terms.[73]

Mystery and Paradox

Another area in which Van Til articulates his doctrine of incomprehensibility is in distinguishing between Christian and non-Christian views of "mystery" and issues of "paradox"[74] in theology. We have already spoken of the concept of "mystery" in relation to other matters in chapter 4. First, Van Til stressed that God is not subject to "possibility." Rather, "possibility" is subject to God. Second, God's rationality and being are coterminous. Hence, he is not ontologically or epistemologically dependent on anything, including any ultimate "mystery" or chance, within himself or from without. In short,

---

72. For a more recent emphasis on the importance of the incarnation for the relation between God's knowledge and man's knowledge, see: Oliphint, *Reasons*, 238, 245.

73. Hunt, "An Introduction," 88–89.

74. It has been suggested by some that a better term would be "hyperdox" (i.e., affirming the teaching of Scripture though it transcends human reasoning) rather than "paradox," which could imply categories of rationalism or irrationalism. Instead of beginning with human reason as far as it will go and leaving the "yet to be rationalized" to mystery, we *begin* with mystery in that we begin with God's transcendent knowledge (Stoker, "Reconnoitering Theory," 30; Van Til, *Common Grace*, 2nd ed, xxxvii-xxxviii).

while all things end in mystery for man in terms of incomprehensibility,[75] there is no mystery for God, who comprehends all things.

Intelligibility

All things are ultimately *intelligible* to God, and this intelligibility is not dependent upon man or anything else outside of God. In contrasting the apologetic approach of Romanism and Protestantism regarding the reference point for knowledge, Van Til states that "man's consciousness of self and of objects presupposes for their intelligibility the consciousness of God."[76] Van Til further observes that "it is not because God is irrational that we cannot comprehend him; it is because God is rational, and in the nature of the case, ultimately rational, that we cannot comprehend him."[77] In other words, God is incomprehensible to man because he rationally comprehends all things in relation to himself, not because he is in part or wholly an irrational mystery to himself. Our rationality as creatures *depends* on his ultimate rationality. There is no ultimate mystery or chance which is unknown to God. One could say that in light of God's comprehensive knowledge, Christian epistemology holds to an ultimate rationalism in God while non-Christian epistemology holds to an ultimate irrationalism.[78]

One may detect an antithesis here between how Van Til understands intelligibility and how Kant and those influenced by him have understood it. For Kant, intelligibility *depends* on the shaping of raw reality by the human mind and its categories.[79] For Van Til, intelligibility depends on the mind of God and his exhaustive self-knowledge. We see how diametrically opposed they are in terms of the source of intelligibility. On Kant's view, a God beyond human experience is *unknowable* and functions only as a limiting, but not actual, concept.[80] The only knowable God is shaped by the human mind.[81] Ultimately, this means that man only knows according to *his* self-knowledge, not in relation to God's. From a Christian worldview, God is distinct from human experience, but is knowable because God knows

---

75. Van Til, *Sovereignty*, 27; *Theory of Knowledge*, 37.
76. Van Til, *Christian Apologetics*, 97, 99–100.
77. Van Til, *Systematic Theology*, 33.
78. Van Til, *Defense of Faith*, 64–65; *Systematic Theology*, 35; *Apologetics*, 172.
79. Kant, *Prolegomena*, 78–79, 116, 124. Kant's scheme actually presupposes that divine, intelligible pre-interpretation revealed to man, is impossible.
80. Kant, *Critique*, 116, 188–90; Van Til, *Systematic Theology*, 261.
81. Kant, *Prolegomena*, 121–24; *Critique*, 368–72.

himself and has revealed himself in creation and Scripture. As a result, God and creation are ultimately intelligible and man is able to know him.

Christian vs. Non-Christian Mystery

Let us now unpack Van Til's idea of *mystery* a bit further as it relates to the topic at hand. One contrast between the Christian and non-Christian concept of mystery is that the latter "holds that there is either no mystery for God or man [i.e., rationalism] or there is mystery for both God and man [i.e., irrationalism]."[82] Both ideas are involved in one another. In discussing Paul's preaching in Athens (Acts 17), Van Til points out that though Paul singles out the altar to an unknown god, he does not endorse either the known or unknown gods as posited by the Greeks. This is perhaps due to the underlying principle "that their doctrine of the unknown god was involved in their doctrines of known gods."[83] Essentially, this principle is grounded in a monistic assumption—that all reality is of one kind of being. Known gods were of the same level of being, even if they were higher on the scale of that being. On the other hand, unknown gods were utterly unknowable and indeterminate, for man is finite. This raises important questions. How would one know if there is an unknown god? What is the relationship between the gods one claims to know and the god one does not know? If there is an unknowable god, can one really know with certainty of such a claim? Again, this pursuit is problematic in that it is impossible to know anything unless one knows everything, which is a problem for finite man but not for the infinite God.[84] The unknown god concept functions as a sort of ultimate irrational mystery, occupying a place in reality and inevitably influencing that reality epistemologically. This renders even the known parts suspect. If there is ultimate irrationalism somewhere in the universe, it will *never* be overcome.[85] Consequently, "Christians and non-Christians cannot pool or trade their mysteries as long as they are true to their positions."[86]

Another contrast between views of mystery is in terms of truth. Van Til explains:

> In effect, non-Christian thought argues that, because man cannot *comprehend* something in its knowledge, to that extent his

---

82. Van Til, *Defense of Faith*, 35; *Christian Epistemology*, 49–50; *Theory of Knowledge*, 50.

83. Van Til, *Paul at Athens*, 4–6.

84. Van Til, *Paul at Athens*, 8.

85. Van Til, *Psychology*, 75.

86. Van Til, *Systematic Theology*, 366.

knowledge is not true. Christians say that we as creatures do not need to and should not expect to comprehend anything fully. God comprehends fully, and that is enough for us. God's full comprehension gives validity to our partial comprehension.[87]

Partial knowledge is not a problem in the Christian system, because God has full comprehension. As such, true partial knowledge is not only possible but a reality due to God's revelation. In understanding anything, we either see it surrounded by God's rational comprehension or unintelligible mystery. We either bow to God or to the void.[88] Notice the difference here with Hirsch's view of validity. For Hirsch, validity is the probable (not certain) consensus regarding the intent of the human author.[89] For Van Til, validity of knowledge, and by implication, interpretation, is dependent upon God's certain comprehension.[90]

Van Til speaks of issues of *paradox*[91] as being involved in the very fact that man can never have comprehensive knowledge, and since man cannot have a fully comprehensible knowledge of God, "we are bound to come into what seems to be contradiction in all our knowledge."[92] In other words, our analogical knowledge must be related to God's absolute system of knowledge, yet we cannot fully comprehend that system.[93] It is important to note that Van Til is not saying that every Christian doctrine can be both affirmed and denied at the same time and in the same way. Rather, he is speaking of paradox in a broad sense, emphasizing the Creator-creature distinction and the element of mystery inherent in finite man trying to understand an infinite and immutable God who works in and through temporal creation.[94] He is saying that there are *apparent* contradictions or antinomies in theological affirmation. While man cannot resolve them, God does—in his own perfect coherence of knowledge. There is no real contradiction in such cases. To conclude that real contradictions exist would be to acknowledge not only incomplete coherence in our thinking, but also to conclude that God lacks

87. Van Til, *Systematic Theology*, 61 (emphasis his).
88. Van Til, *Systematic Theology*, 61. He uses the example of an atom.
89. Hirsch, *Validity*, ix–xi, 4.
90. Van Til, *Psychology*, 142–43.
91. It is important to note that Van Til uses *paradox, apparent contradiction*, and *antimony* interchangeably in his works (e.g., *Defense of Faith*, 67–69; *Common Grace*, 9–10). Along with the concept represented by these designations, he also speaks of being "fearlessly anthropomorphic" (i.e., affirming biblical evidence without denial of any one aspect as a result of abstract deduction) (e.g., *Common Grace*, 73, 187).
92. Van Til, *Defense of Faith*, 67, 384–85.
93. Van Til, *Defense of Faith*, 68.
94. See Oliphint's comments (Van Til, *Defense of Faith*, 384n6).

coherence and is not consistent with himself.[95] Furthermore, justifying a real contradiction involving God would assume an exhaustive knowledge of the necessary and sufficient conditions for what constitutes the divine being and abilities.[96] Some examples of antimonies Van Til highlights include the following: time and eternity; the one and the many;[97] the decrees of God and prayer;[98] divine sovereignty and human responsibility;[99] and glorifying God, who is not dependent on creation for glory.[100] There are two possible responses to these antimonies. Either the human mind solves them and concludes that unless it succeeds, there is no valid knowledge of such things available to man, or they must ultimately be solved in God or man's thinking would be meaningless altogether (not just regarding an issue which seems to be a mystery).[101]

Van Til suggests that antitheistic thought, in one sense, has actually *created* these antimonies. By seeking the false ideal of human knowledge (full comprehension) as an alternative to equivocity, man concludes that he must solve such antimonies in order to have true and adequate knowledge. He uses the Greek philosophers and Kant as examples of those who have endorsed such a false antithesis, introducing a natural epistemological separation between God and man, resulting in an all or nothing approach to truth. Van Til argues that the remedy to this type of thinking is found in a clear understanding of God as an exhaustively self-conscious being on whom man is dependent, not only for what seems to be paradoxical, but for any true knowledge.[102] Only then can man know truly without bearing the impossible burden of an exhaustive knowledge of all things.

Limiting Concepts

Related to the issues of mystery and paradox is Van Til's idea of a *limiting concept*.[103] Drawing upon Kant's terminology concerning the functional

---

95. Van Til, *Defense of Faith*, 68–69.
96. Crisp, *Revisioning Christology*, 7.
97. Van Til, *Christian Epistemology*, 60. The Trinity as three-in-one provides the ultimate ground for the inevitability of paradox for finite human reasoning (Johnson, "Can God?," 87).
98. Van Til, *Defense of Faith*, 68.
99. Geehan, *Jerusalem*, 399.
100. Van Til, *Common Grace*, 9.
101. Van Til, *Christian Epistemology*, 60.
102. Van Til, *Christian Epistemology*, 60–64, 102, 108–9; *Great Debate*, 20.
103. He also uses "supplemental concepts" interchangeably with "limiting concepts"

import of his *noumenal* realm, Van Til self-consciously redefines its meaning according to biblical presuppositions. There are two antithetical notions of this concept related to mystery. The non-Christian notion is purely negative, constructed on the basis of a non-Christian concept of mystery—the irrational, unknown aspect of reality yet to be rationalized. It has no positive content, but rather functions to limit thought, whether it actually exists or not (e.g., God). Yet, on a deeper level, such a god concept is seen as limited by creation and vice versa.[104] The Christian notion of a limiting concept is based on the Christian notion of mystery. The creature seeks to receptively-reconstruct the revelation of the Creator in a systematic form, resting upon the presupposition of the self-contained being of God revealed in Scripture (i.e., not correlated or dependent upon what man knows or does not know).[105] Theologically, the Christian seeks to formulate doctrine in a way that allows various aspects of biblical teaching to balance and inform each other,[106] rather than allowing one doctrine to override an apparently contradictory doctrine.[107] Van Til is emphasizing that man is finite. Therefore, his theological concepts are limiting in the sense that his concepts never exhaust the essence of the thing as known by God.[108] For example, consider Christ's full humanity and full deity. Christians affirm both truths together as taught in Scripture, while recognizing the mystery being professed in such a formulation.[109] Van Til employs limiting concepts to emphasize the actual *reality* of the self-contained God and what he has revealed in a way which does not allow man to solve or override that which is only comprehended by God, through a process of logical deduction based on human autonomy.[110]

(Frame, *Van Til*, 167).

104. E.g., the idea of pure rationality or pure fact (Van Til, *Christian Apologetics*, 186).

105. Van Til, *Common Grace*, 11.

106. In his recent work on paradox, Bosserman argues that Van Til and his followers have not sufficiently attended to how apparently contradictory doctrines do not merely "limit," but actually *require* one another in the Christian system (Bosserman, *Trinity*, 164–65).

107. E.g., General revelation and special revelation limit each other in that the former provides the context for the latter. However, both are ways in which God *freely* relates to creation (Van Til, *Christian Apologetics*, 75; "Introduction," 30–31). So, while general and special revelation "limit" each other, they do not limit God.

108. Frame, "Theological Paradox," 326, 329.

109. Van Til, *Systematic Theology*, 68; *Christian Epistemology*, 20; Tipton, "Triune Personal God," 136–37; Frame, *Van Til*, 165–75.

110. Loder and Neidhardt, *Knight's Move*.

Clark Revisited

Van Til's concept of mystery and paradox runs contrary to Clark, at least in how Clark expressed himself. He was skeptical of paradox and preferred to label such matters as merely something one does not understand and has *yet* to resolve through careful reasoning and logic.[111] Appeals are made to *a priori* principles of reason in general, apart from revelation in seeking solutions.[112] For example, in the divine sovereignty and human responsibility issue, Clark claims to have provided a logical solution.[113] However, as the minority report pointed out in the debate, his solution is unsatisfactory in that it eliminates a key element of the issue (i.e., free agency) in order to solve it.[114] In addition, Van Til claims that Clark's method actually denies sovereignty from the start in that it seeks to use logic outside the context of revelation. Clark seeks a methodological consistency that is recognized by all, Christian and non-Christian alike, but not predicated upon revelation from the start.[115] A Christian form of logical deduction would be used in *submission* to the teachings of Scripture from the start.[116]

Corroboration

Others have corroborated Van Til's general approach to the issue of paradox. Frame suggests that how one conceives of paradox reveals one's methodological commitments. All doctrines, even those with a seeming paradoxical relationship, must be understood as a system of truth grounded in God's systematic and exhaustive knowledge of himself and the world. Hence, even *prolegomena* must be subject to Scripture as any other theological doctrine rather than done apart from or prior to it.[117] Each major doctrine provides a perspective on the whole system. "All doctrines are 'apparently contradictory' in that none exhausts the fullness of truth, and their non-exhaustive character limits our ability to demonstrate formal logical consistency."[118]

---

111. Horton, "Consistently Reformed," 143; Clark, "Apologetics," 161. Clark does mention the importance of God as the source of all truth in the midst of his logical pursuits. The question is whether his view and use of logic is consistent with this fact.

112. Clark, *Christian Philosophy*, 49.

113. Clark, "Determinism," 13–23.

114. Orthodox Presbyterian Church, "Minutes of Thirteenth," 80.

115. Van Til, *Systematic Theology*, 278–79.

116. Frame, "Theological Paradox," 322–25.

117. Frame, "Theological Paradox," 299–300.

118. Frame, "Theological Paradox," 329.

However, they are not actually contradictory but true and intelligible as they are rooted in God's comprehension. Anderson asserts that if human knowledge is analogous to God's knowledge, it *must* be paradoxical. This is due to paradox being an implication of the Creator-creature distinction and incomprehensibility.[119]

Some Objections

Some have objected to the notion that all Christian truth is ultimately paradoxical. One such objection is that Van Til is paradoxical in handling of paradox (denying paradox in the very assertion of it). The basic claim is that Van Til is opposed to rational explanation *because* it is rational.[120] For example, Sproul et al. argues that Van Til affirms paradox in the doctrines of election and reprobation (i.e., Scripture teaches both), yet rationally explains that in order to be disobedient and punished for sin, man must be confronted with God in all he does.[121] Much could be said in response, but I will mention two key flaws. First, Van Til is not against rational analysis as such but, rather, rational analysis in general, without conscious regard for the Creator-creature distinction. This involves recognizing creaturely limits of reason which cannot be imposed on the divine mind as revealed in Scripture. Second, their discussion of reprobation leads to a straw man of Van Til's argument which stems from ignoring an important distinction found in the context of quotes drawn from his work, *Common Grace and the Gospel*.[122] In context, it is clear that Van Til is making a distinction between the decretive will of the Creator and the responsibility of the creature. On the one hand, he states that Adam ultimately could not have chosen not to sin in light of the divine decree. On the other hand, he could choose not to sin in a proximate, creaturely sense. Ignoring this distinction results in pitting the two against each other on the *same level* of being. Overlooking this distinction accounts for their conclusion that Van Til makes God out to be arbitrary and irrational. Curiously, his objectors conclude the following: "Divine 'control' and significant human choices hardly constitute a rational difficulty or apparent contradiction, not to mention paradox."[123] However, they give no explanation concerning how this is not a "rational difficulty."

---

119. Anderson, *Paradox*, 5–6, 311–12.
120. Sproul et al., *Classical Apologetics*, 287–88.
121. Sproul et al., *Classical Apologetics*, 290.
122. Van Til, *Common Grace*, 138, 140; Sproul et al., *Classical Apologetics*, 289–90.
123. Sproul et al., *Classical Apologetics*, 291.

A second and related objection stems from a false assumption. Reymond recognizes that paradox is a hermeneutical category in terms of the need to harmonize Scripture with Scripture.[124] However, he opposes the notion that all Christian truth is ultimately paradoxical to man. After acknowledging that Van Til holds to *apparent* contradictions, he proceeds to argue *as if* Van Til held to irreconcilable, *actual* contradictions set forth in Scripture.[125] This undercuts any sense of success in his argument. His reasons for denying Van Til's idea of paradox exhibit a fundamental and problematic assumption: argumentation according to *one level of being*.[126] For example, he states that Van Til's definition of paradox is problematic in that it rules out the possibility of being "reconciled before the bar of human reason" at some point in the future.[127] However, Van Til's whole point is that paradox cannot be exhaustively reconciled in the human mind, but only in God's mind. Reymond claims the coup de grâce to apparent contradictions is that if truth may appear in the form of irreconcilable contradiction, we give up the possibility of ever detecting falsehood. Why not accept truth claims contrary to Scripture as merely an apparent contradiction?[128] While all truth is ultimately paradoxical, not all truths are equally apparent in terms of this ultimate paradox. We are enabled to grow in understanding and to detect falsehood according to Scripture by the aid of the Holy Spirit. The problem is that Reymond does not consistently recognize that Van Til's concept of paradox is in terms of the Creator-creature distinction, not growth in creaturely knowledge (though he certainly does not rule this out). If growth in creaturely knowledge diminished paradox, it would imply a *one*-level ontology on which man could move up the scale toward God-like knowledge. To the contrary, man may grow in knowledge and harmonization of biblical truth in developing a *creaturely* replica of God's ultimate system, but never in a way which diminishes the Creator-creature distinction regarding paradox. Any progress is dependent on divine knowledge and God freely revealing truth to creatures, not on man's logical abilities to reduce paradox. Much like Clark, Reymond ends up confusing the truth known with the mode of knowing when evaluating paradox.[129]

---

124. Reymond, *Systematic Theology*, 103.

125. Reymond, *Systematic Theology*, 104–7. Basinger makes the same mistake (Basinger, "Biblical Paradox," 207–9, 211).

126. Granted, this is an *inconsistency* in Reymond, not a view he explicitly endorses (*Systematic Theology*, 115–16).

127. Reymond, *Systematic Theology*, 105.

128. Reymond, *Systematic Theology*, 106–7.

129. It may be added that often the law of non-contradiction is invoked against paradox (e.g., Basinger, "Biblical Paradox," 213). However, even this law is rooted in

Hermeneutical Implications

We conclude our discussion of Van Til's doctrine of incomprehensibility by sketching out some important hermeneutical implications. Each will pick up on a particular emphasis in his formulation.

First, his emphasis on the Creator-creature distinction highlights the need to address the mode of thought as it pertains to *subjective* knowing. Attention is often given to either the human author or reader of the Bible to the exclusion of the divine author in this regard, especially in terms of the limits of comprehension. In light of the current emphasis on the limits of human comprehension, a Christian hermeneutic would avoid choosing between alternatives which are inconsistent with a biblical incomprehensibility (e.g., must know everything to know anything truly or one knows nothing truly) in order to establish a foundation for truth and meaning. This problematic pursuit either seeks a presumptuous form of comprehension and certainty in terms of historical-grammatical concerns, or a subjective pragmatism often based on common sense dictated by the interpreter.[130] Neither escapes the pitfalls of seeking to transcend the limits of human knowledge. For example, man does not have to comprehend authorial intent or historical context in order to interpret truly, for God comprehends it all. God's intent revealed in Scripture will not contradict creation or history as such, but it cannot be reduced to them. God's knowledge and control of all things go hand in hand. He cannot fully know that which he does not exercise full control over. Based on revelation, God indeed knows all that is involved in interpretation: knowing subjects (God and man) and all objects of knowledge. In fact, if God does not know all things involved in interpretation, he can give no authoritative interpretation of anything at all, including his own Scripture.[131] However, as true interpretation is rooted in God and not dependent upon creation to supply such meaning (for itself or God), not only is God self-interpreting, but his word (as canon) is also self-interpreting.

Second, the doctrines of God's simplicity and exhaustive self-knowledge provide the basis and ground for true knowledge in interpretation.

God, and is to be imaged in the logic of man. It is not a tool to judge the veracity of God's revelation or to rule out certain truths seemingly incompatible with human reason. It is to be understood according to a two-level ontology, not adhered to by God and man in the same way, but rather as Creator and creature.

130. Apologetic arguments for the existence of God based on the phenomenon of consciousness (e.g., J.P. Moreland) reveal similar flaws related to seeing man's consciousness rather than God's as the reference point for knowledge (Sutanto, "Covenantal Apologetics," 777–91).

131. Van Til, *Theory of Knowledge*, 221.

The fact that God is the ultimate reference point for our interpretation of the Bible should direct how meaning is conceived and sought. Generally speaking, God is the ultimate context or category of creaturely interpretation.[132] Even God's revelation in Scripture, which is in part (for God has not revealed *all* things in the Bible), still expresses *his* intent through the human authors. Hence, his intended meaning is infinite in nature.[133] This is due to his mode of knowing and its close relationship to simplicity and self-knowledge. The goal is creaturely understanding, with the divine, self-exhaustive help of the triune God (1 Cor 2:10–14; Col 2:3), his intent expressed through the human authors' intent. God's intent necessarily transcends that of the human authors.

However, far from introducing a problematic separation between divine and human meaning, we have a relationship resembling that of the two natures of Christ, in which the meaning of Christ follows along the parameters charted by Chalcedon.[134] It is interesting to note that the intent of the human authors, as inspired by God (2 Pet 1:20–21; 2 Tim 3:16), actually directs the reader to consider divine intent (1 Pet. 1:10–12) which necessarily transcends them. For example, in John 17, we cannot limit ourselves to John's human intent because, in the text, he directs the reader to consider the intent of the Son. So, to do justice to John's intent, we must go *beyond* his own comprehension.[135] If this transcendence of comprehension is not dealt with in biblical interpretation, meaning will inevitably be distorted and reduced to mere human categories, undermining not only the divine intent, but also the human intent as carried along by the Spirit.

In short, divine intent may be considered, not merely in a vague or ambiguous way, but more specifically. Who God is in terms of incomprehensibility-type categories which Van Til articulated could be used to provide further insights into the nature of meaning found in biblical texts. Moreover, in order to appreciate divine intent in the Bible, one must go beyond the limitation of humanity without negating it. The only way in which to do this, in a properly controlled manner, is to attend to all that *God* has revealed when interpreting a text. Canonical context is necessary to do justice to the comprehensive knowledge of God which is incomprehensible to man. It is a revealed window into the comprehension of God (though not identical with it), transcending the comprehension of the particular human authors and readers as time-bound participants in history.

---

132. Van Til, *Defense of Faith*, 67.
133. Poythress, *God-Centered*, 77–79.
134. Poythress, *God-Centered*, 78–80.
135. Poythress, *God-Centered*, 79.

Third, Van Til's observations concerning intelligibility also have hermeneutical significance. Interpreting the Bible according to its content involves the recognition that the apprehension and knowability of God's revelation are to be presupposed by creatures. This is involved in God's self-knowledge. Intelligibility of God's revelation in the Bible would be impossible if God did not fully know himself.[136] Here we have an example of how our doctrine of God and interpretation inform one another. Scripture comes to us as already intelligible because it comes from the mind of God. It is not dependent upon the mind of man to make it intelligible according to a standard of reason or hermeneutic without reference to God and not subject to his revelation.

Frame has also pointed out that intelligibility is closely related to application. Formulating the message of the Bible along theological lines is to ask how it *applies* (2 Tim 3:16–17). Theologians summarize the teachings of Scripture for a particular purpose (e.g., to answer questions). Consequently, Frame defines *theology* as "the application of Scripture, by persons, to every area of life."[137] When we look for the meaning of a passage, we are looking according to a purpose or application to our lives on some level. We do not understand the meaning of a text until we know what to do with it.[138] What does this have to do with intelligibility? Frame argues that if interpretation and application are so closely related, "then the question of intelligibility becomes the question of whether a consistent pattern of application is possible."[139] God has eternally known what to do with everything he knows. He understands the full import and meaning of everything he has revealed. What he has revealed is a system of truth inherently involved in its application in order to be understood. Intelligibility in interpretation involves application at some level or texts are not understood according to their divine and human intent. In other words, it is rightly known in a particular *way*, in relation to how God knows it.[140]

Fourth, Van Til's doctrine of incomprehensibility helps to understand *our* level of comprehension in interpretation. This is where his observations concerning correspondence and coherence factor into the discussion. God's comprehensive coherence provides the basis for our correspondence and coherence, not the other way around. Clearly man does not possess

---

136. Van Til, *Systematic Theology*, 268–69.
137. Frame, *Systematic Theology*, 6–8.
138. Frame, *Systematic Theology*, 660; Poythress, *God-Centered*, 73, 76–77.
139. Frame, "Theological Paradox," 328.
140. As SAT and TIS have rightly emphasized, this necessarily involves personal and ethical aspects.

this level of comprehension in either respect and cannot achieve a comprehensive interpretation of any text of Scripture because it is connected to God.[141] Man cannot know himself or anything exhaustively unless he knows God exhaustively. "All our ingenuity cannot exhaust the humanly inexhaustible rationality of God."[142] Our interpretations are not only finite, they are also fallible. Only God, in the self-authenticating Christ, whose person and work is explained in the divinely inspired Bible, has infallible interpretation of his revelation. Sinful and finite men cannot produce an infallible interpretation and are in need of Christ for their interpretive activity.[143] Our finite interpretation is always growing and approximating the infallible interpretation revealed in Scripture.[144] At no point is there an exact replica, but it is at every point analogical of God's system.[145] This only becomes problematic for man when he seeks an autonomous interpretation without reference to God's self-authenticating, comprehensive pre-interpretation.[146] Man's apprehension through interpretation, while adequate, inevitably varies in terms of precision and clarity.[147] We may be uncertain of our interpretive reconstruction at particular points, but absolutely certain that God's pre-interpretation is certain and precise. This implies avoiding what Anderson calls "inflexible univocality" in our approach to interpretation and, instead, embracing an analogical perspective.[148] In light of God as incomprehensible, we must avoid reductionistic tendencies regarding meaning in terms of precision.

Fifth, Van Til's notions of mystery and paradox have implications for biblical interpretation. First, there is no ultimate mystery to be found in the Bible which God does not comprehend. This gives us confidence that what he has revealed and interpreted for us in Scripture is true, even if not comprehensively revealed. Moreover, the Spirit helps us in our interpretation by

---

141. Van Til, *Theory of Knowledge*, 36; *Defense of Faith*, 67; *Systematic Theology*, 60–61.

142. Van Til, *Common Grace*, 10; *Systematic Theology*, 269.

143. Van Til, *Calvinism*, 145; Poythress, "Savior of Interpretation," 321.

144. Van Til, *Theory of Knowledge*, 162.

145. Van Til, *Systematic Theology*, 292.

146. Rushdoony argues that when this autonomous enterprise is pursued, any system is conceived of as an ideal, not as reality (i.e., non-Christian limiting concept) (*By What Standard?*, 105).

147. Van Til argues that the perspicuity of general and special revelation is in no way opposed to mystery. Rather, perspicuity and mystery are involved in one another only as they are understood in light of God as self-contained and exhaustively comprehensible to himself with absolute clarity (*Doctrine of Scripture*, 7–9).

148. Anderson, *Paradox*, 240–41.

renewing our knowledge (Col 3:10) according to his divine comprehension of the godhead and all things (1 Cor 2:6–16). Second, Van Til's notion of paradox provides a fruitful ground for comparing Scripture with Scripture, doctrine with doctrine, and text with text, implying an acute canonical awareness. When dealing with particular texts, Van Til's categories related to incomprehensibility drive the interpreter to consider larger contextual factors, both textual and *metaphysical*. Hermeneutics, like prolegomena and other doctrines, must be subject to Scripture rather than done from the outside. The *that* of hermeneutics must be involved in the *what* (i.e., nature and content) of Scripture.

Conclusion

Our discussion of Van Til's doctrine of incomprehensibility raises important considerations for understanding the divine author in relation to hermeneutics. In conjunction with insights from SAT and TIS, Van Til's summary of the Christian system or worldview provides more categories to pursue. In light of contemporary hermeneutical concerns, a distinctly Christian hermeneutic necessarily moves away from a mere human focus and its reductionist tendencies. A Van Tillian hermeneutic reflects the ultimate realities revealed in Scripture which, while expressed through human authors, actually point beyond them. In the next chapter, we will discuss another important contour of Van Til's doctrine of God which will help to provide and refine relevant hermeneutical categories regarding the divine author and meaning.

Chapter 6: **Ontological Trinity**

Introduction

A THIRD MAIN CONTOUR in Van Til's doctrine of God is the *ontological Trinity*. As we have already seen, each doctrine is inseparable from the others, and when one is spoken of, the others are always in the background. His articulation of the ontological Trinity touches upon many issues which resonate even more directly with certain contemporary hermeneutical categories and concerns. By stressing the *ontological* Trinity, he sought to avoid correlating the Trinity in any way with creation. This, as Van Til sees it, contrasts with all non-Christian thought, which thinks of God as merely one aspect of the universe.[1] This is an all-important point, even with respect to interpretation.[2] Van Til often makes reference to the ontological Trinity as the most basic principle of interpretation for all reality,[3] and especially for Scripture in terms of the self-interpreting nature of its divine author.[4] This is due to the fact that God is ultimately independent and active within himself as Trinity, apart from creation.[5] As such, he is absolutely self-explanatory. "It is this notion of the ontological Trinity that ultimately controls a truly Christian methodology."[6]

Before proceeding, a word may be said about Van Til's emphasis on God as *absolute personality*. For the most part, he uses this designation synonymously with the ontological Trinity.[7] However, he does seem to use *absolute*

---

1. Van Til, *Systematic Theology*, 353. Here, Van Til cites Bavinck regarding the importance of the ontological Trinity (*Reformed Dogmatics*, 2:296).

2. Frame, *Van Til*, 64–65. While recognizing essential continuity between the two, Van Til highlights the importance of thinking of the ontological Trinity before the economic Trinity in order to avoid blurring the Creator-creature distinction (*Defense of Faith*, 37; "Introduction," 23).

3. Van Til, *Christian Apologetics*, 30; *Common Grace*, 64; *Christian Epistemology*, 62.

4. E.g., Van Til, "Introduction," 22–23; *Theory of Knowledge*, 19; *Defense of Faith*, 396; *Reformed Pastor*, 76.

5. Van Til, *Christian Apologetics*, 29

6. Van Til, *Defense of Faith*, 122.

7. E.g., Van Til, *Christian Apologetics*, 128; *Defense of Faith*, 75, 236; *Systematic*

personality to preserve certain truths. He sought to guard against setting notions of an *absolute* and *personality* in opposition to one another. Rather, with God, "there is no distinction between absoluteness and personality."[8] He does not limit himself (ceasing to be absolute) in order to relate to another. His essence and being are coterminous, as is his essence and personality.[9] Van Til emphasizes that men are like God in terms of being persons, but unlike him in that we are not absolute, but finite, persons.[10]

In this chapter, we will look at four main ways in which Van Til nuances this doctrine with an eye toward hermeneutical significance: the philosophical issue of the *one and the many*; *personalism*; the ontological Trinity as the *archetype* for human communication; and *perspectivalism*.

The One and the Many

Perhaps the most fundamental and enduring issue in the history of philosophy is the *one and the many problem*. Is reality ultimately one or many? What is prior, unity or diversity? How does the one relate to the many and the many to the one? Where do the one and many come from to begin with? In light of Van Til's emphasis on the Creator-creature distinction, ultimacy belongs to the Creator. This distinction precludes the possibility that the space-time universe can be a source of independent or absolute particularity or unity. As a creation of God, the space-time universe's particularities and universals are rooted in the nature and plan of God.[11] The ontological Trinity has direct bearing on the answer to this problem of the one and the many. In God, unity and plurality, the one and the many, are *equally ultimate*, independent from creation.[12] Van Til explains:

> Unity in God is no more fundamental than diversity, and diversity is no more fundamental than unity . . . In God's being there are no particulars not related to the universal, and there is nothing universal that is not fully expressed in the particulars.[13]

Theology, 348.

8. Van Til, *Systematic Theology*, 346.
9. Van Til, *Systematic Theology*, 346, 364.
10. Van Til, *Defense of Faith*, 33.
11. Van Til, *Psychology*, 58.
12. Van Til, *Systematic Theology*, 59, 348; *Defense of Faith*, 31, 34; Bavinck, *Reformed Dogmatics*, 2:300, 332; Gunton, *One, Three*.
13. Van Til, *Defense of Faith*, 48–49.

The ontological Trinity does not depend upon creation for unity, particularity, or for their relationship to one another at any point. Rather, the persons of the Trinity are "mutually exhaustive of one another and therefore of the essence of the Godhead."[14] The one and the many in God are exhaustively related to one another.[15]

Failure to see the equal ultimacy of the one and the many in the ontological Trinity leads to unstable forms of philosophical tension. Van Til suggests that "all heresies in the history of the church have in some form or other taught subordinationism," and that "all 'heresies' in apologetic methodology spring from some sort of subordinationism."[16] However, there is no ontological subordination among the persons of the Trinity, or between the unity and plurality of God.[17] The unity of God does not surrender to or subordinate the diversity of the three persons.[18] Apologetic methodology which fails to maintain this point undermines what it seeks to defend—the triune God.[19] Christian hermeneutical methodology avoids contradiction insofar as it does justice to this point. For example, if there is any level of ontological subordinationism in the persons of the Trinity, there is no complete self-consciousness as the foundation of epistemology. To whatever extent there is subordinationism, God is "to that extent no longer the sole interpretive category of all reality."[20] Non-Christian philosophies and non-Trinitarian religious thought exhibit a tension between the one and the many. Either they are conceived of as two ultimate principles in a dialectical relationship[21] or one is more ultimate than the other, making the subordinate principle

---

14. Van Til, *Systematic Theology*, 348.
15. Van Til, *Systematic Theology*, 372–73.
16. Van Til, *Defense of Faith*, 48.
17. Frame helpfully nuances this point by recognizing that while there is no subordination in the divine nature shared by the persons of the Trinity, there is a subordination of roles involved in the distinctiveness of each person. This provides essential continuity between the ontological and economic Trinity, while maintaining God's independence from creation (*Doctrine of God*, 720).
18. Rushdoony, "One and Many," 345. Giles wrongly cites Van Til in support of his argument that no subordination in the Trinity means there are no distinctive roles (Giles, "Evangelicals," 323–38). This overlooks Van Til's emphasis on *ontological* subordination as the issue to avoid, not with regard to roles. For Giles, it seems that role differentiation necessitates ontological subordination. Hermeneutically, he neglects the distinction between canon and history, leaving the meaning of Scripture ultimately dependent upon man and historical context (see his book, *Trinity and Subordinationism*).
19. For an example of a theistic argument which presupposes the Trinitarian foundation for the one and the many, see: Anderson, "If Knowledge," 61–64.
20. Van Til, *Christian Epistemology*, 102.
21. Rushdoony, "One and Many," 342; *One and Many*, 3–8, 356.

CHAPTER 6: ONTOLOGICAL TRINITY

illusionary and incapable of differentiation from the other. If the triune God is not the ultimate interpretive category, then eternal and temporal categories are not distinct but, rather, parts of the same reality.

There is an interesting connection between concepts of subordinationism and being-in-general which appears in some forms of Trinitarian theology. For example, some have argued that Karl Rahner's identification of the economic and ontological Trinity[22] tends toward making God a part of creation. His Christology exhibits a blending of deity, humanity, and humanity in general, with the result of correlating God and man's experience in order for God to reveal himself. The ontological Trinity becomes illusory and reduced to human experience, leaving a kind of general ontology in its wake, in which *both* God and man participate.[23] LaCugna, influenced by Rahner, argues that "economy and theology are two aspects of *one* reality: the mystery of divine-human communion."[24] To the contrary, Molnar rightly warns against allowing any principle of relationality to be defined according to a general ontology founded upon some form of correlation with creation *prior* to considering how the economic Trinity can enrich that ontology.[25] This disregards God's independence, freedom, and authority. In terms of hermeneutical methodology, this cautions against assuming a principle of relationality (e.g., between the reader and the author[s] or between a text and a reader) prior to consideration of the ontological Trinity.

We have seen that in philosophical hermeneutics, there has been a tendency to assume a being-in-general (whether it is conceived of as being, experience, language, or history) which is more ultimate and somehow provides a unity to the plurality of things. However, certain problems arise. For instance, if all reduces down to one type of being (personal or not), how can an interpreter of reality (or of a text) distinguish particulars in relation to universals? How can an interpreter even *know* that all is essentially "being" if he or she is merely reducible to that same being? Does not all such interpretation end up saying that being is being? The same could be said of opting for ultimate plurality. Interpretation would merely end in saying "that all is all."[26] Explanation becomes a mirage, with no progress in understanding. Van Til's assertion that "every type of heresy is, in

---

22. Rahner, *Trinity*.
23. Gunton, *Yesterday and Today*, 11–15; Molnar, *Divine Freedom*, 85–92.
24. LaCugna, *God for Us*, 222, 228.
25. Molnar, *Divine Freedom*, 312. In Rahner's case, there is a tendency to subordinate the many to the one in a kind of modalism, which depends upon God *in relation to creation* for "personality" (Rahner, *Trinity*, 109–10).
26. Poythress, *Redeeming Philosophy*, 40–41.

last analysis, an attack upon the Trinity"[27] is applicable to hermeneutics in terms of metaphysical assumptions. This becomes especially evident in the one and many problem.

Generally, human beings seek to organize information in terms of generality and particularity.[28] Non-Christian thought tends toward either pole as if on what Frame calls a ladder of *abstraction*. Either one moves up the ladder (from particular to general) in order to seek the essence of things through more abstraction, *or* one moves down the ladder (from general to particular) in order to reduce things down to their most detailed components. As one moves *up*, there is a loss of actual content in that it is stripped of all particulars, so that there is nothing left but an empty concept or essence. As one moves *down*, the small components become much like the essences of things (like moving up). For example, the smallest components of a text may be marks on a page and whiteness and blackness. Yet, these visual experiences of a text do not tell us anything meaningful about it. Some unifying principle must tie these various experiences together in order to understand its meaning. So, whether going up or down the scale, there is a loss of actual content and meaning.[29] Frame summarizes:

> In the end, there is no difference between "being in general" [abstract unity] and "ultimate matter" [abstract particularity].[30] Both concepts are empty, uninformative, and unintelligible. If abstract being is the ultimate reality, then there is no particularity. If abstract particularity is the ultimate truth, then there is no unity in the world. If both are somehow true, then all is chaos, and nothing is true.[31]

There is a need for *both* for intelligibility and meaning. Van Til has pointed out that the kind of thinking presented above comes out of man's desire to achieve exhaustive knowledge of reality, which ultimately ends in futility. Abstract concepts of unity and particularity are idolatrous in that they are sought *within* creation, rather than in the triune God. These abstract concepts

---

27. Van Til, *Systematic Theology*, 352–53.

28. For the following discussion, see: Frame, *Van Til*, 72–76.

29. E.g., Scientific metaphysics, as a means of getting to the bottom of what is real and what is not, is ultimately reductionistic (Poythress, "Three Modern Myths," 328).

30. Generally speaking, the former is characteristic of modernism (i.e., the one over the many), while the latter is characteristic of postmodernism (i.e., the many over the one). Van Til also speaks of abstract particulars as *brute facts* and abstract universals as *abstract laws* (*Common Grace*, 75).

31. Frame, *Van Til*, 74.

CHAPTER 6: ONTOLOGICAL TRINITY

are not only empty in terms of content, but they also cannot be meaningfully related to one another.[32] This leads us to our next consideration.

The one and many of *creation* is dependently derivative of the equally ultimate one and many found in the Trinity. In his discussion of temporal unity and plurality as created by God, Van Til argues the following, based on the fact that the created one and many are both equally dependent on God for their being and sustainment:

> The particulars or facts of the universe do and must act in accord with universals or laws . . . the laws may not and can never reduce the particulars to abstract particulars or reduce their individuality in any manner. The laws are but generalizations of God's method of working with the particulars . . . thus there is a basic equality between the created one and the created many, or between the various aspects of created reality [in relation to God].[33]

This means that not only is there an ultimate correspondence of the created one and many with that of triune God's inner coherence, but there is also a consequent irreducibility of the one and many in creation. In addition, this irreducibility corresponds to the particulars exhaustively related to the universal in God. Hence, created particulars are not unrelated and unknowable in that they are inherently correlative to universals. We do not have to abstract the one from the many or the many from the one because they are not inherently opposed to one another. Bahnsen summarizes:

> The Christian worldview, therefore, does not face the problem of irrational particulars (which cannot be interpreted according to unifying categories, generalizations, or laws) standing over against abstract universals (blank formalities, empty of any detailed content regarding the concrete particulars).[34]

These realities have implications for all levels of knowledge. Consider *history*, a significant concept for contemporary hermeneutics. For there to be a history or an interpretation of a fact of history, there must be recognition of both particulars and universals in order for a pattern to be articulated (i.e., a philosophy of history and of reality).[35] However, these must not be abstract and impersonal or else history loses purpose and direction. Non-Christian concepts of history are often impersonal, making purposeful

---

32. Frame, *Van Til*, 74. Moreover, abstract concepts within creation are impersonal principles which cannot account for personal aspects of reality.

33. Van Til, *Defense of Faith*, 50; *Systematic Theology*, 364–65; *Common Grace*, 64.

34. Bahnsen, *Van Til's Apologetic*, 241.

35. Van Til, *Christian Apologetics*, 19; *Common Grace*, 2–9.

and directional claims suspect in terms of their foundation.[36] One must get behind the facts of history to find their meaning.[37] For example, if one takes historical relativism as a starting point, no mere series of historical facts can itself raise problems or questions in that there is no intelligible relation between the elements of the series. Even if the series had meaning in and of itself, all the elements of the series would lack a larger intelligible context, fully comprehended, from which to discern the relative value of each element, not to mention any larger contour of history from which to discern a climax of the whole.[38] Non-Christian philosophy, including hermeneutical philosophy, often seeks the meaning of history *within* history.[39] Such a pursuit, due to its assumption of brute, unrelated facts and abstract, impersonal universals leads to a denial of history, offering no final interpretation.[40] On non-Christian presuppositions:

> No philosophy . . . can offer any true interpretation of history, for history cannot supply the key to its own meaning, and the human mind cannot impose its subjective interpretation upon objective factual data. History is neither self-originating nor self-sustaining and time cannot exist in and of itself.[41]

Neither is history nor any historian intelligibly self-interpreting. Rather, the meaning of history, if we remain consistent with special revelation, is found in the eternal one and the many. Only a *theology* of history is fit for the task, not only for historiography, but also for any hermeneutical method that would seek to do justice to history—as revelation of God. Forms of both, historical relativism and positivism, run contrary to the Christian worldview in that they assume man is an autonomous and a self-interpreting interpreter.

Consider the broader implication of the one and the many as it pertains to the general and particulars of the hermeneutical enterprise. If one cannot emphasize unity to the expense of diversity and vice versa, then the particular is always related to the whole and the whole to the particular. Knowledge of one truth is always in relation to other truths.[42] Of course

---

36. Van Til, *Theistic-Evidences*, 94–110; McIntire, "Ongoing Task," 54–59.
37. Van Til, *Psychology*, 87.
38. Van Til, *Psychology*, 42. An ironic result of historical subjectivism is that history is not the past at all but, rather, the present inward teleology of the mind (Singer, "Problem," 66–67).
39. E.g., Collingwood, *Idea of History*.
40. Rushdoony, "One and Many," 346–47; Singer, "Problem," 58.
41. Singer, "Philosophy," 330.
42. Poythress, *Symphonic Theology*, 46; "Truth and Fullness," 212.

this is only perfectly and comprehensively known by God, in relation to himself and his plan. Modernist tendencies to exalt unity over diversity and postmodern tendencies to exalt diversity over unity (in Scriptural exegesis or in terms of hermeneutical possibility) ultimately run contrary to the ontological Trinity. As mentioned in chapter 1, Poythress detects the errors of Unitarianism and polytheism present in hermeneutical approaches which either collapse elements of communication (author-text-reader) into one or multiply and set meanings in opposition to one another through a denial of unity in favor of diversity.

Another implication of the one and the many being equally ultimate in the ontological Trinity is the hermeneutical *spiral*. In God's knowledge, there is no process or spiral between knowing the particular in relation to the whole and the whole in relation to the particular. This is another way of saying that God has pre-interpreted all things in terms of the one and many in relation to his own being. However, finite man *does* grow through the spiral with the help of the Spirit as he learns to think God's thoughts after himself with regard to the one and many.

Personalism

We now turn to perhaps Van Til's most controversial theological formulation. The ontological Trinity is the very foundation of his concept of *personalism*. We have already seen that being and personality are coterminous in God, as are the three persons exhaustive of one another, without correlation with anything outside of himself. Van Til boldly asserts:

> We speak of God as a person; yet we speak also of three persons in the Godhead . . . each of the persons of the Trinity is exhaustive of divinity itself, while yet there is a genuine distinction between the persons . . . God is a one-conscious being, and yet he is also a tri-conscious being.[43]

Later, he states plainly, "we do assert that God, that is, the whole Godhead, is *one person*."[44]

Not surprisingly, he received sharp criticism for his deviation from traditional formulation.[45] We will briefly mention three prominent ones. First, some have objected to the *uniqueness* of the formulation. Clark labeled it as

---

43. Van Til, *Systematic Theology*, 348.
44. Van Til, *Systematic Theology*, 363 (emphasis mine).
45. For the following discussion, see: Hunt, "An Introduction," 71–73, 89–92.

a novelty, out of step with the theological heritage of the church.[46] Robbins branded it as a new Unitarian heresy, opposed to the Westminster standards.[47] In addition, Clark argued that Van Til imported his irrational view of incomprehensibility into his doctrine of Trinity, involving a clear violation of the law of non-contradiction.[48] Second, some have objected to supposed roots in British absolute idealism for such language as "one-conscious," "tri-conscious," and speaking of equal ultimacy of unity and diversity.[49] Lee Irons also sees the influence of Idealism, concluding that Van Til falls prey to modalism.[50] Third, some have complained that, while orthodox in his intention, his formulation suffers from the limitations of human language. Letham warns that the one person-three person rendering could be taken in one of three problematic directions: the being of God as a fourth person related to the other three, the being of God related to another being, or the three persons "reduced to the attributes of the one absolute person."[51] The key issue is whether Van Til intends that God is one and three in the *same* sense. Even if not, why abandon the difference stressed in church history expressed through the use of different terms (e.g., one *substance*, three *persons*)? Has he not confused the matter?[52]

Responding to the above criticisms in turn will give us at least a greater sense of Van Til's rationale and purpose for his innovation. First, the charges of novelty or heresy can be dismissed upon closer inspection of the context of Van Til's statements. His rationale is self-consciously orthodox. Out of an appreciation for even the earliest historical developments of the doctrine, he especially draws upon Calvin's emphasis on *autotheos* with regard to the Son and Hodge's emphasis on *perichoresis*.[53] The concept of *autotheos* (deity of himself) stresses that each person is equally underived and consubstantial, yet at the same time, not denying actual personal distinctions in the Godhead. This opposes any hint of subordination or mixing the eternal with the

---

46. Clark, *Trinity*, 88.

47. Robbins, *Man and Myth*, 20–21.

48. Clark, *Trinity*, 84–88; Reymond, *Systematic Theology*, 108–9; Plantinga, "Three/Oneness," 50–53.

49. Vander Stelt, *Philosophy and Scripture*, 231–33.

50. Smith, *Paradox and Truth*, 119–23.

51. Letham, *Holy Trinity*, 181, 462.

52. Others have expressed reservations about referring to God as *one person* (e.g., Torrance, *Christian Doctrine*, 102–3, 155–61; Henry, *God Who Stands*, 209–12).

53. Van Til, *Systematic Theology*, 356–60. The concept of *perichoresis* goes back much earlier than Hodge, being present in the early church, at least by the time of Athanasius. This term was used later by St. Hilary and John of Damascus (Kelly, *Systematic Theology*, 489; Twombly. *Perichoresis*).

CHAPTER 6: ONTOLOGICAL TRINITY   167

temporal.⁵⁴ This influence explains Van Til's emphasis on each person as exhaustive of the essence of the Godhead. The concept of *perichoresis* emphasizes the unity of the three persons as they mutually indwell one another. On the basis of *perichoresis*, Charles Hodge pointed out that the three persons are one God, with one will and one mind as opposed to three intelligences, wills, and efficiencies. In light of this, he and others have spoken of God in unipersonal terms, though not inconsistent with tri-personality, thus steering clear of modalism.⁵⁵ It may be that Reymond's criticism is indicative of his own hesitation to affirm the doctrine of *perichoresis*.⁵⁶ Rather than being *doctrinally* innovative, Van Til merely made explicit what was already implicit through the use of *autotheos* and *perichoresis*.⁵⁷ He re-summarizes the doctrine in a way which highlights that God is personal, *both* in his unity and diversity. God is not an essence that has a *personality* attached to it. Rather, he is exhaustively personal.⁵⁸

Second, Vander Stelt's claim that Van Til was influenced by British idealism is unfounded. The substance of Van Til's treatment displays the marks of Calvin and Old Princeton, *not* philosophical idealism. In fact, there is no positive reference to British idealists in his most concentrated treatment of the subject.⁵⁹ Rather, Van Til's emphasis on God as an absolute personality runs contrary to British idealism's concept of the *absolute*, which *transcends* personal and impersonal categories.⁶⁰ Elsewhere, he clearly opposes idealism's concept of the absolute as contrary to the Christian God.⁶¹ Any similarity is merely formal in nature.

Lastly, if prone to misunderstanding, why did Van Til choose this manner of expression? Letham has rightly warned against possible dangers related to the language used. However, Tipton has pointed to the apologetic contexts in which Van Til was working to highlight certain advantages of this particular summary of the Trinity. He argues that Van Til purposely brought

---

54. Van Til, *Christian Epistemology*, 101.

55. Hodge, *Systematic Theology*, 1:461–62; Hodge, *Evangelical Theology*, 102–3; Bavinck, *Reformed Dogmatics*, 2:300, 302–3; Torrance, *Trinitarian Perspectives*, 33; *Doctrine of God*, 161, 173, 175.

56. Reymond, *Systematic Theology*, 321–22; Letham, Review, 316–19.

57. Tipton, "Triune Personal God," 53, 87.

58. Van Til, *Systematic Theology*, 364. This would oppose Clark, who saw God as tri-conscious in his diversity but *not* one-conscious in his unity (Clark, *Trinity*, 106–7). Tipton has argued that on Clark's notion, any self-consciousness in terms of God's unity would imply a *fourth* person (Tipton, "Triune Personal God," 36, 74).

59. E.g., Van Til, *Systematic Theology*, 351–61; Tipton, "Function," 304.

60. E.g., Cunningham, *Idealistic Argument*, 110, 140.

61. Van Til, *Christianity and Idealism*, 7–34; *Defense of Faith*, 229–31

the incomprehensibility of the Trinity to the foreground in order to expose univocal reliance upon a non-Christian notion of the law of non-contradiction, one to which God must conform. Van Til creatively summarized the doctrine of the Trinity in order to guard against unbiblical rationalism and univocal thought. Moreover, God, as fully conscious and personal in his unity and diversity rules out any uninterpreted facts, since God creates out of his exhaustive and personal consciousness and pre-interpretation.[62] Van Til uses the term, "person," in *two different senses*—with regard to unity and diversity. It is better to think of Van Til's contribution as a supplement, *not* a replacement of the traditional formulations.[63] Once misconceptions are dispelled, it becomes merely another tool with which systematic theology can confront unbelief. However, because of the longstanding traditional formulation, caution should be taken in using the one-person concept.

This brings us to Van Til's broader view of God and creation in terms of a *personalistic worldview*, flowing out of his emphasis on the exhaustively personal nature of the Trinity. All worldviews must deal with personalism at some point. Van Til states that:

> In the last analysis every theology or philosophy is personalistic. Everything "impersonal" must be brought into relationship with an ultimate personal point of reference. Orthodoxy takes the self-contained ontological trinity to be this point of reference. The only alternative to this is to make man himself the final point of reference.[64]

This can readily be seen, even in materialistic worldviews where there is a struggle to account for *mind, consciousness,* and *personality* within an otherwise impersonal system.[65] Non-Christian thought assumes that a personal fact must be *unipersonal* in that any personal fact or action is ultimately surrounded by impersonal reality.[66] This begs the question of whether there can be such a personal fact or action if there is no other to relate to on a personal level. Making man the final reference point rather than the triune God results in seeking to explain reality in temporal terms.[67] Van Til sums up man's situation:

---

62. Tipton, "Function," 301–2.
63. Tipton, "Function," 289, 295, 298.
64. Van Til, "Introduction," 66.
65. Plantinga, *Where Real Conflict*.
66. Van Til, *Systematic Theology*, 230; *Christian Epistemology*, 78.
67. Van Til, *Christian Epistemology*, 96–97, 129.

> A finite personality could function in none other than a completely personalistic atmosphere, and such an atmosphere can be supplied to him only if his existence depends entirely upon the exhaustive personality of God.[68]

Elsewhere, Van Til defines *personalism* as:

> That form of idealism which gives equal recognition to both the pluralistic and monistic aspects of experience and which finds in the conscious unity, identity and free activity of personality the key to the nature of reality and the solution to the ultimate problems of philosophy.[69]

Again, we see how his description is informed by his understanding of the ontological Trinity in terms of unity, plurality, and personality. The ontological Trinity stands behind creation as the personal and relational atmosphere for the meaning of reality, including the interpretation of special revelation. Consequently, the structures and relations within created reality necessarily reflect the ontological Trinity.

A related concept is Van Til's lesser known *representational principle*. This affirms that relations within the ontological Trinity *and* between the ontological Trinity and man are *exhaustively personal*, with the latter relation (free) founded upon the former (necessary). Moreover, relations among humans are exhaustively personal on the ontological basis of the Trinity.[70] Each person of the Trinity is exhaustively representational of one another. As a result, Van Til argues that "it was impossible for God to create except upon the representational plan."[71] In other words, God's creation and plan are necessarily consistent with his triune, personal nature. Consequently, as a creature in the image of the triune God, man is in a representational relationship with God. Of course, as a finite creature, this representation in terms of thinking, feeling, and doing is not *exhaustively* representational of God, but analogously so. Man cannot help but exist and function in an atmosphere of representational personalism.[72]

This principle affirms both God's aseity and his condescension in terms of being personal in nature. The biblical concept of *covenant* especially captures the nature of his condescension.[73] The triune God is

---

68. Van Til, *Christian Epistemology*, 97.
69. Van Til, *God of Hope*, 304.
70. Tipton, "Triune Personal God," 118, 141.
71. Van Til, *Christian Epistemology*, 78–79.
72. Van Til, *Theory of Knowledge*, 208; *Theistic Ethics*, 49.
73. Van Til, "Covenant Theology," 306.

"covenantally operative in all of the facts of the world."[74] This includes the fact that *Scripture* is to be conceived of as exhaustively personal—as special revelation involving the personal relation between the divine and human.[75] With regard to both general and special revelation, every fact man encounters puts him face to face with God and, hence, must "deal covenantally with every fact of history."[76] He argues that "the covenant idea is nothing but the expression of the representational principle consistently applied to all reality."[77] In sum, the representational principle brings together the doctrines of Trinity and covenant, along with their ontological and epistemological implications.[78] The only metaphysical alternative, according to Van Til, is utter impersonalism. "A completely Christian theistic epistemology can allow for no impersonalism anywhere along the line of the transaction between God and man."[79]

One implication Van Til draws out in many of his works is the unavoidable covenantal relation that all men have with God. Man cannot but exist and function in an *ethical* environment. "To speak of man's relation to God as being covenantal at every point is merely to say that man deals with the personal God everywhere."[80] He ultimately classifies men as either *covenant breakers* or *covenant keepers*. Covenant breakers are those who are fallen in Adam. In rebellion against God, they confuse the Creator-creature distinction and tend to reason as if uncreated (Rom 1:18–32; Gen 3:5, 22). Incidentally, Van Til argues that one philosophical characteristic of this rebellion is the notion that ultimate coherence lies in a general ontology, which envelopes both man and God (if any God were to exist at all). Covenant keepers are those who are redeemed in Christ, the One who keeps covenant, obeying where Adam fell, and serves as their representative head (Rom 5:12–21). In this broad sense, *all* men are covenantally responsible to God at every point. This revelational atmosphere is inherently authoritative as it is the revelation of *God*.[81] This ultimate personalism of the Trinity is opposed to the non-Christian notion of impersonal ethical determinism or man's self-determined ethic in the midst of an ultimately impersonal

---

74. Van Til, *Doctrine of Scripture*, 67.
75. Van Til, *Doctrine of Scripture*, 24, 27.
76. Van Til, *Christian Epistemology*, 97; *Theory of Knowledge*, 29.
77. Van Til, *Christian Epistemology*, 96.
78. Tipton, "Triune Personal God," 159–65.
79. Van Til, *Christian Epistemology*, 68.
80. Van Til, *Common Grace*, 69–70; *Christ and Jews*, 25–26.
81. Krabbendam, "Cornelius Van Til," 130–33.

environment.⁸² On the presupposition of the ontological Trinity, there is no room for man to construct an ethic in a void of impersonalism, for there is no impersonalism to be found.⁸³

Recently, Bosserman has argued that Van Til failed to carry forward his representational principle with respect to why God is necessarily *tri*-personal in nature.⁸⁴ This stems from almost agnostic-sounding passages found in Van Til's works which emphasize God as *multi*-personal and *uni*-personal but not as *tri*-personal.⁸⁵ With all his emphasis on the ontological Trinity as the necessary presupposition for the Christian worldview, it is surprising that he did not delve more directly into this matter, though it is clear that he affirms only three persons. If the Trinity is the key interpretative concept for all reality in terms of unity and plurality, then it cannot be a unity or plurality *in general*.⁸⁶ Though he often speaks against forms of unity-in-general, it is the issue of plurality which seems to receive the least attention in Van Til.⁸⁷ Moreover, in terms of paradox, he focused on how apparent contradictions (like the one and three of the Trinity) *limit* one another but not on how they *require* one another, failing to follow his own method of implication to its logical conclusion.⁸⁸ Bosserman helpfully discusses how various multi-personal alternatives to the tri-personal nature of God (e.g., unitarian, binity, and quadrinity) introduce impersonal elements which undermine the representational principle.⁸⁹ He concludes:

> to add or subtract from the number of three divine persons is to compromise an ultimately personalist view of reality, by making God identical with, or subordinate to, an impersonal context. Such a God could not speak with authority . . . because He would not "know" himself solely with reference to His own person.⁹⁰

God must be one *and three* from a covenantal personalist view of reality.

---

82. Van Til, *Defense of Faith*, 84–85; *Theistic Ethics*, 33–35.

83. Van Til, *Case for Calvinism*, 97. Elsewhere, Van Til speaks of the error of seeing the human personality as an accomplishment of man in the midst of an impersonal environment (*Psychology*, 105).

84. Bosserman, *Trinity*, 152.

85. E.g., *Systematic Theology*, 364; *Christian Epistemology*, 97.

86. Bosserman, *Trinity*, 157.

87. Perhaps, this is due to his emphasis on God as "one person."

88. Bosserman, *Trinity*, 165, 171.

89. Bosserman, *Trinity*, 178–82.

90. Bosserman, *Trinity*, 181.

Van Til unfolds his brand of personalism on the assumption that the idea of covenant is fundamental to the idea of exhaustive personal relationship found in the ontological Trinity. In doing so, he boldly asserts that "since the internal relationships of the triune God are covenantal, God's relation to mankind is also covenantal."[91] Curiously, he does not give explicit justification for this assumption. Whatever the reason, it is likely that he is not proposing any novel doctrine out of step with traditional Reformed theology.[92] In light of his discussion, it would seem that he is merely stressing the *continuity* between the personal relations *ad intra* and God relating personally *ad extra*. In other words, he is saying that God does not relate to man in a way which is inconsistent with his own personal triune nature. He is *not* saying that the personal relations of the Trinity *ad intra* are somehow correlated or dependent on creation, with the persons necessarily relating to one another in ways identical to covenantal relations between God and man. Rather, how God relates personally *ad extra* is consistent with how he relates *ad intra*—the difference being that the latter is between infinite, indivisible, and inseparable persons and is necessary, while the former is with finite creation and free.[93]

In light of how Van Til articulated his notion of personalism, there are at least two significant hermeneutical implications. First, all of our interpretive efforts are done in an exhaustively personal atmosphere, not personality in general but in relation to the triune God of Scripture. As such, we are immediately confronted with God's authority and man's *ethical* relationship to his Creator at every point. All hermeneutical work is personal and ethical in nature.[94] All knowledge is inherently personal and covenantal in nature. Indicative of this fact is that man, in Christ, is being renewed in knowledge (Eph 4:24; Col 3:10).[95] Moreover, one can see the consistency of man's personal knowledge and the knowledge God has with regard to his simplicity—his knowledge and attributes are coterminous with his eternal

---

91. Van Til, "Covenant Theology," 306.

92. E.g., In discussing the *Pactum Salutis*, Bavinck says that "the pact of salvation makes known to us the relationships and life of the three persons in the Divine Being as a *covenantal life*, a life of consummate self-consciousness and freedom" (Bavinck, *Reformed Dogmatics*, 3:214) (emphasis mine).

93. Van Til, *Defense of Faith*, 227–79. There has been recent debate over whether God takes on "covenantal properties" that are *new* in his condescension or whether they are *prior* to his condescension. The debate revolves around Oliphint's book on divine condescension (*God with Us*). One should consult articles by Helm, Dolezal, Oliphint and Shannon posted on reformation21.org and Helm's blog at paulhelmsdeep.blogspot.co.uk.

94. Van Til, *New Hermeneutic*, 117.

95. Van Til, *Christian Apologetics*, 94–97.

and exhaustive triune relations. True knowledge implies proper *relating*. This necessarily confronts impersonal and detached notions of meaning.[96] This raises the question, in light of the personal and ethical environment of man in relation to God, can meaning be established prior to or separate from application? It would seem that a sharp distinction between meaning and application is unwarranted, for it would treat meaning as a relatively *neutral* concept, apart from proper relating of that meaning to God.

In discussing the attitude of modern man (i.e., autonomous man) toward Scripture, Van Til highlights a tendency to think that the human personality is somehow violated by an all-knowing and powerful Creator. Hence, autonomous man rejects God's exhaustively personal control in favor of freedom—one self-identified in an impersonal environment.[97] Van Til concludes that:

> both in religion and science the modern temper is impersonalist in its conception of some abstract super-personal law and personalist in that in practice even this impersonal law is interpreted in terms of the standards that are within man himself apart from God. Thus there is no personal confrontation of man with either God or Christ. Both of these become impersonal ideals that man has set before himself.[98]

These ethical observations related to the ontological Trinity resonate with the concerns of theological interpretation of Scripture (TIS).[99] Zimmerman argues that theological hermeneutics provides the principles for "interpretation to be truly ethical and character forming, the very things that both philosophical hermeneutics and radical postmodern hermeneutics strive for."[100]

These observations related to the Trinity also speak to the concerns of speech-act theory (SAT), with ethics and responsibility inherent in interpretation with respect to the divine author speaking through his word.[101] Vanhoozer's work in this area has emphasized the importance of the Trinity, as the ultimate personal communicator, in connection with man's response to Scripture, exploring the personal and ethical nature of this response through

---

96. Poythress takes Vanhoozer and Hirsch to task for implying that "human authors' intentions are meaningful apart from God's personal involvement in their acts" (Poythress, Review, 128).
97. Van Til, *Theory of Knowledge*, 70.
98. Van Til, "Introduction," 28.
99. See chapter 3.
100. Zimmerman, *Recovering*, 322.
101. E.g., Vanhoozer, *Is There?*, 367–441.

the metaphor of *Theo-drama*.[102] However, for all his helpful insights, Vanhoozer primarily emphasizes the economic Trinity as a paradigm for communication, choosing not to explore the relevance of the ontological Trinity for hermeneutics.[103] With his emphasis on the ontological Trinity, Van Til creatively summarized important aspects of theology proper which may prove to be helpful in Vanhoozer's concern to unmask what he calls, "interpretive idolatry." In particular, the ontological Trinity more clearly exposes forms of correlativism in methods which make God's personal communication, recorded in Scripture, dependent upon creation, including history and human authors/readers. Van Til's emphases further refine and complement biblical concerns of both SAT and TIS related to the Trinity.

Second, Van Til's personalism has relevance for what is often referred to in hermeneutical discussions as the I-it/I-thou dichotomy. Van Til saw this distinction as an unbiblical metaphysical assumption with roots in the dualism of the Greeks (form-matter), Greek influenced scholasticism (nature-grace), and Kant (nature-freedom)[104]—one unknown to the Reformers.[105] Perhaps the most obvious implication is that exhaustive personalism precludes any dichotomy between impersonal and personal knowledge. For example, Buber uses this scheme to argue that God's revelation bypasses impersonal information and propositions through a truly personal encounter.[106] This dichotomy often pits science (I-it) against revelation (I-thou).[107] Again we find the assumption of a more ultimate metaphysic which subordinates and displaces a biblical ontology, informed by the ontological Trinity.[108] However, even the so-called I-it dimension is wholly under God's authority, to which man is ethically responsible if one assumes the ontological Trinity as integral to a proper metaphysic.[109] Van Til goes to great length to show that whether we are dealing with general or special revelation, the

---

102. Vanhoozer, *Drama of Doctrine*, 41–43, 63–68; *Is There?*, 161, 456–59.

103. Vanhoozer, *First Theology*, 168.

104. Frame, *Van Til*, 356–57; Van Til, *Sovereignty*, 87.

105. Van Til, *Sovereignty*, 56.

106. Buber, *I and Thou*, 109–20; Brunner, *Revelation and Reason*, 5–6; *Philosophy of Religion*, 183–91.

107. Van Til, *Case for Calvinism*, 5, 10, 13.

108. E.g., Van Til, *New Modernism*, 40–41; *Christ and Jews*, 35. Van Til argues that this more ultimate metaphysic includes the notion of ontological correlation between God and man that transcends the Creator-creature distinction (*Christ and Jews*, 47–48). Buber's assumed metaphysic expresses itself through allegorizing the history of the OT à la Philo (influenced by Greek philosophy), eschewing Christ as the hermeneutical key to the OT (*Christ and Jews*, 22, 56).

109. Van Til, *Case for Calvinism*, 104–5.

CHAPTER 6: ONTOLOGICAL TRINITY   175

personal component is always and everywhere present as God is personally involved in nature, man, and with respect to himself.[110] Van Til saw this dichotomy as essentially an unbiblical counterfeit of the covenantal relationship between God and creation. He calls this broad covenantalism between God and creation the "Christian I-Thou scheme." True personal dialogue is "covenantal interaction with the God of Scripture," not one which is inherently opposed to information or science.[111]

Interestingly, Zimmerman, like Vanhoozer, opts to focus on the economic Trinity, the incarnation, and human relations to the neglect of the ontological Trinity when discussing the personal I-thou relation.[112] Certainly, it is important to give attention to the incarnation and the human relational context of the interpreter but not to the exclusion of the ontological Trinity nor its relationship to each of those doctrines. Indicative of this neglect are statements about God's relation to reality which border on being *necessary*. For example, in his discussion of Bonhoeffer, Zimmerman says that God "entered ontology in the incarnation" and cites approvingly that "there is only one reality and that is the God-reality in the reality of the world which was revealed in Christ . . . participating in Christ we are at the same time in God-reality and in world reality."[113] Perhaps, consideration of the ontological Trinity would clarify such comments.

In sum, our view of God implies a definite conception of his relation to creation *and* of everything in creation, which necessarily includes consideration of his triunity.[114] To be consistent with the content of Scripture, it is incumbent that our hermeneutical method takes these considerations into account.

Archetype for Communication

Van Til sees the ontological Trinity as the necessary, eternal archetype for all communication. God's self-sufficient personality is the foundation and background for man's personality.[115] It naturally follows that "for God, the object and the subject of knowledge are coterminous as far as his own person is concerned."[116] This truth also follows from God's omniscience

---

110. Van Til, *Systematic Theology*, 121–222.
111. Van Til, *Christ and Jews*, 36, 55–56.
112. Zimmerman, *Recovering*, 304–5.
113. Zimmerman, *Recovering*, 280, 283, 307.
114. Van Til, *Defense of Faith*, 32, 247.
115. Van Til, *Psychology*, 70–73, 161.
116. Van Til, *Systematic Theology*, 230. By *object* he means the thing known and by

and incomprehensibility. There is no disjunction between the subject and object of knowledge, nor is there mystery concerning his own exhaustive self-knowledge and his knowledge of all things. The subject and object of knowledge in God are also *equally ultimate*. God is the ultimate subject and object.[117] As the archetype for human knowledge, all created relationships (i.e., object-object, subject-object, and subject-subject), find their source and foundation in the ontological Trinity. They cannot exist independently of the free will and plan of the triune personal God.[118] Discussing the existence and relation between the subject and object of knowledge, Van Til comments on human interpretation:

> the *existence* and *meaning* of the human interpreter must be brought into a relation of subordination to God as the ultimate interpreter . . . in him [God], existence and interpretation are coextensive . . . it follows from this that any human interpreters would have to be *derivative* interpreters or reinterpreters . . . the interpretation that man would give to anything in this world can therefore never be comprehensive and exhaustive.[119]

Unless a perfect coherence exists in the ontological Trinity as the foundation, our knowledge in terms of subject and object is incoherent. Human interpretation can never exhaust the meaning of anything, including Scripture. The key issue regarding the subject of knowledge is whether one sees human consciousness as functioning apart from God or not. If one assumes independence, human subjectivity will inevitably undermine any hope for certain interpretation.[120] It is not a matter of the object being opposed to the subject, nor objective knowledge being opposed to subjective knowledge per se, as if they are naturally in tension with one another. Rather, both aspects of knowledge find their perfect coherence in the self-knowledge of the triune God, with human knowledge corresponding to that foundation on a *creaturely* level of being. Hence, neither the subject nor object trumps the other, nor does objectivity trump subjectivity. Man, as subject, knows an object insofar as that knowledge corresponds to God, as Subject, who knows himself and that object. In other words, man knows derivatively as a creature in the ultimate context of the knowledge of his Creator. In terms of redemption, Van Til sees sin affecting both the created object and subject, with the redemption of both being brought into a right relationship with each other

---

subject he means the knower.

117. Van Til, *Christian Epistemology*, 133.
118. Van Til, *Systematic Theology*, 57–59, 122.
119. Van Til, *Systematic Theology*, 60 (emphasis his), 66.
120. Van Til, *Christian Epistemology*, 136, 221–22.

and ultimately God through Christ. Man needs special revelation and God's Spirit to enable this right relationship.[121] Van Til concludes:

> The whole contention of the Christian theistic position is that what is called the subject-object relation, that is, the possibility of having knowledge of any object whatsoever, is unintelligible except upon the presupposition that every subject of knowledge, since subjects are from this point of view also objects, owes its existence and its connotation, in last analysis to God.[122]

In discussing non-Christian conceptions of the subject-object relation, Van Til again points out that a general ontology is being assumed prior to the consideration of the Trinity. For example, naturalistic and idealistic systems deal with the subject-object relation without contact with personality (i.e., without relation to God and his relation to man). In discussing Brunner's view of human psychology, he argues that without God as the starting point, revelation, for instance, must come to man through subject-object relationships which are ultimately impersonal categories. Consequently, revelation cannot be received for what it is—personal communication in an exhaustively personal atmosphere.[123] Van Til argues that Brunner seeks personal correspondence with God through correlation, such that God's consciousness and being are ultimately related to man rather than within the ontological Trinity.[124]

Regarding the new hermeneutic, Van Til sees an ontological correlativity being assumed between the subject and object of faith, which replaces the idea of both being related in the ontological Trinity with God and man being related ontologically in terms of subject and object on the same level of being.[125] This is where the primacy of the I-thou relation seems to take hold with regard to the subject-object relation. The I-thou scheme seeks to lead to a deeper layer of reality than that of mere subject and object.[126] This deeper layer is prior to such conceptual categories as subject and object.[127] So, for communication to take place between God and man, an *event* must take place which transcends subject-object categories, engaging

---

121. Van Til, *Christian Epistemology*, 122–23, 184. Van Til points out that even in redemption, the objective aspect (Christ) and the subjective aspect (Holy Spirit) are never separated (*Psychology*, 151, 154).

122. Van Til, *Christian Epistemology*, 131; 217.

123. Van Til, *New Modernism*, 249–50.

124. Van Til, *New Modernism*, 254.

125. Van Til, *New Hermeneutic*, 18.

126. Van Til, *Christ and the Jews*, 47.

127. Thiselton, "New Hermeneutic," 83.

the interpreter's subjectivity beyond cognition wherein the text "*actively grasps him as its object.*"[128] "Truth has us ourselves as its object."[129] Yet, this event of language is construed as *being*, which is somehow shared by both God and man, with both being interdependent.[130] Van Til's interaction with the new hermeneutic reveals an ontological focus, which speaks to present hermeneutical concerns.

For all its insights concerning the subjective involvement of the interpreter, especially as it pertains to being interpreted *by* a text (something all the more relevant when dealing with a divinely authoritative text), the new hermeneutic reveals stark differences with the doctrine of the ontological Trinity. First, it assumes a metaphysic of being, which not only compromises the Creator-creature distinction, but also the inner personal relations of the ontological Trinity, including objectivity and subjectivity. It assumes an ontology which is more ultimate than the theological categories of the ontological Trinity. Second, the question of *what* exactly is communicated in such an event which transcends conventional linguistic categories persists. As Van Til emphasized, the triune God is self-contained *fullness*, highlighting the fact that God is able to reveal positive qualities he actually possesses, not being a transcendent blank or merely an extrapolation of finite reality.[131] Third, being is conceived of as an ultimate unity without ultimate diversity, leaving personal relatability dependent upon man's encounter with being or God. The hermeneutical concern for communicative engagement with contemporary readers through the Bible finds an answer in the fully communicative ontological Trinity, who does not need such engagement to become communicative, but was so from all eternity in himself.[132]

One hermeneutical implication from this is that since Trinitarian knowledge involves both the object and the subject in perfect, personal coherence, one can expect to find similar analogous insights in modernist and postmodern hermeneutics, while at the same time, recognize that neither is correct at the ultimate metaphysical level.[133] Frame has observed that every epistemology which seeks to do justice to knowledge in terms of subject, object, and criterion (logic) apart from the ontological Trinity tends to deify or absolutize one of the three aspects. For instance, exalting the subject in

---

128. Thiselton, "New Hermeneutic," 92 (emphasis his).

129. Thiselton, *Two Horizons*, 345.

130. Thiselton, "New Hermeneutic," 94–95; Van Til, *New Hermeneutic*, 106.

131. Frame, *Van Til*, 54. By *positive*, we mean actual content as opposed to pure negation.

132. Westphal's answer to this concern is notably lacking in Trinitarian emphasis ("Philosophical/Theological View," 86).

133. Poythress, *God-Centered*, 67.

CHAPTER 6: ONTOLOGICAL TRINITY

communication is found in various forms of subjectivism, while exalting the object is found in forms of empiricism. Without the triune God, there is no guarantee that these three aspects will ultimately cohere.[134] Each, like the persons of the Trinity, are distinct but inseparable.[135] The archetypal object (God) as the context for all knowledge is *also* exhaustive personal subjectivity.[136] Van Til's emphasis on the equal ultimacy of subject and object avoids hermeneutical idolatry which either deifies one over the other, or seeks to transcend them both in favor of a more ultimate metaphysic. Both run contrary to one informed by the ontological Trinity.

Poythress has not only affirmed archetypal coinherence of subject and object in God's triune self-knowledge,[137] but has also pointed out that Trinitarian coinherence between speaker, speech, and hearer (associated with the Father, Son, and Holy Spirit, respectively) grounds our own speech. Each provides a perspective on the whole of communication. Not only does this Trinitarian coinherent triad provide intelligibility and grounding for human communication, it also highlights the fact that none of the three components are intelligible in isolation. Any theory of interpretation which pits one against the others ends up distorting the truth and deifying one aspect at the expense of others.[138]

It is worth noting one more contemporary concern to which the ontological Trinity as an archetype for human communication can help nuance. Vanhoozer has explicitly stated his concern to "take God's Trinitarian self-communication as the paradigm of what is involved in all true communication." Also, he contends that "the undoing of interpretation rests on a theological mistake."[139] However, he proposes to combat secular literary theories ("anti-theologies") by emphasizing the *economic* Trinity in redemption. Certainly, this is not inappropriate, but it is incomplete in terms of ontology, and begs more ultimate questions, such as: where does personal speech originate? In a chapter on the metaphysics of communication, it is surprising that Vanhoozer would neglect to mention the ontological Trinity beyond an implicit reference.[140] In a later work, he relegates the immanent Trinity to a mere footnote, given his emphasis on God's self-revelation on

---

134. Frame, *Knowledge of God*, 110.
135. Frame, *Knowledge of God*, 107.
136. Poythress, "Christ," 321; *God-Centered*, 25.
137. Poythress, *Redeeming Philosophy*, 247.
138. Poythress, *God-Centered*, 102–4.
139. Vanhoozer, *Is There?*, 199–200.
140. Vanhoozer, *Is There?*, 201–65.

the stage of history.[141] Yet, he makes the point that the gospel is unintelligible apart from Trinitarian theology, for only such a theology "adequately accounts for how those who are not God come to share in the fellowship of the Father and Son through the Holy Spirit."[142] It would seem that Van Til's emphasis on the ontological Trinity could round out Vanhoozer and provide nuances which speak to his concerns about intelligibility and keeping those who are not God distinct from the self-sufficient Trinity.

Perspectivalism

Though he does not explicitly use the term *perspectivalism*, the concept is present in Van Til's writings.[143] As we saw in chapter 1, perspectivalism seeks to do justice to both the finitude of man and the unified nature of God's system of truth rooted in his triune nature. Van Til's way of looking at the Christian system of truth is to look at various aspects as *related* to one another in unity.[144] This unity is essential in maintaining a proper defense against non-Christian thought. While perspectival triads can be seen in his approach to such topics as ethics,[145] epistemology,[146] revelation,[147] and others, their theological roots lie in his doctrine of the Trinity.[148] Each person of the Trinity is a perspective on the entire Godhead, while remaining eternally distinct (versus modalism).[149] In terms of the unified Christian system of truth, one doctrine is related to another and to the whole. One doctrine cannot be elevated by cancelling out the others, but rather each informs the others. Even the attributes of Scripture (necessity, authority, clarity, and sufficiency) are perspectivally related in that each implies the others, and the nature of Scripture as a whole can be seen from each of the four perspectives.[150] This is another case of God's special revelation having

---

141. Vanhoozer, *Drama of Doctrine*, 42n26.

142. Vanhoozer, *Drama of Doctrine*, 43.

143. He does speak against non-Christian forms of "perspectivism," in which each intellectual system for us is merely a relativistic take on the ultimate, actual mystery of reality (*Defense of Faith*, 148).

144. Van Til, *Christian Apologetics*, 17–18; Frame, *Van Til*, 173–75.

145. E.g., Van Til, *Theistic-Ethics*, 3.

146. E.g., Van Til, *Case for Calvinism*, 96.

147. E.g., Van Til, *Systematic Theology*, 121.

148. Frame, *Van Til*, 170.

149. Van Til, *Systematic Theology*, 348.

150. Van Til, *Systematic Theology*, 222–27. In context, Van Til explicitly makes the connection between the attributes of Scripture and "an absolutely true interpretation" from God "into a world of false interpretation." (227).

Trinitarian qualities. Moreover, creation exhibits Trinitarian characteristics. This can be seen in terms of the one and many phenomena already discussed. Because God's archetypal knowledge is tri-personal, our ectypal knowledge involves multiple perspectives.[151] This does not mean the endorsement of multiple contradictory meanings[152] but rather the further explication of the one *full* sense of any Scripture.[153]

A Van Til-influenced, perspectival hermeneutic would exhibit a number of distinctives. First, it would recognize the value of perspectives for *finite* man seeking to understand God's word as coming from the *infinite* and personal One, whose comprehensive perspective is exhaustive of all perspectives, being both one and many.[154] Second, not only does it make the interpreter more ontologically, epistemologically, and ethically self-conscious, it helps us to better understand the full sense of any one text. Legitimate perspectives in Scripture (e.g., doctrines, themes, and analogies)[155] can provide different looks at the entire canon. In this sense, perspectives promote the unity and deeply contextual nature of Scripture, with conscious roots in the ontological Trinity. Rather than denying absolute truth, perspectives exhibit the *fullness* of truth encountered by finite interpreters.[156] Third, the use of multiple perspectives serves to prevent theological blind spots from forming due to a dominant focus on certain ones to the neglect of others. This may contribute to more fruitful dialogue with other theological perspectives while exposing forms of reductionism and heresy.[157]

Recently, some evangelical scholars have employed similar perspectival-like triads in hermeneutics. Köstenberger employs history, literature, and theology as his hermeneutical triad of choice. While this triad provides complementary insight into the interpretive enterprise, it is not self-consciously Trinitarian. As such, it lacks explicit ontological and epistemological foundations. Desiring to balance each aspect in the face of various forms of imbalance in the history of interpretation, Köstenberger curiously suggests that while theology is the goal of interpretation, appreciation of history and literary features are essential and foundational.[158] Clearly this assertion needs

---

151. Frame, *Van Til*, 170–71; "Multiperspectivalism," 190–92.
152. Jacobsen, "Rise of Evangelical," 325–35.
153. WCF 1.9.
154. Poythress, *Symphonic Theology*, 51; *In the Beginning*, 166.
155. Certain perspectives are more prominent and pervasive than others.
156. Poythress, *Symphonic Theology*, 45–46.
157. E.g., some are mono-perspectival reductions, which make one perspective into a godlike origin for everything else (Poythress, *Redeeming Philosophy*, 87).
158. Köstenberger and Patterson, *Invitation*, 67–79.

to be nuanced. Is it consistent with the ontological Trinity to privilege history as more foundational than theology in interpretation? In light of our survey in chapters 2 and 3, such ontological concerns must be addressed in order to meet the demand of contemporary hermeneutics.

Treier, argues that TIS uses multiple lenses to integrate multiple perspectives into a fuller, unified picture of God and his call in Scripture. This not only aids our finite and fallen capacities through expanded appreciation but also corrects them.[159] However, while the metaphors of *lenses* and *maps* are helpful to a point, they do not provide the deeper and particular foundation of the ontological Trinity. In order to defend against opposing worldviews and articulate a distinctly Christian hermeneutic, it is necessary to address metaphysical assumptions. Trinitarian considerations on this level would only contribute to the otherwise Trinitarian-oriented TIS movement.[160]

Conclusion

We have seen how Van Til's summary of the ontological Trinity, in terms of four main categories, provides insight and application to contemporary hermeneutics. In particular, these insights speak to concerns of both SAT and TIS but in ways that develop and nuance them. As with all of Van Til's emphases in his doctrine of God, there is benefit in assessing issues related to metaphysics from a consistently Christian worldview. Not only is this a pressing matter due to how hermeneutics has come to be defined (chapter 2) and how its relationship to metaphysics has been construed (chapter 3), but also in how few have offered such a self-conscious Christian ontology to meet the need.

We have looked at macro-hermeneutical observations of Van Til throughout our discussion, in light of contemporary hermeneutical concerns (i.e., scope and metaphysics). We also addressed the three main contours of Van Til's doctrine of God with their respective implications for interpretive method. In the next chapter, we will more specifically seek to apply insights from Van Til's doctrine of God to a relevant contemporary issue: *the NT use of the OT.*

---

159. Treier, *Theological Interpretation*, 203–5.

160. Treier not only emphasizes the importance of the doctrine of the Trinity for interpretation, but also sees the need for articulating the right relation between TIS and biblical theology. He mentions that some are fearful that TIS might involve a theology based on a philosophy *in general* (Treier, "Biblical Theology," 20–29). Van Til's thought would not only address Trinitarian concerns, but also combat forms of "philosophy in general" found in various hermeneutical approaches.

Part III: **Van Til's Doctrine of God Applied**

Chapter 7: The NT Use of the OT

Introduction

IN PART I, WE saw how hermeneutics is inextricably linked with metaphysical assumptions. Van Til's relevance comes out of his concern to articulate and defend Christianity as a worldview, including a biblical metaphysics. In part II, we discussed the centerpiece of his Christian worldview—the doctrine of God, *the* basis for a Christian ontology. In particular, we looked at three main contours which Van Til emphasized in evaluating apologetic method. It is our contention that not only does every ontology imply an epistemology,[1] but every ontology also implies a *hermeneutic*. To put a hermeneutical twist on a phrase from Van Til, "we cannot choose hermeneutical methods like we do hats."[2] Our method of interpretation must match the content of Scripture.[3] This consistency involves taking into account the revealed nature of God.

It is important to note that the Bible teaches that fallen man's tendency is to confuse God with creation, seeking to reason autonomously in the place of God (Gen 3; Rom 1), according to some more ultimate criteria than what God has revealed. We discussed this in terms of how a general ontology is often assumed in hermeneutics which precludes theological consideration and ends up correlating God with creation at some point. This creates tension between interpretive method and the theological content of Scripture. In what follows, we will seek to apply Van Til's macro-hermeneutical concerns to the contemporary debate over the NT use of the OT. It is our aim that this brief case study will shed light on the issue by approaching it from a different angle, one which self-consciously takes the implications of a biblical ontology into account.

---

1. Van Til, *Christian Epistemology*, 15. Lillback suggests that "at the heart of the hermeneutical crisis there is an epistemological crisis that denies men the certainty of divine knowledge" (Lillback, "Infallible Rule," 313).

2. Van Til, *Christian Epistemology*, xiv.

3. Van Til, *Christian Epistemology*, 4–6; *Reformed Pastor*, 45; *Psychology*, 148–49.

NT Use of the OT: *An Overview*

It would be impossible to deal with the complexity of this issue in the present chapter.[4] For our purposes, we will only highlight aspects which more directly intersect with Van Til's macro-hermeneutical concerns. One helpful way to navigate is to recognize the central questions involved in the discussion. Lunde suggests that the central issue in making sense of the NT's use of the OT concerns *the relationship between the OT and the NT authors' intended meanings.*[5] Of the other orbiting questions which revolve around this central question,[6] the ones more directly related to *method* will concern us here: *what was the source of the NT authors' hermeneutical methods? Are we able to replicate such methods?* We will look at questions regarding meaning and method in turn. However, the two are interrelated. Hence, there is inevitable overlap, and neither can be discussed in a purely discrete fashion.

Relation between Human Authors' Intended Meanings?

Not only does this question involve the relationship between OT and NT authors' intent in terms of correspondence, it also involves the relationship between original and modern meaning (e.g., the first century for the NT authors and their audience). Among evangelical scholars, there have been three main views of this relationship.[7]

Single Meaning, Unified Referents

First, some have argued that there is no difference between what was intended by the OT author and what the NT author intends.[8] This single intent extends to the referents of the text. In other words, "in addition to prior reference, the OT writer is to be understood as ultimately having the same people or events in mind when he writes his text as the NT author does when he refers that text to Jesus and the community defined by him."[9] Did the OT authors know the future meaning of their texts? Did the NT authors

---

4. For a good introduction, see: Beale, *Right Doctrine*.
5. Lunde, "An Introduction," 10–12.
6. E.g., *sensus plenior*, typology, and contextual sensitivity.
7. The following three main views represent general categories, not all their variations.
8. Kaiser, "Single Intent," 55–68. For example, the OT prophets only claimed ignorance to the timing of their prophecies, not their content.
9. Lunde, "Introduction," 40.

go beyond the human intent of older Scripture? In essence, the answer is *yes* to the former and *no* to the latter question.[10] Kaiser has argued that this single intended meaning of the human author can be accessed by the usual literary conventions but *without* introducing any prejudice or pre-understanding.[11] Moreover, this intent can only include revelation *prior* to the historical context of the original author.[12] Christian theology is bracketed out for a later stage in the process and not to be used until that point.[13] In each of these emphases,[14] there is a concern to provide controls which secure meaning in the *human* intent of the original author, often in contrast to other approaches—primarily, subjectivism and Roman Catholic tradition under the guise of *sensus plenior*.[15]

There are a number of problematic features to this approach to meaning. First, there is a de-emphasis on the divine author to the point that, rather strikingly, the human author's intent is *equated* with the divine author's intent. This seems to stem from Kaiser's emphasis on general hermeneutics in establishing objective meaning.[16] He asserts that "the superiority of the Scriptures over other books does not come in the *manner* we interpret it but in its *matter* and grand source."[17] Yet his method (manner), based on general hermeneutics, shows itself to be inconsistent with the message (matter) of Scripture, especially if the divine author's intent is considered to be the same as the human author's intent.[18] Erickson observes that "here is the adoption of a methodology without due attention to the compatibility of its presuppositions with those of the Christian biblical tradition."[19] By largely treating the Bible like any other book, Kaiser sets up a playing field which makes

---

10. Kaiser, "Single Meaning," 65.
11. Kaiser, "Single Intent," 67–68.
12. Kaiser, *Exegetical Theology*, 133–34.
13. Kaiser, *Exegetical Theology*, 140.

14. This includes Hirsch's distinction between meaning (unchanging) and significance (changing) (Kaiser, "Legitimate Hermeneutics," 117). For a discussion of problematic aspects of this distinction for the NT use of the OT, see: Moo, "The Problem," 198–200.

15. Erickson, *Evangelical Interpretation*, 11–12. For the classic Catholic treatment of this concept, see: Brown, *'Sensus Plenior'*; "Sensus Plenior," 262–85.

16. Kaiser, "Legitimate Hermeneutics," 112–18.
17. Kaiser, "Legitimate Hermeneutics," 116.

18. Erickson, *Evangelical Hermeneutics*, 13, 18–19. Kaiser boldly asserts that "God did not exceed the intention of the human author either through a retrojection of the whole of the canon on an earlier text or by means of a hidden freight of meaning which awaited our discovery of it centuries later" (Kaiser, "A Response," 445–46).

19. Erickson, *Evangelical Hermeneutics*, 30.

it impossible to affirm the biblical relationship between human authorship and divine inspiration he seeks to endorse. Erickson observes:

> a built-in contradiction continues to surface. The antisupernaturalist (or at least nonsupernaturalist) assumptions eliminate any meaning conveyed by a divine coauthor of which the human author would not be consciously aware.[20]

By anchoring meaning in the human author, it becomes necessary to establish objective control and comprehension of that meaning on a human level, which, as we discussed earlier (chapter 4), seeks to transcend the limits of human reason, regarding both the human author *and* reader.

Second, OT authors end up being endowed with superhuman comprehension in order to save objective meaning from subjectivism and uncertainty. While this seeks a sort of comprehensive knowledge in the human mind, it ironically limits modern meaning for the human reader. Unchanging *meaning* is locked in the past, while only a changing *significance* is left for the modern reader. It has been suggested that this lesser significance may even prove to be an open door for responding to the text in a way which exhibits a different value system than the one found in Scripture.[21] Kaiser's reliance upon Beecher's concept of "generic prophecy" proves unpersuasive.[22] With it, he hopes to affirm that the prophets saw the whole complex of future events and all parts with their various intervals involved in their prophecy, yet with the caveat that they may apply indifferently to various parts or the whole. Can we say that the prophet knows the whole of his prophecy if his knowledge is ultimately *generic* and *may* include certain applications to various parts *or* the whole? It would seem like he is confusing what is often labeled as the *prophet perspective* (i.e., seeing a complex of events as happening together)[23] with a comprehensive and determinate one. Other questions remain. For instance, what about prophecy regarding the future which has yet to be fulfilled for the contemporary reader?[24]

Third, only taking into consideration that which was known or available to the human author of an OT text, besides being an inexact science,[25]

---

20. Erickson, *Evangelical Hermeneutics*, 30–31.
21. Poythress, "Divine Meaning," 247.
22. Beecher, *Prophets and Promise*, 130.
23. Hoekema, *Bible and Future*, 9; Waltke, *Old Testament*, 822–24.
24. Erickson, *Evangelical Hermeneutics*, 29.
25. E.g., books of the OT with which there is debate over dating, authorship, editing? In addition, how much do we know about the human authors of Scripture, in terms of their *intent* in using previous canonical material (e.g., which portions?), and what their historical context was and how much it influenced their intent? (Poythress,

actually *decontextualizes* a text (along with a portion of the canon) from the completed canon. Theological meaning associated with an OT text must be detached from the canon in order to be rightly understood.[26] This is problematic if divine authorship is to be maintained. One wonders if theology, considered merely as a secondary tack-on, will ever find true compatibility with that from which it has been excluded from the start.[27] Contrary to avoiding the analogy of faith until the end of the exegetical process, Payne suggests that in limiting meaning to the human author's intent, "we would have no basis for using the analogy of Scripture to check present-day interpretations that conflict with other teachings of Scripture."[28]

Fourth, after being decontextualized from the canon, an OT text, in essence, is *re-contextualized* within the more ultimate limiting factor—in this case, *history*. On a human level, this is something to which the author and reader are bound. Kaiser's method demands historical restrictions on meaning which are inconsistent with his doctrine of divine inspiration. In short, divine intent ends up being ultimately bound by historical constraints.

Fuller Meaning, Single Goal

Enns has endorsed a view which sees NT authors intending *new* meanings in OT texts which were not necessarily intended by the original authors. If Kaiser sees no distinction between OT and NT authors' intent, Enns sees a separation between the two. Enns affirms the role of divine inspiration with *both* OT and NT authors, but for him, this does not mean there is no difference in intent. There are things which the NT authors intend regarding the OT that are not actually found in the OT. In other words, reading the OT by itself, using the grammatical-historical method, does not lead to the NT reading of it.[29] According to his view, the NT authors' intent does not match the OT context.[30] The NT authors were *not* concerned with staying true to the OT authors' intent. Rather, they were concerned to explain what the OT

"Dispensing," 481–96).

26. This would seem to be inconsistent with what Kaiser says elsewhere concerning the theological presuppositions of the OT authors which necessarily point *forward* to NT fulfillment ("Response to Bock," 153–54). Are such theological presuppositions to be bracketed out in understanding OT intent or not?

27. This would be akin to a sort of hermeneutical *block-house* method discussed in chapter 4.

28. Payne, "Fallacy," 81.

29. Enns, "Apostolic Hermeneutics," 271, 283; *Inspiration and Incarnation*, 115.

30. Enns, "Fuller Meaning," 215; *Inspiration and Incarnation*, 115, 156–60.

means in light of Christ.³¹ In other words, they were concerned with modern meaning (in the first century), not so much with original meaning.³²

This approach is also problematic. First, while seeking to get beyond intended meaning being trapped in the past via the Hirschian *meaning/significance* distinction, it ends up disconnecting OT and NT intent, and then reconnecting them via an extra-biblical historical and hermeneutical context.³³ This raises an important question: *where does the hermeneutical authority of Scripture ultimately reside?* Enns seems to provide an answer to this when he says, "There is no absolute reference point to which we have access that will allow us to interpret the Bible stripped of our own cultural context."³⁴ Certainly, the Bible is culturally conditioned, but its meaning is not culturally bound. In terms of biblical hermeneutics as a dialogue with God as the ultimate authority, Enns' approach seems more like a dialogue with a second opinion. He conceives of extra-biblical evidence as a "vital 'conversation partner' for thinking through what the Bible is."³⁵

Second, Enns' use of the incarnational analogy is not only ambiguous but also breaks down at points. Generally, this analogy affirms that like Christ who is fully divine and fully human at the same time, so also is the Bible. Though the analogy is helpful if this general point is maintained,³⁶ he speaks of it in a way which would lead one to think that the Son did not merely take up humanity in service of his sovereign mission but actually was *dependent* upon it in order to make sense of his mission. For instance, his emphasis on the extra-biblical, historical, and cultural context of Jesus and the NT authors as the key to understanding their use of the OT shows that "the Bible is not unique to its environment."³⁷ This leads Carson to conclude that Enns endorses an Arian understanding of Scripture (i.e., the human trumps the divine).³⁸ Contrary to Enns, Tipton helpfully summarizes the value of the incarnational analogy:

---

31. Enns, *Inspiration and Incarnation*, 116.

32. Though he claims to not abandon the proper instinct to respect original intent, he ends up focusing on *another* context in order to make sense of the NT use of the OT—namely, an extra-biblical, Second Temple Jewish context (*Inspiration and Incarnation*, 114–17).

33. Enns, *Inspiration and Incarnation*, 132.

34. Enns, *Inspiration and Incarnation*, 169.

35. Enns, "Apostolic Hermeneutics," 287.

36. Bavinck, *Prolegomena*, 380, 432–43; Gaffin, *God's Word*, 15, 40, 46.

37. Enns, *Inspiration and Incarnation*, 20.

38. Carson, *Collected Writings*, 270. It may also be noted that though Enns accuses evangelicals of docetism (denying the humanity of Scripture), one could charge him with a functional Ebionitism in return (denying deity of Scripture).

The incarnational analogy ought to yield both a theology of Scripture and a hermeneutic that take into account the primarily theological and hermeneutical significance of the Holy Spirit's agency, on the one hand, and the *subordinate* theological and hermeneutical significance of human agency on the other hand. The primacy of the divine in pneumatology finds a clear analogue in the primacy of the eternal person of the Son of God.[39]

A proper use of the incarnational analogy will recognize that the humanity of Christ is not primary, nor are the two natures equally ultimate. Rather, the Creator-creature distinction remains fully intact in the hypostatic union. Here, Enns fails to do justice to the doctrine of *enhypostasia*, as endorsed by the church at Constantinople II (553).

Third, according to Enns' view, biblical theology fails to "serve as buffer between the NT and the interpretive practices of the world in which the NT writers lives."[40] In other words, he cuts the cord of organic revelation, in which earlier parts are inherently related to later parts, so that NT authors do not develop the original intent of OT texts.[41] Rather, an *inorganic* context becomes the link that holds the meaning of the OT and the NT together. This sets up an unstable dichotomy between *contexts* of revelation and the *climax* of that revelation in Christ, leaving the latter a climax of something to which it has no substantive relation.

Single Meaning, Multiple Contexts, and Referents

Third, Bock argues for a single unity of meaning between OT and NT authors when texts are cited. However, in this unity of meaning, the OT texts take on new dimensions as they apply to new contexts and referents that unfold in the larger canonical context.[42] In many cases, the OT authors were not fully conscious of these new referents. This view seeks to allow the original context of an OT passage to resonate with the NT context in terms of canonical development, with the former as the starting point, setting trajectories for the latter.[43] Hence, there is a consideration of *both* contexts

---

39. Tipton, "Incarnation, Inspiration," (emphasis mine); Berkouwer, *Person of Christ*, 311.

40. Enns, "Response," 10–11.

41. Beale, *Erosion of Inerrancy*, 105.

42. This is similar to Vanhoozer's notion of "thick description'" (*Is There?*, 313–14).

43. Bock, "Single Meaning," 106–7. Similarly, Francis Watson argues for what he calls *dialectical unity* (vs. *discrete witness*, implying independence) of the testaments in which the voice of each "can only be properly heard on the assumption of their

in the larger context of the canon. In order to do justice to issues of intent and context, the *theological* presuppositions of the OT and NT authors must be considered. Though there is some difference of opinion on exactly what these presuppositions were, this approach recognizes their integral role in method.[44] Some directly point to the doctrine of God in terms of inspiration, the unity of special revelation, and a sovereign plan for the progress of history.[45] The concern "is that the movement of a text through its scriptural, temporal development of salvation history must always be kept in mind as work with meaning in the early church citation."[46] This means that development between earlier and later OT texts must be taken into account when seeking to understand the NT use of them. Recognition of this development *within* the OT may explain the strange use of earlier OT passages. It has been argued that NT authors cite such passages with the later development in mind, making their use of them consistent with the passage in its larger context.[47] Indeed, what often seems to be an atomistic treatment actually proves to be more *deeply contextual*,[48] through the consideration of larger context, development, and theological and eschatological expectations of the authors.[49] In short, meaning develops throughout the canon but does so in ways which complement and expand upon it, not in ways which flatten or contradict it. This view embraces the standard evangelical notion of the

---

interdependence" (Watson, "Old Testament," 227–28).

44. Bock, "Single Meaning," 111; Snodgrass, "The Use," 37–40. For a summary of seven main presuppositions involved in NT authors' interpretation of the OT, see: Beale, *Handbook*, 95–102.

45. One of the helpful contributions of N.T. Wright is his emphasis on the importance of *story* for understanding knowledge and worldview, highlighting the role of interpretation regarding facts (vs. uninterpreted or atomistic facts). However, he is unclear on the role of authorial intention in textual interpretation. While affirming a concept of *sensus plenior*, he does not explain how God's relationship to meaning factors into his critical realism. He seems to prefer a sort of hermeneutical syncretism, in which he draws together aspects from a variety of approaches (Moritz, "Critical but Real," 180–92; Wright, *New* Testament, 31–144). Carson has criticized Wright's emphasis on the functional authority of Scripture through the kingdom of God (i.e., authority as a *sub-branch* of other theological categories), which does not address the question of what is the essence of scriptural authority in itself (vs. God's authority *through* it) (Carson, *Collected Writings*, 299–300; Wright, *Last Word*, 17, 22, 37).

46. Bock, "Single Meaning," 141.

47. Beale, "Cognitive," 263–93; Silva, "New Testament Use," 161; Goldsworthy, *Christ*-Centered, 148–49.

48. Dodd convincingly shows that OT citations in the NT were being used as signposts to larger, assumed OT contexts (Dodd, *According to Scriptures*).

49. LaSor, "*Sensus Plenior*," 61; Bush, "Apostolic Hermeneutics," 291–307.

grammatical-historical method but is not limited to a strict version of it in light of the canonical dynamics in meaning.

This third view is the most persuasive in that it places an emphasis on canonical context, theological presuppositions,[50] and an appreciation for the fullness of meaning, which transcends the human author but does not contradict original intent. However, in this view, there is often little explicit attention paid to the *divine* author's relation to meaning, at least according to a biblically informed ontology and epistemology. The following discussion will flesh out this concern according to emphases in Van Til's doctrine of God.

A Van Tillian Critique of Meaning: The Deeper Question

Behind our brief evaluation of the three views, there is a deeper question than the central one suggested above. Namely, *what is the relationship between God and the OT and NT authors' meanings?* In the current discussion, there are very few references to ontology, even in the midst of epistemological considerations. Van Til's emphasis can help to address many of the concerns and questions regarding the above views. By focusing on the divine author as *the* context for the human authors, their message, and subsequent audiences, one finds biblically stable ground on which to stand.

First, in light of Van Til's extensive discussions of the Creator-creature distinction, the question of the relationship between the OT and NT in terms of authorial intent is dependent upon *God's intention* mediated through them. Each of the three views fails to make this explicit to one degree or another, with Kaiser most blatantly confusing the Creator-creature distinction in his understanding of authorial intent. God's personal intent through a text of Scripture necessarily involves that intent being related to his exhaustive self-knowledge and knowledge of all things, according to his comprehensive plan for creation. Ultimately, *God* is the context for meaning.[51] Poythress points out that divine intent includes not only his revelation *through* the human author to the original audience but *also* to subsequent audiences. His intent includes both particular texts and the whole canon.[52] Before stability of meaning is established, it is important to note that *all* involved in understanding the NT use of the OT (e.g., humans, texts, and so on) necessarily

---

50. However, as Beale points out, larger hermeneutical assumptions related to the continuity or discontinuity of the testaments factor into which theological presuppositions are emphasized or not (Beale, *Handbook*, 96–97).

51. Poythress, *In the Beginning*, 86–90.

52. Poythress, *God-Centered*, 109–22.

depend on God for meaning. Rather than canceling out the actual intent of the human authors in the process, God's intent establishes it.

Another Creator-creature category highlighted by Van Til is the *incarnation*, especially in its Chalcedonian formulation. As we saw with Enns, the incarnational analogy can be helpful in setting forth the relationship between the divine and human qualities of Scripture, but it can also provide a corrective for Christological heresies expressed in hermeneutical form. The most salient dangers among evangelicals in trying to understand and find controls for meaning in the NT use of the OT are hermeneutical Arianism or Nestorianism (Enns) and Monophysitism (Kaiser)—a tendency to ignore the divine author, separate divine and human intent, or confuse them, respectively. Consideration of the divine and human authors involves a recognition that we are dealing with *two* levels of being in order to avoid a taking away from one in order to establish the other. Only God exhaustively knows the relationship between the divine and human natures in the person of the Son, and only he knows that relation as it is present in Scripture. However, does this leave us then with a kind of hermeneutical agnosticism in *our* understanding?

Van Til spent much time articulating the biblical relationship between general and special revelation, seeing the latter as God's authoritative (inspired and inerrant) interpretation of reality. Just as God is absolute, self-contained, and self-attesting, so also is his word.[53] Contrary to Enns, "the Bible itself must determine for us what the Bible is."[54] General revelation and special revelation are not opposed to one another nor do they function without one another, as they come from the same authority. However, after the fall, there is a sinful tendency to pit the two against one another,[55] often under the guise of doing justice to the historical and cultural context. Special revelation, as divine interpretation, is not opposed to what actually happened in the past but is opposed to correlating God's interpretation of reality with creation in a way which undermines it. The question of authority factors into the situation. God's word is revealed in history, but its (and history's) origin is not in history. According to Scripture, history is not the master category for interpretation. This is not to say that history is not involved, but that the *divinely* inspired canon, with its own inner-hermeneutic, is the master category which, of course, has God himself as its origin and foundation. Historical facts, much like evidence in apologetics, are always in touch with and informed by their philosophical and theological

---

53. Van Til, *New Hermeneutic*, 158.
54. Goldsworthy, *Hermeneutics*, 271.
55. Van Til, "Nature and Scripture," 273.

foundations.[56] Non-inspired interpretation (e.g., Second Temple Judaism midrash, Qumranic pesher, or contemporary methods) cannot impose any category of theological understanding not derived from the canon itself.[57] NT interpretation of the OT as special revelation is distinct and authoritative for all interpretation. Hence, it is *not* like first century interpretive methods in this sense.

Oliphint, citing Muller, has observed that the basic protestant hermeneutical principle in the seventeenth century was that Scripture's unity must be given priority over the interpretation of particular texts. He describes this priority as "ontological" and rooted in the aseity of God. In other words, we are "not to impose an extrabiblical conception of God on the text so it will say what we, in our preconceived assumptions, want it to say."[58] From another direction, this raises the question: *do some views of the NT use of the OT compromise the aseity of God?* VanGemeren has observed that OT prophetic interpretation in Scripture begins and ends with God who is free from any correlation with human interpretation (e.g., false prophets).[59] This is just one example of the ontological priority of the aseity of God *within* the divine interpretation revealed in Scripture.

Second, Van Til's emphasis on the incomprehensibility of God opposes grounding meaning in the comprehension of the human authors, or in readers for that matter. Meaning and hermeneutical control only become problems if they are grounded in man and his finite limitations. Inevitably, one runs into the complications of the rationalistic-irrationalistic dialectic, as well as a reductionistic view of meaning discussed in chapter 4. Kaiser's approach tends toward the autonomous ideal of human comprehension, creating more problems than it solves. The uncertainties regarding intent and historical gaps find their intelligibility and comprehension in the mind of God, not man. Van Til's emphasis on the connection between the mode and content of God's knowledge prevents the reduction of meaning to the human level. In addition, God's comprehension does justice to legitimate postmodern concerns about human limitations without losing touch with objective meaning, while avoiding the rationalistic pitfalls of modernism. Following Van Til, finite, creaturely interpretation is not a problem to be overcome. Rather, it is an issue of creaturely submission to God's special

56. Van Til, *Christian Apologetics*, 19.
57. McCartney, "New Testament's Use," 116.
58. Oliphint, *God with Us*, 27–28; Muller, *Divine Essence*, 451–52.
59. VanGemeren, "Prophets," 98. This would oppose attempts to seek ontology in the *encounter* between God as the *source* of meaning and the reader as the condition of its *possibility* (hence, correlating God and man in meaning) (e.g., Huelin, "Toward Theological," 223–26).

revelation (and its own inner-hermeneutic), with its content providing the necessary ontological presuppositions.

Positively, Van Til's emphasis on the incomprehensibility of God coupled with his articulation of the ontological Trinity can inform an appreciation for the *fullness* of meaning found in a text, which is not truncated by grounding it in the human author alone. In his discussions of mystery and apparent contradictions, along with his perspectival approach to the Trinity, Van Til lays out ontological foundations which can be employed in service of understanding OT texts in light of their NT use without stifling legitimate intertextual connections or leaving blind spots created by allowing one finite perspective (e.g., human intent of author or reader) to limit other legitimate perspectives divinely intended in Scripture (e.g., NT author's intent concerning an OT text).

To answer the question posed earlier, we are *not* left with an agnostic stance about the divine intent of Scripture. While not possessing divine comprehension, we most clearly see God's intent from a finite, analogous perspective, in the larger canonical context—organically transcending the original human author but not violating original intent.[60] Within the canon, we have divinely revealed theological presuppositions which we are to embrace in order to understand particular texts in their contexts, both narrow and broad. The theological presuppositions are not completely hidden from us as they are derived from OT trajectories and expectations.

Third, Van Til's Trinitarian emphasis helps to evaluate questionable distinctions and dichotomies.[61] First, Kaiser's concern to isolate and provide control for meaning through Hirsch's distinction ends up steering attention away from the divine aspects of meaning—namely, knowing in *relation* to God. This inherently relational meaning rooted in the ontological Trinity would seem to undermine the sharp distinction between meaning and significance. To correspond to God's knowledge (on a creaturely level), one must take into account how God relates to what he knows and analogously match that relation on a creaturely level. This implies that knowing the meaning of a text of Scripture as the intent of God through the human author's intent involves *applying* or responding to it properly (e.g., knowing as *covenant-keepers*). Second, the ontological Trinity involves coinherence between the one and many. Meaning is inherently contextual and resists hermeneutical isolation, whether in the human author or in a bracketed-out portion of history or the canon. Third, it would seem that Kaiser endorses

---

60. Vanhoozer, *Is There?*, 263–65; Gaffin, "Redemptive-Historical View," 89–110; Beale, "Positive Answer," 401.

61. Poythress, *God-Centered*, 82–83.

a concept of meaning which privileges the one over the many. Meaning is an unchanging one, with the many as changing and dependent upon history and creaturely context. This ends up ignoring the Trinitarian fullness of meaning and the one and many being equally ultimate in the intent of God.

Can We Follow the NT Authors' Methods of Interpreting the OT?

We will consider two main approaches to answering this second main question. Each view involves important macro-hermeneutical concerns which resonate with Van Til's emphases in apologetics. After summarizing the two and providing some brief critique, we will consider more explicitly how Van Til speaks to the issues raised.

Negative Answer

Longenecker has argued that the exegesis of the NT is *not* normative and should *not* be followed to the degree that it deviates from standard, contemporary historical-grammatical exegesis.[62] His approach is built on the assumed distinction between the transcultural truth or *message* of NT authors and the cultural, time-bound *methods* they used to communicate and support that message in the first century. In light of this distinction, he sees the former to be normative and the latter as not normative for exegetical method.[63] The NT is not meant to be a textbook for hermeneutics and should not be treated as one. In other words, the NT authors got the right doctrine but from the wrong texts. This approach is not entirely uncommon among evangelical scholars, though in varying degrees.[64]

What accounts for the cultural, time-bound methods used in the NT? Longenecker highlights four main types of Jewish exegesis present in the first century: literalist, midrashic, pesher, and allegorical. He concludes that while there is some presence of literalist and occasional allegorical use of the OT, pesher is representative of Jesus' early disciples, and midrashic exegesis is prevalent in Paul and the author of Hebrews.[65] The latter two (along with

62. Longenecker, *Biblical Exegesis*, 198; "Major Tasks," 54.
63. Longenecker, "Evangelical Hermeneutic," 48.
64. E.g., Enns, "Apostolic Hermeneutics," 281–82; Ellingworth, *Hebrews*, 63; Greidanus, *Preaching Christ*, 186–91, 269.
65. Longenecker, "Negative Answer," 380–83. *Pesher* is characterized by seeking to identify one's present situation with what is depicted in OT Scripture (i.e., *this is that*), while *midrash* is characterized by a desire to contemporize earlier revelation with

allegorical) are characterized largely by *non*-contextual usage of the OT.[66] Moreover, it is argued that Jesus himself adhered to the same methods and actually taught them to his disciples.[67]

While the issues involved are admittedly complex and require more detailed attention than what is possible here, we will look at some concerns related to Longenecker's approach. First, many have questioned the uniform nature of Jewish exegesis during the Second Temple period,[68] specifically with regard to its non-contextual nature.[69] Others have noted that the NT is more contextual in its use of the OT than much rabbinic exegesis.[70] On a mere research methodology level, it would seem that such diversity should guard against the decisive conclusions which Longenecker reaches. This brings us to another related concern. Apart from the diversity issue, the presence of similarity does *not* necessarily entail dependence.[71]

Second, it would seem that the general notion is that the apostles' methods were culturally bound to the first century in a sort of relativism, necessarily dependent on the determining influences of their environment.[72] However, Longenecker and others, at the same time, seem to take a detached stance in their critique which Weeks calls an "illogical Modernism." It is illogical in that their assessment and hermeneutical standards (e.g., grammatical-historical) are not applied to the present.[73] In other words, the relativism necessarily involved in the past is not operative in the present. They proceed to attach definitive significance to their own methodology. Hays contends that Longenecker wrongly grants an arbitrarily privileged status to first century interpretation of the OT which is deemed inappropriate for today, leaving Scripture in a past we cannot participate in.[74] Beale has argued that Enns, on the one hand, cautions against using modern standards of determining truth and error to evaluate whether Scripture contains truth or error; on the other hand, Enns fails to account for what standards

---

regard to the historical context of the interpreter (i.e., *that* has relevance for *this*).

66. Longenecker, "Negative Answer," 381–85.

67. Longenecker, *Biblical Exegesis*, 36–62; Enns, *Inspiration and Incarnation*, 132.

68. Weeks, *Sufficiency of Scripture*, 183–93; Neusner, *Rabbinic Traditions*; Beale, *Erosion*, 92–96; Enns even recognizes this lack of uniformity when he observes that "there are *Judaisms* but no 'Second Temple Judaism'" (P. Enns, "Pseudepigrapha," 652).

69. Beale, "Positive Answer," 388–89; Brewer, *Techniques and Assumptions*.

70. Moo, "Sensus Plenior," 193; Silva, "New Testament Use," 159.

71. Weeks, "Ambiguity," 233.

72. Hughes, "Truth of Scripture," 175.

73. Weeks, "Ambiguity," 235.

74. Hays, *Echoes of Scripture*, 181.

of truth and error *were* present in the past. Hence, his position becomes non-falsifiable.[75]

Third, notions regarding the use of the OT by Jesus and Paul raise concerns. First of all, Jesus is depicted as one who is just as culturally determined as the apostles in his use of the OT. This is another problem with the way Enns confuses his incarnational analogy. He uses it to emphasize the humanity of Scripture in the culturally bound method of Jesus and the apostles, but presses it to deny that the divine nature is expressed through Jesus' hermeneutic in particular, as it is truly expressed in other ways (e.g., miracles).[76] This clearly goes against traditional formulations of the incarnation which guard against separating out the human from the divine in terms of Christ's actions and teaching.[77] Indeed, one of the things Jesus taught (i.e., his message) was that the OT Scriptures spoke of him (Luke 24:25–27, 44–47; John 5:39, 46–47). Both Longenecker and Enns agree that the method of the apostles expressed in the NT was the method taught to them by Christ himself.[78] What was the nature of this method? While there are some formal similarities, Jesus' exegesis of the OT *differed* significantly from his Jewish contemporaries in that he displayed a greater fidelity to the sense of OT passages, namely with regard to the OT finding its *fulfillment* in him.[79] This approach involves the larger redemptive-historical context, including the groundswell of trajectories and expectations within the OT itself, not adding new meaning that is somehow disconnected from what the OT says.[80] The same methodology is seen in the apostles.[81] France concludes that "the source of the distinctive Christian use of the Old Testament was not the creative thinking of the primitive community, but that of its founder."[82]

Concerning Enns' treatment of Paul's exegesis, Carson insightfully asks why is it that Paul and his non-Christian Jewish colleagues reach *different* conclusions from the same texts, if they employed the *same* method? Are only his conclusions different because of his conversion or is it that they

---

75. Beale, *Erosion*, 54. Following Van Til, we might add that only God's knowledge and interpretation of truth is non-falsifiable.

76. Beale, *Erosion*, 120; Enns, *Inspiration and Incarnation*, 17–21, 114–15, 132; "Fuller Meaning," 202–4.

77. Macleod, *Person of Christ*, 188–89; Berkhof, *Systematic Theology*, 322–23.

78. Longenecker, *Biblical Exegesis*, 36, 61–62; Enns, *Inspiration and Incarnation*, 132.

79. France, *Jesus*, 200–1.

80. Contra Enns, who sees such trajectories not in the OT but in extra-biblical Jewish texts of the Second Temple period (*Inspiration and Incarnation*, 120).

81. France, *Jesus*, 223–26.

82. France, *Jesus*, 226.

stem from a hermeneutical change as well, one that *"warrants* the Christological readings of the Old Testament he adopts?"[83] It would seem that the difference is a hermeneutical one, not merely regarding the fruits of it. A Christian reading of the OT involves a number of theological presuppositions which feed into the interpretation of it and is dependent upon the Spirit's work (1 Cor 2:6–16; 2 Cor 3:14–16). One could argue that believers today not only experience the enabling work of the Spirit to see Christ in the OT, but also stand in the same redemptive-historical vantage point in relation to the OT as the NT authors (i.e., between the comings of Christ).[84] As Hays and others have shown, the apostolic message and doctrine cannot be cleanly extracted from apostolic exegesis, for the message is rooted in Spirit-led intertextual reflection.[85] Hays concludes:

> Scripture interpretation is the theological matrix within which the kerygma took shape; removed from that matrix, it will die. Longenecker would like to pluck and preserve the flower of apostolic doctrine, but severed from its generative hermeneutical roots that flower will surely wither.[86]

Could the Spirit inspire the NT authors in a way which comes to the right conclusions from going down the wrong paths? To claim to follow the former, while opposing the latter is like saying, "I will follow you wherever you go, so long as you go in my direction."[87]

Fifth, there seem to be problems with Enns' argument for following the apostles' hermeneutical *goal* without following their methods. Herein is the difference between himself and Longenecker. Where Longenecker draws a distinction between exegetical *methods*, Enns draws a distinction between methods and *goals*. The former distinguishes between types of methods which can be employed today, and which ones cannot, favoring the literal, grammatical-historical method. The latter distinguishes between methods and goal, endorsing only the use of the apostles' hermeneutical goals for today (*Christo-telic* hermeneutic).[88] Enns wants to maintain an apostolic hermeneutical standard which is still relevant. Yet, goals are not unrelated to methods. "Methods are chosen according to what produces

---

83. Carson, *Collected Writings*, 279–80.
84. Beale, "Positive Answer," 399.
85. Hays, *Echoes of Scripture*, 182.
86. Hays, *Echoes of Scripture*, 182.
87. McCartney and Clayton, *Let the Reader*, 65.
88. Enns, "Apostolic Hermeneutics," 282.

results in line with what is already known or what makes sense of a text."[89] The NT authors' goal determined their method. That goal was the center of redemptive history—Jesus Christ's person and work. Moreover, the NT is the hermeneutical goal of the OT.[90] It is ironic that Enns endorses McCartney's emphasis on the goal, but fails to acknowledge its inherent connections with method, something for which McCartney argues.[91]

Another problem with separating conclusions or goals from methods is the *apologetic* fallout. How can we defend theological truths which are not inherently connected to method or interpretation present in Scripture? Apart from divine inspiration on par with the NT authors themselves, how would we proceed?[92] Indeed, Van Til was concerned with not severing this vital connection between content and method.

Another blind spot present in the argument for a Christo-telic hermeneutic is that it is usually portrayed as following the apostles' pattern of interpretation in *hindsight*. The apostles, upon being convinced that the eschaton had dawned in Christ's coming and subsequent resurrection, went back to the OT with a Christ-centered focus, which was *not* present in the OT itself prior to the change in themselves.[93] However, one of the very texts Enns uses in support of this point (Luke 24:45) has a context which undermines such use. Before the opening of the minds of his disciples to understand the OT, Jesus told them that they were responsible for understanding the OT as pointing to himself *before* his resurrection because his person and work were *already in the text* of the OT (24:25–26, 44) (i.e., not a brand new meaning absent from the OT text).[94] To take this a step further in terms of connections with theology proper, Van Til argued that because Christianity is a unified system of truth, a definition of Christ's work would necessarily involve a certain doctrine of God.[95] Hence, not only does the OT inherently speak of Christ's work, it is also connected to a particular doctrine of God and, in turn, should influence interpretive method, even in making sense of the NT use of the OT.

---

89. McCartney and Clayton, *Let the* Reader, 66.
90. McCartney, "New Testament's Use," 116.
91. E.g., Enns, "Apostolic Hermeneutics," 276n31.
92. Beale, "Positive Answer," 404.
93. Enns, "Apostolic Hermeneutics," 275, 277; *Inspiration and Incarnation*, 119–20; Ericson, "NT Use," 341.
94. Carson, *Collected Writings*, 281–82.
95. Van Til, *Christian Apologetics*, 18.

Positive Answer

Many scholars have argued that we *should* follow the hermeneutical methods of the NT authors, not merely their conclusions or Christ-centered goal. It is suggested that even the more puzzling uses of the OT found in the NT can be explained when the larger context of Scripture is taken into account.[96] However, it is recognized that NT authors cite the OT in a variety of creative ways which do not readily fit into how the grammatical-historical method is often understood today.[97] Often, *multiple* contexts are involved, with the OT context (narrow and broad) of a passage resonating with the context of the NT citation in ways which go beyond, but also reinforce the use of the cited text.[98] These ways include the following: direct fulfillment, indirect fulfillment, typology, analogical, illustrative, symbolic, abiding authority, proverbial, rhetorical, prototype, alternate textual use, assimilated use, and ironic use.[99] Yet, in each use, there is a contextual connection on some level which reveals the NT use as *organically* related to the meaning of the OT text. This qualified concept of *sensus plenior*, contrary to various abuses, does not violate "the integrity of earlier texts but rather develops them in a way in which is consistent with the Old Testament author's understanding of the way in which God interacts with his people."[100] LaSor uses the analogy of a *seed* containing everything related to its subsequent development and being organically related to its eventual branch, leaf, and flower.[101] This approach steers clear from "scientific" methods—which seek to either collapse the historical development of textual meaning or separate a text from it—and from subjectivist methods. Similarly, with typology and other patterns, there is an appreciation for history which avoids non-contextual allegory but, at the same time, appreciates legitimate expansion of meaning in light of redemptive history. The "extension of the data base being exegeted does not mean we are no longer exegeting but only that we are doing so with a larger block of material."[102] Put differently, typology, biblical theology, and systematic theology are merely doing different types of exegesis at the canonical level.

---

96. Beale, "Positive Answer," 389.
97. Bock, "Single Meaning," 149–50.
98. C.f. Beale and Carson, Commentary, xxiii–xxviii.
99. Beale, *Handbook*, 55–93; Bock, "Single Meaning," 118–21.
100. Beale, "Positive Answer," 393; Moo, "Sensus Plenior," 201–11.
101. LaSor, "Prophecy, Inspiration," 55–56; Vos, *Biblical Theology*, 7, 16–18.
102. Beale, "Positive Answer," 401.

It is acknowledged that *our following* of the interpretive method of the NT authors is not itself divinely inspired. Hence, our certainty regarding exegetical conclusions is not on the same level. However, we must not confuse certainty with method from our side of things.[103] This would be akin to saying that we cannot follow the method of the inspired writers because we do not have *divine* certainty. However, this is only a problem if we are seeking to have such divine certainty for ourselves in the first place. In essence, a false dilemma is set in place: only follow the inspired methods if you can have divine certainty (as a creature).[104] This would seem to preclude following a divine pattern and growing in it with God's help, without seeking to get beyond the Creator-creature distinction. It is important to note that while the writers of Scripture are unique, they were not endowed with divine qualities. Rather, we affirm *dual* authorship of Scripture. In every case and at every point, the Creator-creature distinction is maintained.

Beale argues that it is not only improper to separate method from conclusions derived from method, but the issue has bearing on theology and theological method in general. The NT use of the OT is the key to the *theological* relation between the testaments, which is necessarily broader than the select citations of the OT found in the NT.[105] Using the larger contextual method, patterned after the NT authors, we can grow in our understanding of the divine intent, creatively summarizing what is already expressed in the canon, much like the apostles, with the help of the Spirit. In sum, we should follow the methods of the NT authors.

The positive answer view to the question about method is more persuasive and less problematic than the negative answer. Van Til's macro-hermeneutical insights clearly resonate with the fundamentals of this view. For example, this view seeks to appreciate and follow the methodology of the NT authors as part of the divinely inspired inner-hermeneutic across the canon, rather than seeking to impose a method based on a framework, foreign to the canon. That being said, there is room for further refinement. For instance, there is some concern whether the treatment of epistemological issues is consistent with a biblical ontology stemming from the nature of God and his relation to creation. In particular, how consistent is Hirsch's approach to meaning, and Wright's critical realism, with not only the nature of the divine author (see chapters 1–3), but also the positive answer view regarding method? Van Til's emphases can help to defend

---

103. Beale, "Positive Answer," 399, 402.

104. This is similar to seeking the autonomous ideal in terms of knowledge (i.e., comprehensive), which Van Til opposed in his writings.

105. Beale, "Positive Answer," 404.

against unbiblical presuppositions present in the negative answer view, and provide a more nuanced understanding of worldview, thus strengthening the case for the positive view.

A Van Tillian Critique of Method: The That and the What Involved in One Another

In addition to the critique offered above, Van Til's emphasis on the inherent connection between method and the message of the Bible will now be considered with regard to some of the deeper issues raised.

First, Longenecker's fundamental distinction between transcultural truth and culturally bound method concerns a deeper issue which Van Til often addressed, albeit in a different context. Longenecker's separation of message and method *in* the NT raises three deeper hermeneutical questions. Apart from the problems associated with a "canon-within-a-canon" mentality, if we cannot follow the hermeneutic present in Scripture because of this separation, then *where do we get the hermeneutic which establishes it?*[106] Closely connected is the issue of authority. By what authority is this separation *the* lens through which the method found in the NT is understood? Longenecker is fairly straight forward in his response to this last question, citing Vermes:

> We have, as a result, three cognate schools of exegesis of the one message recorded in the Bible, and it is the duty of the historian to emphasize that none of them can properly be understood independently of the others.[107]

As his works shows, there is a loss of methodological authority among certain cultural and historical influences, with no one school more authoritative than the others in terms of contextualizing the message in the first century (i.e., the NT) *and* today. There is also a distinct tendency to confuse and correlate special revelation with general revelation in the post-fall situation, leaving redemptive history recorded in the canon ultimately indistinguishable from history in general.[108] This brings up a related tendency seen in contemporary hermeneutics—to separate theology from history, especially as it pertains to method. When this is done, the pride of place often goes to

---

106. This assumes that there is a self-sufficient and self-contained principle of interpretation apart from that which is found in Scripture (Van Til, "Nature and Scripture," 283).

107. Longenecker, *Apostolic Exegesis*, xxii; Vermes, "Qumran Interpretation," 85–97.

108. Longenecker, "Evangelical Hermeneutic," 55–56.

history as a more ultimate reality.[109] As Van Til has demonstrated, all facts of history find their meaning in relation to God and his plan. Therefore, all history is not only dependent upon God as triune Creator, but also derives its meaning and intelligibility from him. From the beginning, general revelation was to be informed by special revelation, and all the more since the fall.[110] God's word as canon is the divinely authoritative, self-contained interpretation of reality.[111] We simply cannot withhold theological reflection when considering history and understand that history properly. As it relates to the issue at hand, Silva aptly concludes:

> If we refuse to pattern our exegesis after that of the apostles, we are in practice denying the authoritative character of their scriptural interpretation—and to do so is to strike at the very heart of the Christian faith.[112]

If we do not receive our hermeneutic from Scripture, then *where* do we get it? If God's word is self-attesting because God himself is, then this includes a self-attesting hermeneutic present within it.

A second related question concerns the relationship between method and content. *If method can be removed from content without affecting that content, what informs the method?* It is in the answer to this question that unstated presuppositions come to bear in Longenecker's approach. Not addressing this question, he seems to be working from what he might deem as self-evident assumptions, or at least ones which convey that as we study such matters, we all start with the historical facts in the first century and allow the evidence to lead us to the right assessment of methods present in Scripture. However, Van Til's insistence is that because of God's very nature, our methods are involved in our conclusions.[113] Ontologically speaking, "one's theory of being and one's theory of method are interrelated."[114] Even if we grant the historical arguments regarding facts related to the comparative study of Second Temple Jewish exegesis and what is found in Scripture, we must still consider one's philosophy of fact rooted in *the*

---

109. E.g., Perrin faults Waters for allowing his theological presuppositions influence his evaluation of history in his critique of N.T. Wright (Perrin, "Some Reflections," 142, 146). Wolfhart Pannenberg seeks to ground the resurrection in historical scholarship, apart from revelation, rendering it uncertain at best, waiting for the end of history to verify or falsify such claims (Pannenberg, *Apostles' Creed*, 108–9; *Metaphysics*, 166).

110. Van Til, *Doctrine of Scripture*, 120.

111. Van Til, *Reformed Pastor*, 74–75, 189.

112. Silva, "New Testament Use," 164.

113. Van Til, *Christian Epistemology*, 4–6; *Defense of Faith*, 122.

114. Van Til, *Systematic Theology*, 28.

Fact that determines them all—the triune Creator. As Van Til has argued, the Bible gives us both history *and* a philosophy of history.[115] While there is considerable attention paid to Longenecker's dealings with the facts of history by his critics, there is considerably less attention paid to deeper assumptions related to a philosophy of history, involving the interplay between ontology and method.[116]

Third, *if methods are borrowed from extra-biblical sources to convey the message, but are not part of that message, does this not leave them virtually neutral in their adaptability?* What governs and informs hermeneutical method if disengaged from the message? *What standard is used,* if not the Bible and its message? This is where Van Til's insistence upon both the pre-interpretation of God (as Creator) concerning all reality and creation as exhaustively personal (related to the ontological Trinity) render such supposed neutrality a mirage. If method is not neutral in its adaptability or contextualization, and is inherently involved in its conclusion,[117] then in Longenecker's argument we have a two-fold error in terms of context. Rather than recognizing a distinct and authoritative context for divine intent for *both* message and method, he *decontextualizes* both through separation and then seeks to *re-contextualize* the message in a non-canonical context (i.e., later historical contextualization down to the present day).[118] He even goes so far as to say that it is impossible to retrieve the methods found in the NT because "they lack the power to convince in different cultures, circumstances, and situation of today."[119]

Due to the inherent connection between method and message, one wonders how Longenecker's approach ends up distorting the transcultural message (through de-contextualization) he seeks to preserve. One way is by denying the presence of a built-in hermeneutic rooted in theological

---

115. Van Til, *Christian Apologetics*, 20.

116. Van Til, *Christian Apologetics*, 18.

117. We see evidence of this in how scholars have recognized theological presuppositions of the NT authors related to their method. While one may see some overlap with what can be seen in the Qumran community and first century Jewish exegesis, this does not necessarily entail dependence. A stronger case can be made for the origin of these presuppositions being in the OT itself, with the NT unique in its divine inspiration and authority, and extra-biblical manifestations of them as testifying to the very presence of those ideas in the OT. This just shows that in the latter case, exegetes were working with the same texts.

118. Van Til observed that in general, non-Christian thought is *atomistic* (*Apologetics*, 154–55). Such atomistic understanding is often falsified by context—whether in terms of scriptural context or God as the ultimate context for understanding reality (Frame, *Knowledge of God*, 53).

119. Longenecker, "Evangelical Hermeneutic," 55.

presuppositions derived from the progressive revelation of God. Such redemptive-historical progress is not merely retroactive in direction, but also pro-active through the forward-looking trajectories of the OT. To borrow from Enns' terminology, the first and second *readings* are organically related in *both* message and method. Another way it distorts the message is by making it *dependent* upon extra-biblical sources for re-contextualization and modern meaning. An example of this can be seen in Longenecker's use of the "new wine and fresh wineskins" metaphor from Matthew 9, which is ultimately unconvincing and ironic.[120] Not only does he end up correlating the biblical message (new wine) and extra-biblical cultural context (fresh wineskins) in terms of authority, but he also undermines his very purpose in using the metaphor. For as the context shows, Jesus is opposing the old wineskins of *Judaism* (i.e., the matrix of first century Jewish religion and its attendant hermeneutic) which does not recognize Christ as the bridegroom having come. Actually, the fresh wineskins would correspond more with the inner-hermeneutic of inspired Scripture that Jesus himself appeals to in his own teaching and what he taught to his disciples [121]

Related to the issue of relying upon an extra-biblical context in interpretation is Van Til's evaluation of unbelieving Jewish interpretation of the OT law.[122] According to Van Til, their fundamental hermeneutical flaw consisted in the reliance upon an unwritten Torah as a way to provide modern meaning for the ancient written Torah. It ended up functioning as an unwritten authority on par with Scripture, a sort of continuous revelation. He points out that this approach involves deeper questions of epistemology and metaphysics.[123] It is tied to their understanding of God's revelation and man's response to it (epistemology), as well as their concept of God and his control of history and man's response to this control (metaphysics). He argues that their unwillingness to see that the OT spoke of Christ exhibits a desire to preserve the autonomy of man's ethical consciousness rather than to submit to the ultimate ethical authority of God's word.

---

120. Longenecker, "Evangelical Hermeneutic," 55.

121. Carson, "Matthew," 227–28; France, *Mark*, 142.

122. Van Til, *Christ and Jews*, 70–85.

123. McCartney has argued that hermeneutical method is a product of worldview, including method being bound up in one's view of what a text *ought* to say ("New Testament's Use," 103–7).

Conclusion

We have seen how the issues of meaning and method have been conceived and understood with regard to the NT use of the OT. Views have been proposed *within* evangelicalism which, upon evaluation, exposed the need to ask deeper questions related to metaphysics. Van Til's potential contribution to this issue is the need to evaluate and promote a hermeneutic rooted in the self-contained authority of Scripture. Some of the more problematic features of certain views were able to be addressed according to Van Til's doctrine of God, drawing from the three main contours discussed in chapters 4–6.

It is clear that a Christian hermeneutic consistent with the theology it affirms will include a strong *canonical emphasis*. This emphasis reflects the nature of Scripture as God's self-contained interpretation of reality, implying that it is also self-interpreting (reflecting the nature of God as both Creator and ontological Trinity).[124] It also involves seeing meaning as ultimately *God's* intention which transcends the comprehension of man (incomprehensibility). Moreover, a canonical emphasis will take into account redemptive-historical development found throughout the canon. Though indirect in much of his treatment of method, Van Til seems to show an acute awareness of redemptive history in his discussions of revelation,[125] the new hermeneutic,[126] and non-Christian Jewish hermeneutics.[127]

This hermeneutical approach is not opposed to or in violation of history per se, but rather seeks to understand it according to its created nature and place in the plan of God. The self-interpreting word of God, while involving history, is not dependent upon it in terms of intent and meaning. Hence, any hermeneutical method which assumes a prior and more ultimate metaphysic (e.g., history)[128] than the one revealed in Scripture sets a playing field on which the message of Christianity is denied from the start—if one reasons consistently from this false starting point. For example, if apostolic exegesis is dependent upon *history* for its method and meaning, it is rendered merely

---

124. This would include the potentially fruitful categories under both of these truths which were explored—*Creator-creature*: fact/possibility/interpretation, inerrancy, analogy, antecedent being, person of Christ, sovereignty/election, and the fall as rebellion against the Creator-creature distinction; *Ontological Trinity*: one and the many, personalism, archetype for communication, and perspectivalism.

125. E.g., Van Til, *Systematic Theology*, 126–27, 209–12.

126. E.g., Van Til, *New Hermeneutic*, 214.

127. E.g., Van Til, *Christ and Jews*, 36, 56.

128. Van Til mentions this particular assumption as a tendency of unbelieving thought ("Intellectual Challenge," 40, 11).

a product of its time, severed from divine intention and control. Van Til, in discussing hermeneutical methods of his day, observed:

> the grandest self-deception of modern times is found among Christian theologians who build their theological structure on top of the sinking structure of modern science and philosophy.[129]

Such is the case with a history metaphysically conceived of apart from and prior to the ontology revealed in Scripture.

The Bible contains an authoritative inner-hermeneutic, which functions as a "regulative principle of hermeneutics," not just for itself, but also as a lens of special revelation through which reality is rightly understood. This is merely one implication of *Sola Scriptura*.[130] No extra-biblical criteria are needed for it to function as such. Nor is there an extra-biblical authority to which the Bible must correspond to in order to be and function as the word of God. The central message of Scripture, Jesus Christ, is self-identifying as revealed in Scripture.[131] He is not dependent upon creation in order for him to be explained, nor is he dependent upon any outside criteria to which he must measure up to in order to explain himself. Though revealed in the incarnation and through inspiration of the human authors of Scripture, the message conveyed did not *depend* on the creature for its meaning.

Our task is to seek to match the Bible's own hermeneutic, with the help of the Holy Spirit. Much like a child tracing the inner-structure of a leaf with pencil on paper through the help of a parent, so we are to proceed. While our interpretation and theological formulation is provisional in that we are not inerrant and authoritative on the same level as Scripture, God's word and its inner-hermeneutical rule are *not* provisional.[132]

Methodology, whether apologetic or hermeneutical, can be fruitfully evaluated according the doctrine of God revealed in Scripture. The aim, in this case, is consistency between theology and method, with the goal of thinking God's thoughts after himself *about hermeneutics*. Also included in this evaluation is the detection of rational and irrational elements indicative of the fallen mind which may be present in a given hermeneutic to one degree or another. Due to his emphasis on a biblical ontology rooted in the doctrine of God, Van Til's critique of the new hermeneutic is replete with references to the unstable combination of rationalism and irrationalism.

---

129. Van Til, *New Hermeneutic*, 43.

130. Lillback, "Infallible Rule," 301–2, 305, 323. By *Sola Scriptura*, we mean that Scripture is the primary authoritative norm for doctrine, with doctrinal and hermeneutical tradition as a useful but subordinate and derivative norm.

131. Van Til, *New Hermeneutic*, 65, 158, 215.

132. Lillback, "Infallible Rule," 330.

The main contours of Van Til's doctrine of God help to provide a test of consistency for contemporary hermeneutics from a Christian worldview, in order to avoid undermining the very message it seeks to interpret.

Conclusion

Cornelius Van Til's work in the field of apologetics has relevance for contemporary hermeneutics in terms of the interplay between doctrine and method. We may summarize our findings along chapter lines as follows.

In chapter 1, we saw how Van Til has been brought into the hermeneutical discussion but often quickly dismissed without due consideration. We briefly surveyed some examples of macro-hermeneutical statements found throughout his works and discussed some hermeneutical contributions of those who have been consciously influenced by him in their work. We concluded with the question: if Van Til *has* a place in contemporary hermeneutics, *where*?

In chapter 2, we began answering this question by first discussing how *hermeneutics* has come to be defined in the literature. We found that, while implicit throughout the history of biblical interpretation, the contemporary definition is explicitly holistic in nature, on par with worldview. This includes considerations of metaphysics, epistemology, and ethics. In particular, there has been a desire to provide a general theory of understanding which can account for meaning while still recognizing limits of the human mind. This raised the question: what are the necessary presuppositions to account for such a theory of understanding? Worldview and presuppositions were the focus of Van Til's work in apologetics and direct us to his place in the hermeneutical discussion.

In chapter 3, we took a closer look at the curious relationship between metaphysics and hermeneutics. We found a distinct tendency in the literature to assume a general ontology as *prior* to and *more ultimate* than the theology found in Scripture. In addition, when it comes to biblical interpretation, there has been a tendency to *decontextualize*, making it dependent upon history and culture. It is evident from this survey that there is a need for a Christian hermeneutic articulated at the level of worldview. Van Til has provided a significant contribution to this need through his work in apologetics. He argued that methodology is involved in ontology. Theology proper was the foundation for Van Til's conception of a biblical ontology. This provides the necessary presuppositions for a biblical theory of understanding. Lastly, we acknowledged recent developments in contemporary evangelical hermeneutics. We argued that Van Til's thought can be considered complementary to concerns of both SAT and TIS, while also providing further refinement.

In chapter 4, we began tracing the main contours of Van Til's doctrine of God, beginning with the *Creator-creature distinction*. This distinction is paramount for the Christian worldview, providing a *two*-level ontology as opposed to the one-level variety most often assumed in hermeneutics. This distinction also informs concepts of *fact, possibility*, and *interpretation*—whether they are conceived as *created* or *uncreated*. This affects whether the interpreter or text is ultimately *de-contextualized* and *re-contextualized* in a different metaphysical environment from the one revealed in Scripture. One cannot do justice to the facts biblically without God as *the* Fact providing the true philosophy of fact. Without a two-level ontology, man treats God as a co-interpreter of brute facts, which are ultimately *uninterpretable*. A two-level ontology is opposed to a hermeneutical *blockhouse* method which seeks to build Christian theology on top of a general ontology uninformed by that theology. It is also opposed to any shaping of meaning based on the assumption of indeterminate facts. In Scripture, we find finished authoritative interpretation which requires *receptively reconstructive* interpretation rather than constructing meaning. A two-level ontology entails two levels of interpreters—Creator and creature.

Since the fall, man tends to deny and suppress the Creator-creature distinction in favor of a one-level ontology, even in hermeneutics. Assuming the autonomy of the human mind, fallen man seeks to go beyond the creaturely limits of reason and ends up with an unstable mix of rationalism and irrationalism. Van Til sought to expose this *rationalistic-irrationalistic dialectic* in evaluating various philosophies from a Christian worldview. With respect to hermeneutics, the debate is not so much between modern and postmodern schools but rather between the deeper issues of autonomy and monistic metaphysics in *both*. It was argued that Van Til's notion of a rationalistic-irrationalistic dialectic can provide a helpful diagnostic tool for evaluating hermeneutical theory and methodology from a Christian worldview.

In chapter 5, we explored a second main contour in Van Til's doctrine of God—*incomprehensibility*. This truth moves interpretation away from reductionist preoccupation with the human author and reader and toward an appreciation for the divine author as the ground of meaning. Interpretation and knowledge are dependent upon God's certain comprehension as opposed to mere human limitations or probable consensus. Some hermeneutical implications from God's incomprehensibility are as follows:

the need to address the mode of thought; God is the ultimate reference point for knowledge and interpretation; Scripture comes to us already exhaustively intelligible to God; intelligibility involves application; there is no ultimate mystery; and hermeneutics must be subject to Scripture rather than being done from the *outside*.

In chapter 6, we discussed the third main contour in Van Til's doctrine of God—the *ontological Trinity*. The one and many of the Trinity is equally ultimate, without subordination. This is opposed to *being-in-general*, which seeks to provide unity to the plurality of things either through meaningless abstraction or through allowing a principle of relationality to function as logically prior to the ontological Trinity. The ontological Trinity is also opposed to any notion of a personal encounter with a text which is itself impersonal (e.g., propositional) prior to this encounter. The personalism of the Trinity precludes any I-it/I-thou dichotomy. The Trinity implies that interpretation is exhaustively personal and ethical in nature. Moreover, the ultimate coherence of the subject-object relationship is found in the ontological Trinity (not one at the expense of the other). The Trinitarian origin and nature of the canon, as a whole, lends itself to perspectival study. Since man comes to Scripture with a limited, finite perspective, multiple (yet, legitimate and compatible) perspectives should be sought in order to appreciate the depth of meaning found in the canon.

In chapter 7, we provided a brief case study, applying insights from Van Til's doctrine of God to one contemporary hermeneutical issue among evangelicals: *the NT use of the OT*. In light of the main questions raised, we looked at how a Van Tillian critique of *meaning* and *method* might inform the issue.

In terms of *meaning*, a Van Tillian hermeneutic would press the deeper question: *what is the relationship between God and the OT and NT authors' meanings* (vs. merely the relationship between the OT and NT authors' meanings)? This would take into account God's intention mediated through the intentions of the human authors in both the OT and NT, while preserving the Creator-creature distinction. Authority in interpretation follows, with the canon's divine origin (God) as the master category, not history or man. Van Til's articulation of the incomprehensibility of God opposes grounding meaning in the comprehension of the human authors or readers, which is finite. If comprehension is sought on the human level, a rationalistic-irrationalistic dialectic ensues, often tending toward reductionism in meaning. Emphasis on incomprehensibility promotes an appreciation for the fullness of meaning. For example, we looked at how the ontological Trinity provides a foundation for legitimate forms of perspectival analysis of the content of Scripture. This is opposed to allowing one finite perspective (human intent of the author or reader) to limit other legitimate perspectives *divinely* intended in Scripture (e.g., NT use of the OT). A Van Tillian hermeneutic would emphasize canonical considerations as essential in appreciating other legitimate perspectives, because it is in the divinely inspired canon that we most clearly appreciate divine intent, which transcends human intent. Moreover, Van Til's Trinitarian emphasis highlights our knowing in *relation* to God. Knowing is inherently tied to application. Also, meaning is inherently contextual due to the nature of the ontological Trinity, in terms of unity and diversity being equally ultimate. This is opposed to conceiving meaning as an unchanging *one*, with a changing *many*, due to its dependence on history and creaturely context.

In terms of *method*, a Van Tillian hermeneutic would give particular attention to how method and content are involved in one another. By keeping in mind the close relationship between the two, three particular questions arose in our discussion of Longenecker. His distinction between the transhistorical truth and culturally bound methods (endorsing the former but not the latter as normative for today) begged the question: *where do we get the hermeneutic which establishes this distinction?* Secondly, *if method can be removed from content without affecting that content, what informs the method?* Thirdly, *if methods are borrowed from extra-biblical sources to convey the message, but are not part of that message, does this not leave them virtually "neutral" in their adaptability?* Van Til's doctrine of God exposes such neutrality as illusory. Longenecker's approach unwittingly exhibits a two-fold error in terms of context. First, he *decontextualizes* the method from the message. Then, he *re-contextualizes* the message in non-canonical context. Not only does he deny the presence of a built-in hermeneutic with its necessary theological presuppositions found in Scripture, he also makes the message dependent upon extra-biblical sources for re-contextualization and modern meaning (not unlike unbelieving Jewish interpretation of the OT).

The strong *canonical* emphasis of a Van Tillian hermeneutic would more clearly highlight God's intention in terms of meaning. It would not be opposed to or in violation of history but would rather seek to understand it as created. The self-interpreting canon certainly involves history but is not ultimately dependent on it for its meaning. A Van Tillian hermeneutic is opposed to any assumed metaphysic prior to or more ultimate than the one revealed in Scripture. The canon reveals an authoritative inner-hermeneutic, which functions as a lens through which reality, including history, is rightly understood. While *our* interpretation and theological formulation is finite and provisional in nature (i.e., growing), *God's* interpretation and attendant inner-hermeneutical rule is not.

CONCLUSION

Van Til's doctrine of God as articulated along its three main contours provides not only a helpful diagnostic tool for evaluating contemporary approaches for consistency between theology and method, it also further articulates concerns of SAT and TIS, providing necessary theological grounding in the process. This grounding proves to be a more ontologically and epistemologically self-conscious one than what is commonly found in both SAT and TIS, with careful examination at the presuppositional level. This would seem to meet the demands of the contemporary discussion. Van Til's contribution also calls for a proper awareness of *antithesis*—the contrasting spiritual opposition between believers and unbelievers, whatever hermeneutical theory is in view. Any legitimate insights should be appreciated in terms of common grace and *borrowed capital*,[1] with a cautious eye toward the principle of *antithesis*. There is more work to be done, both in formulating a more nuanced Christian hermeneutic and in evaluating not only more reader-response approaches, but even grammatical-historical ones used by evangelicals.

This study has established that Van Til *is* relevant to developments in contemporary hermeneutics. These developments not only include worldview considerations in general, but the relationship between ontology and hermeneutics in particular. Van Til's unique approach to apologetic methodology stressed consistency between theology and method, especially concerning the doctrine of God found in Scripture. This approach has proved to be transferrable and particularly suited to face pressing hermeneutical issues that emerged from our survey. The three contours of his doctrine of God highlighted in this study exposed certain foundational biblical truths necessary for worldview considerations. Positively, they provide the necessary foundations not only of a Christian apologetic, but also a Christian *hermeneutic*. Negatively, they provide a helpful framework to evaluate attempts to answer the deeper hermeneutical questions related to meaning and method. Not only is Van Til's doctrine of God relevant to contemporary hermeneutics, it also implies its own hermeneutical method, a presuppositional, Van Tillian hermeneutic.

---

1. Chapter 1, p. 32.

Bibliography

Adam, A. K. M. "Poaching on Zion: Biblical Theology as Signifying Practice." In *Reading Scripture with the Church*, edited by A. K. M. Adam, Stephen E. Fowl, Kevin J. Vanhoozer, and Francis Watson, 17–34. Grand Rapids: Baker, 2006.

Aichele, George, Peter Miscall, and Richard Walsh. "An Elephant in the Room: Historical-Critical and Postmodern Interpretations of the Bible." *Journal of Biblical Literature* 128 (2009) 383–404.

Allen, Diogenes. *Philosophy for Understanding Theology*. Louisville: Westminster John Knox, 1985.

Ameriks, Karl. "The Critique of Metaphysics: The Structure and Fate of Kant's Dialectic." In *The Cambridge Guide to Kant and Modern Philosophy*, edited by Paul Guyer, 269–302. Cambridge: Cambridge University Press, 2006.

Anderson, James. "Cornelius Van Til and Alvin Plantinga." http//www.proginosko.com/docs/cvt_ap_comp.html.

———. "If Knowledge, Then God: The Epistemological Theistic Arguments of Alvin Plantinga and Cornelius Van Til." *Calvin Theological Journal* 40 (2005) 49–75.

———. *Paradox in Christian Theology: An Analysis of Its Presence, Character, and Epistemic Status*. Eugene, OR: Wipf & Stock, 2007.

———. "Van Til Frequently Encountered Misconceptions." http://www.vantil.info/articles/vtfem.html.

Anderson, Owen. *Benjamin B. Warfield and Right Reason: The Clarity of General Revelation and Function in Apologetics*. New York: University Press of America, 2005.

The Ante-Nicene Fathers. Edited by Alexander Roberts and James Donaldson. 10 vols. 1885–1887. Reprint. Peabody, MA: Hendrickson, 1994.

Austin, J. L. *How to Do Things with Words*. 2nd ed. Cambridge: Harvard University Press, 1975.

Bahnsen, Greg L. "The Crucial Concept of Self-Deception in Presuppositional Apologetics." *Westminster Theological Journal* 57 (1995) 1–31.

———. "Machen, Van Til, and the Apologetical Tradition of the OPC." In *Pressing Toward the Mark*, edited by Charles Dennison and Richard C. Gamble, 259–94 Philadelphia: OPC, 1986.

———. "Pragmatism, Prejudice, and Presuppositionalism." In *Foundations of Christian Scholarship: Essays in the Van Til Perspective*, edited by Gary North, 241–92. Vallecito, CA: Ross House, 1976.

———. "Socrates or Christ: The Reformation of Christian Apologetics." In *Foundations of Christian Scholarship: Essays in the Van Til Perspective*, edited by Gary North, 191–239. Vallecito, CA: Ross House, 1976.

———. *Van Til's Apologetic: Readings & Analysis*. Phillipsburg, NJ: Presbyterian & Reformed, 1998.

Barker, Kit. "Divine Illocutions in Psalm 137: A Critique of Nicholas Wolterstorff's 'Second Hermeneutic.'" *Tyndale Bulletin* 60 (2009) 1–14.

———. "Speech Act Theory, Dual Authorship, and Canonical Hermeneutics: Making Sense of Sensus Plenior." *Journal of Theological Interpretation* 3 (2009) 227–39.

Barr, James. *Holy Scripture: Canon, Authority, Criticism*. Philadelphia: Westminster, 1983.

Barr, William. "Theology as Hermeneutic." *Lexington Theological Journal* 12 (1977) 1–14.

Barth, Karl. *The Doctrine of Creation*. Vol. III.2 of *Church Dogmatics*. Edited by G. W. Bromiley and T. F. Torrance. Translated by G. W. Bromiley. Peabody, MA: Hendrickson, 2010.

———. *The Doctrine of Creation*. Vol. III.3 of *Church Dogmatics*. Edited by G. W. Bromiley and T. F. Torrance. Translated by G. W. Bromiley. Peabody, MA: Hendrickson, 2010.

———. *The Doctrine of God*. Vol. II.1 of *Church Dogmatics*. Edited by G. W. Bromiley and T. F. Torrance. Translated by G. W. Bromiley. Peabody, MA: Hendrickson, 2010.

———. *The Doctrine of God*. Vol. II.2 of *Church Dogmatics*. Edited by G. W. Bromiley and T. F. Torrance. Translated by G. W. Bromiley. Peabody, MA: Hendrickson, 2010.

———. *The Doctrine of Reconciliation*. Vol. IV.1 of *Church Dogmatics*. Edited by G. W. Bromiley and T. F. Torrance. Translated by G. W. Bromiley. Peabody, MA: Hendrickson, 2010.

———. *The Doctrine of the Word of God*. Vol. I.1 of *Church Dogmatics*. Edited by G. W. Bromiley and T. F. Torrance. Translated by G. W. Bromiley. Peabody, MA: Hendrickson, 2010.

———. *The Doctrine of the Word of God*. Vol. I.2 of *Church Dogmatics*. Edited by G. W. Bromiley and T. F. Torrance. Translated by G. W. Bromiley. Peabody, MA: Hendrickson, 2010.

———. *Protestant Thought: From Rousseau to Rischl*. Translated by Brian Cozens. New York: Harper & Row, 1959.

Bartholomew, Craig G. "Babel and Derrida: Postmodernism, Language, and Biblical Interpretation." *Tyndale Bulletin* 49 (1998) 305–28.

———. *Introducing Biblical Hermeneutics: A Comprehensive Framework for Hearing God in Scripture*. Grand Rapids: Baker, 2015.

———. "Post/Late? Modernity as the Context for Christian Scholarship Today." *Themelios* 22 (1997) 25–38.

———. "Three Horizons: Hermeneutics from the Other End—An Evaluation of Anthony Thiselton's Hermeneutic Proposals." *European Journal of Theology* 5 (1996) 121–35.

———. "Uncharted Waters: Philosophy, Theology, and the Crisis in Biblical Interpretation." In *Renewing Biblical Interpretation*, edited by Craig Bartholomew, Colin Greene, and Karl Möller, 1–39. Grand Rapids: Zondervan, 2000.

Basinger, David. "Biblical Paradox: Does Revelation Challenge Logic?" *Journal of the Evangelical Theological Society* 30 (1987) 205–13.

Bavinck, Herman. *God and Creation*. In Vol. 2, *Reformed Dogmatics*, edited by John Bolt. Translated by John Vriend. Grand Rapids: Baker, 2004.

———. *Prolegomena*. In Vol. 1, *Reformed Dogmatics*, edited by John Bolt. Translated by John Vriend. Grand Rapids: Baker, 2004.

———. *Sin and Salvation in Christ*. In Vol. 3, *Reformed Dogmatics*, edited by John Bolt. Translated by John Vriend. Grand Rapids: Baker, 2006.

Bayer, Oswald. "Theology in the Conflict of Interpretations—Before the Text." *Modern Theology* 16 (2000) 495–502.

Beale, G. K. "The Cognitive Peripheral Vision of Biblical Authors." *Westminster Theological Journal* 76 (2014) 263–93.

———. "Did Jesus and His Followers Preach the Right Doctrine from the Wrong Texts? An Examination of the Presuppositions of Jesus and the Apostles' Exegetical Method." In *The Right Doctrine from the Wrong Texts?*, edited by G. K. Beale, 387–404. Grand Rapids: Baker, 1994.

———. "Did Jesus and His Followers Preach the Right Doctrine from the Wrong Texts? Revisiting the Debate Seventeen Years Later in Light of Peter Enns' Book, *Revelation and Inspiration*." *Themelios* 32 (2006) 18–43.

———. *Erosion of Inerrancy in Evangelicalism: Responding to New Challenges to Biblical Authority*. Wheaton, IL: Crossway, 2008.

———. *Handbook on the New Testament Use of the Old Testament: Exegesis and Interpretation*. Grand Rapids: Baker, 2012.

———. "Positive Answer to the Question." In *The Right Doctrine from the Wrong Texts?*, edited by G. K. Beale, 387–404. Grand Rapids: Baker, 1994.

Beale, G. K., ed. *The Right Doctrine from the Wrong Texts?* Grand Rapids: Baker, 1994.

Beale, G. K., and D.A. Carson, eds. *Commentary on the New Testament Use of the Old Testament*. Grand Rapids: Baker, 2007.

Beecher, Willis J. *The Prophets and the Promise*. Grand Rapids: Baker, 1975.

Berkhof, Louis. *Principles of Biblical Interpretation*. Grand Rapids: Baker, 1950.

———. *Systematic Theology*. Carlisle, PA: Banner of Truth, 1958.

———. *Systematic Theology*. New Combined ed. Grand Rapids: Eerdmans, 1996.

Berkhof, Louis, and Cornelius Van Til. *Foundations of Christian Education*. Edited by Dennis E. Johnson. Phillipsburg, NJ: Presbyterian & Reformed, 1990.

Berkouwer, G. C. "The Authority of Scripture (A Responsible Confession)." In *Jerusalem and Athens: Critical Discussions on the Philosophy and Apologetics of Cornelius Van Til*, edited by E. R. Geehan, 197–203. Phillipsburg, NJ: Presbyterian & Reformed, 1980.

———. *The Person of Christ*. Grand Rapids: Eerdmans, 1954.

———. *The Triumph of Grace in the Theology of Karl Barth*. Translated by Harry R. Boer. Grand Rapids: Eerdmans, 1956.

Bernstein, Richard J. *Beyond Objectivism and Relativism: Science, Hermeneutics and Praxis*. Oxford: Blackwell, 1983.

Blomberg, Craig L. "The Historical-Critical/Grammatical View." In *Biblical Hermeneutics: Five Views*, edited by Stanley E. Porter and Beth M. Stovell, 133–45. Downers Grove, IL: InterVarsity, 2012

———. *The Historical Reliability of the Gospels*. 2nd ed. Downers Grove, IL: InterVarsity, 2007.

Blue, Scott A. "The Hermeneutic of E. D. Hirsch, Jr. and Its Impact on Expository Preaching: Friend Or Foe?" *Journal of the Evangelical Theological Society* 44 (2001) 253–69.

———. "Meaning, Intention, and Application: Speech Act Theory in the Hermeneutics of Francis Watson and Kevin J. Vanhoozer." *Trinity Journal* 23 (2002) 161–84.

Bock, Darrell L. "Single Meaning, Multiple Contexts and Referents." In *Three Views of the New Testament Use of the Old Testament*, edited by Kenneth Berding and Jonathan Lunde, 105–51. Grand Rapids: Zondervan, 2008.

Bosserman, B. A. *The Trinity and the Vindication of Christian Paradox: An Interpretation and Refinement of the Theological Apologetic of Cornelius Van Til*. Eugene, OR: Pickwick, 2014.

Bowald, Mark Alan. "Rendering Mute the Word: Overcoming Deistic Tendencies in Modern Hermeneutics; Kevin Vanhoozer as a Test Case." *Westminster Theological Journal* 69 (2007) 367–81.

Brewer, D. Instone. *Techniques and Assumptions in Jewish Exegesis before 70 C.E.* Tübingen: Mohr Siebeck, 1992.

Briggs, Richard S. "What Does Hermeneutics Have to Do with Biblical Interpretation?" *Heythrop Journal* 47 (2006) 55–74.

———. *Words in Action: Speech Act Theory and Biblical Interpretation*. Edinburgh: Clark, 2001.

Bristley, Eric D. "A Guide to the Writings of Cornelius Van Til, 1895-1987." In *The Works of Cornelius Van Til, 1895–1987*, edited by Eric H. Sigward. Logos Library System. CD-ROM.

Bromiley, Geoffrey W. "The Authority of Scripture in Karl Barth." In *Hermeneutics, Authority, and Canon*, edited by D. A. Carson and John D. Woodbridge, 275–94. Grand Rapids: Zondervan, 1986.

Brown, Colin. *Philosophy & the Christian Faith*. Downers Grove, IL: InterVarsity, 1968.

Brown, Jeannine K. *Scripture as Communication*. Grand Rapids: Baker, 2007.

Brown, Raymond E. "The 'Sensus Plenior' in the Last Ten Years." *Catholic Biblical Quarterly* 25 (1963) 262–85.

———. *The 'Sensus Plenior' of Sacred Scripture*. Baltimore: St. Mary's University, 1955.

Browning, Don S. *A Fundamental Practical Theology: Descriptive and Strategic Proposals*. Minneapolis: Fortress, 1991.

Brunner, Emil. *The Philosophy of Religion*. Translated by A.J.D. Farrer and Bertram Lee Woolf. New York: Scribner's, 1937.

———. *Revelation and Reason*. Translated by Olive Wyon. Philadelphia: Westminster, 1946.

Buber, Martin. *I and Thou*. 2nd ed. Translated by Ronald Gregor Smith. New York: Scribner's, 1958.

Bultmann, Rudolf. *Essays Philosophical and Theological*. London: SCM, 1955.

———. *Existence and Faith: Shorter Writings of Rudolf Bultmann*. London: Collins, 1964.

———. *History and Eschatology*. New York: Harper & Row, 1957.

———. *Jesus Christ and Mythology*. London: SCM, 1960.

———. "The Problem of Hermeneutics." In *Essays: Philosophical and Theological*, 234–61. London: SCM, 1955.

———. *Theology of the New Testament*. 2 vols. Translated by Kendrick Grobel. London: SCM, 1955.

Burnett, Richard E. *Karl Barth's Theological Exegesis: The Hermeneutical Principles of the Römerbrief Period.* Grand Rapids: Eerdmans, 2004.

Busch, Eberhard. *Karl Barth: His Life from Letters and Autobiographical Texts.* Grand Rapids: Eerdmans, 1994.

Bush, L. Russ. "Apostolic Hermeneutics: 'Proof Texts' and the Resurrection." *Criswell Theological Review* 2 (1988) 291–307.

Buswell, J. Oliver. "The Fountainhead of Presuppositionalism." *The Bible Today* 42 (1948) 41–64.

Calvin, John. *Institutes of the Christian Religion.* 2 vols. Edited by John T. McNeill. Translated by Ford Lewis Battles. Louisville: Westminster John Knox, 1960.

Carson, D. A. *Collected Writings on Scripture.* Compiled by Andrew David Naselli. Wheaton, IL: Crossway, 2010.

———. *Exegetical Fallacies.* 2nd ed. Grand Rapids: Baker, 1996.

———. *The Gagging of God: Christianity Confronts Pluralism.* Grand Rapids: Zondervan, 1996.

———. "Matthew." *Expositor's Bible* Commentary, vol. 8. Edited by Frank E. Gaebelein. Grand Rapids: Zondervan, 1984.

———. "Recent Developments in the Doctrine of Scripture." In *Hermeneutics, Authority, and Canon,* edited by D. A. Carson and John D. Woodbridge, 1–48. Grand Rapids: Zondervan, 1986.

———. "Theological Interpretation of Scripture: Yes, But . . . " In *Theological Commentary: Evangelical Perspectives,* edited by R. Michael Allen, 187–207. London: T. & T. Clark, 2011.

———. "Unity and Diversity in the New Testament." In *Scripture and Truth,* edited by D. A. Carson and John D. Woodbridge, 65–100. Grand Rapids: Baker, 1992.

Cassidy, James J. *God's Time for Us: Barth's Reconciliation of Eternity and Time in Jesus Christ.* Bellingham, WA: Lexham Press, 2016.

Childs, Brevard S. *Introduction to the Old Testament as Scripture.* Philadelphia: Fortress, 1979.

———. "On Reclaiming the Bible for Christian Theology." In *Reclaiming the Bible for the Church,* edited by Carl E. Braaten and Robert W. Jensen, 1–15. Edinburgh: T. & T. Clark, 1995.

———. "Speech Act Theory and Biblical Interpretation." *Scottish Journal of Theology* 58 (2005) 375–92.

Clark, Gordon H. "Apologetics." In *Contemporary Evangelical Thought,* edited by Carl F. H. Henry, 137–61. Great Neck, NY: Channel, 1957.

———. "The Bible as Truth." *Bibliotheca Sacra* 114 (1957) 157–70.

———. *A Christian Philosophy of Education.* Grand Rapids: Eerdmans, 1946.

———. "Determinism and Responsibility." *Evangelical Quarterly* 4 (1932) 13–23.

———. *Logic.* Jefferson, MD: Trinity Foundation, 1985.

———. *The Trinity.* Jefferson, MD: Trinity Foundation, 1985.

Clark, R. Scott. "Janus, the Well-Meant Offer of the Gospel and Westminster Theology." In *The Pattern of Sound Doctrine: Systematic Theology at the Westminster Seminaries,* edited by David VanDrunen, 149–79. Phillipsburg, NJ: Presbyterian & Reformed Publishing, 2004.

Collett, Don. "Apologetics: Van Til and the Transcendental Argument." *Westminster Theological Journal* 65 (2003) 289–306.

Collingwood, R. G. *The Idea of History.* Oxford: Oxford University Press, 1970.

Conn, Harvie M. "A Historical Prologue: Inerrancy, Hermeneutic, and Westminster." In *Inerrancy and Hermeneutic: A Tradition, A Challenge, A Debate*, edited by Harvie M. Conn, 15–34. Grand Rapids: Baker, 1988.

Cooper, John W. "Reformed Apologetics and the Challenge of Post-Modern Relativism." *Calvin Theological Journal* 28 (1993) 108–20.

Copleston, Frederick, S. J. *A History of Philosophy*. 9 Vols. New York: Doubleday, 1960.

Corduan, Winfried. "Philosophical Presuppositions Affecting Biblical Hermeneutics." In *Hermeneutics, Inerrancy, and the Bible*, edited by Earl D. Radmacher and Robert D. Preus, 495–513. Grand Rapids: Zondervan, 1984.

———. *Reasonable Faith: Basic Christian Apologetics*. Nashville: Broadman & Holman, 1993.

Corley, Bruce, Steve W. Lemke, and Grant I. Lovejoy. *Biblical Hermeneutics: A Comprehensive Introduction to Interpreting Scripture*. 2nd ed. Nashville: Broadman & Holman, 2002.

Crisp, Oliver D. *Revisioning Christology: Theology in the Reformed Tradition*. Surrey, UK: Ashgate, 2011.

Cunningham, G. Watts. *The Idealistic Argument in Recent British and American Philosophy*. Westport, CT: Greenwood Press, 1969.

Daane, James. *The Theology of Grace*. Grand Rapids: Eerdmans, 1954.

Davies, P. R., *Whose Bible Is It Anyway?* Journal for the Study of the Old Testament: Supplement Series. Sheffield: Sheffield Academic Press, 1995.

Davis, D. Clair. "Inerrancy and Westminster Calvinism." In *Inerrancy and Hermeneutic: A Tradition, A Challenge, A Debate*, edited by Harvie M. Conn, 35–46. Grand Rapids: Baker, 1988.

Davis, Ellen F. "Critical Traditioning: Seeking an Inner Biblical Hermeneutic." *Anglican Theological Review* 82 (2000) 733–51.

DeBoer, Cecil. "The New Apologetic." *The Calvin Forum* 19 (1953) 3–7.

DeBoer, Jesse. "Professor Van Til's Apologetics, Part 1: A Linguistic Bramble Patch." *The Calvin Forum* 19 (1953) 7–12.

Dempster, Stephen. "The Prophets, the Canon and a Canonical Approach." In *Canon and Biblical Interpretation*, edited by Craig G. Bartholomew et al., 293–329. Grand Rapids: Zondervan, 2006.

Derrida, Jacques. "Des Tours de Babel." *Semeia* 54 (1991) 3–34.

———. *Margins of Philosophy*. Translated by Alan Bass. Chicago: Chicago University Press, 1982.

———. *Of Grammatology*. Baltimore: Johns Hopkins University Press, 1976.

———. *Writing and Difference*. Translated by Alan Bass. Chicago: Chicago University Press, 1978.

DeVries, D. "Schleiermacher, Friedrich Daniel Ernst." In *Historical Handbook of Major Bible Interpreters*, edited by Donald McKim, 350–55. Downers Grove, IL: InterVarsity, 1998.

De Vries, Paul. "Martin Heidegger." In *Evangelical Dictionary of Theology*, edited by Walter A. Elwell, 545–46. 2nd ed. Grand Rapids: Baker, 2001.

Dilthey, William. "The Development of Hermeneutics." In *Dilthey: Selected Writings*, edited and translated by H. P. Rickman, 247–63. Cambridge: Cambridge University Press, 1976.

Dockery, David S. *Biblical Interpretation Then and Now: Contemporary Hermeneutics in Light of the Early Church*. Grand Rapids: Baker, 1992.

Dodd, C. H. *According to the Scriptures: The Sub-Structure of New Testament Theology.* London: Nisbet, 1952.
Donfried, Karl P. "Alien Hermeneutics and the Misappropriation of Scripture." In *Reclaiming the Bible for the Church*, edited by Carl E. Braaten and Robert W. Jensen, 19–45. Edinburgh: T. & T. Clark, 1995.
Dooyeweerd, Herman. "Cornelius Van Til and the Transcendental Critique of Theoretical Thought." In *Jerusalem and Athens: Critical Discussions on the Philosophy and Apologetics of Cornelius Van Til*, edited by E. R. Geehan, 74–89. Phillipsburg, NJ: Presbyterian & Reformed, 1980.
———. *A New Critique of Theoretical Thought.* Philadelphia: Presbyterian & Reformed, 1969.
Dreyfus, Hubert. "Beyond Metaphysics: Interpretation in Late Heidegger and Recent Foucault. In *Hermeneutics: Questions and Prospects*, edited by Gary Shapiro and Alan Sica, 66–83. Amherst: University of Massachusetts, 1984.
Ebeling, Gerhard. *Introduction to a Theological Theory of Language.* London: Collins, 1973.
———. *Word and Faith.* Philadelphia: Fortress, 1963.
Edgar, William. "No News is Good News: Modernity, the Postmodern, and Apologetics." *Westminster Theological Seminary* 57 (1995) 359–82.
Ellingworth, Paul. *The Epistle to the Hebrews.* New International Greek Testament Commentary. Grand Rapids: Eerdmans, 1993.
Enns, Peter. "Apostolic Hermeneutics and an Evangelical Doctrine of Scripture: Moving Beyond a Modernist Impasse." *Westminster Theological Journal* 65 (2003) 263–87.
———. *The Bible Tells Me So: Why Defending Scripture Has Made Us Unable to Read It.* New York: HarperCollins, 2014.
———. "Fuller Meaning, Single Goal." In *Three Views of the New Testament Use of the Old Testament*, edited by Kenneth Berding and Jonathan Lunde, 167–217. Grand Rapids: Zondervan, 2008.
———. *Inspiration and Incarnation.* Grand Rapids: Baker, 2005.
———. "Pseudepigrapha." In *Dictionary of the Theological Interpretation of the Bible*, edited by K. Vanhoozer, 652–53. Grand Rapids: Baker, 2005.
———. "Response to G. K. Beale's Review Article of *Inspiration and Incarnation*." *Journal of the Evangelical Theological Society* 49 (2009) 313–26.
———. "Response to Professor Greg Beale." *Themelios* 32 (2007) 5–13.
Erickson, Millard J. *Evangelical Interpretation: Perspectives on Hermeneutical Issues.* Grand Rapids: Baker, 1993.
Ericson, Norman R. "The NT Use of the OT: A Kerygmatic Approach." *Journal of the Evangelical Theological Society* 30 (1987) 337–42.
Evans, Stephen. *Faith Beyond Reason: A Kierkegaardian Account.* Grand Rapids: Eerdmans, 1998.
———. "Tradition, Biblical Interpretation, and Historical Truth." In *"Behind" the Text: History and Biblical Interpretation*, edited by Craig Bartholomew et al., 320–36. Grand Rapids: Zondervan, 2003.
Fackre, Gabriel. "Revelation." In *Karl Barth and Evangelical Theology: Convergences and Divergences*, edited by Sung Wook Chung, 1–25. Grand Rapids: Baker, 2008.
Fair, Ian A. "Disciplines Related to Biblical Interpretation." In *Biblical Interpretation: Principles and Practices*, edited by F. Furman Kearley, Edward P. Myers, and Timothy D. Hadley, 31–49. Grand Rapids: Baker, 1986.

Farrar, Frederic W. *The History of Interpretation*. 1886 Reprint. Grand Rapids: Baker, 1961.
Fish, Stanley. *Is There a Text in This Class? The Authority of Interpretive Communities*. Cambridge: Harvard University Press, 1980.
Flatt, Bill. "The Function of Presuppositions and Attitudes in Biblical Interpretation." In *Biblical Interpretation: Principles and Practices*, edited by F. Furman Kearley, Edward P. Myers, and Timothy D. Hadley, 60–72. Grand Rapids: Baker, 1986.
Forster, Michael N. *Kant and Skepticism*. Princeton: Princeton University Press, 2008.
Fowl, Stephen E. "Further Thoughts on Theological Interpretation." In *Reading Scripture with the Church*, edited by A. K. M. Adam et al., 125–30. Grand Rapids: Baker, 2006.
Frame, John M. *Apologetics to the Glory of God: An Introduction*. Phillipsburg, NJ: Presbyterian & Reformed, 1994.
———. *Cornelius Van Til: An Analysis of His Thought*. Phillipsburg, NJ: Presbyterian & Reformed, 1995.
———. "Divine Aseity and Apologetics." In *Revelation and Reason: New Essays in Reformed Apologetics*, edited by K. Scott Oliphint and Lane G. Tipton, 115–30. Phillipsburg, NJ: Presbyterian & Reformed, 2007.
———. *The Doctrine of the Christian Life*. Phillipsburg, NJ: Presbyterian & Reformed, 2008.
———. *The Doctrine of God*. Phillipsburg, NJ: Presbyterian and Reformed Publishing, 2002.
———. *The Doctrine of the Knowledge of God*. Phillipsburg, NJ: Presbyterian & Reformed, 1987.
———. *The Doctrine of the Word of God*. Phillipsburg, NJ: Presbyterian & Reformed, 2010.
———. "The Problem of Theological Paradox." In *Foundations of Christian Scholarship: Essays in the Van Til Perspective*, edited by Gary North, 295–330. Vallecito, CA: Ross House, 1976.
———. *Systematic Theology: An Introduction to Christian Belief*. Phillipsburg, NJ: Presbyterian & Reformed, 2013.
France, R. T. *The Gospel of Mark*. New International Greek Testament Commentary. Grand Rapids: Eerdmans, 2002.
———. *Jesus and the Old Testament*. Vancouver: Regent, 1998.
Francke, John R. "Reforming Theology: Toward a Postmodern Reformed Dogmatics." *Westminster Theological Journal* 65 (2003) 1–26.
Frei, Hans. *The Eclipse of Biblical Narrative*. New Haven: Yale University Press, 1974.
Frye, Northrop. *Anatomy of Criticism*. Princeton: Princeton University Press, 1957.
Fuchs, Ernst. *Studies of the Historical Jesus*. London: SCM, 1964.
Gadamer, Hans-Georg. "The Hermeneutics of Suspicion." In *Hermeneutics: Questions and Prospects*, edited by Gary Shapiro and Alan Sica, 54–65. Amherst: University of Massachusetts, 1984.
———. *Philosophical Hermeneutics*. Berkeley: University of California Press, 1976.
———. "Reflections on My Philosophical Journey." In *The Philosophy of Hans-Georg Gadamer*, edited by Lewis E. Hahn, 3–63. Chicago: Open Court, 1997.
———. *Truth and Method*. Translated by Garrett Barden and John Cumming. New York: Seabury, 1975.

Gaffin, Richard B., Jr. "Geerhardus Vos and the Interpretation of Paul." In *Jerusalem and Athens: Critical Discussions on the Philosophy and Apologetics of Cornelius Van Til*, edited by E. R. Geehan, 228–37. Phillipsburg, NJ: Presbyterian & Reformed, 1980.

———. *God's Word in Servant Form: Abraham Kuyper and Herman Bavinck on the Doctrine of Scripture*. Jackson: Reformed Academic, 2008.

———. "The Redemptive-Historical Response." In *Biblical Hermeneutics: Five Views*, edited by Stanley E. Porter and Beth M. Stovell, 174–87. Downers Grove, IL: InterVarsity, 2012.

———. "The Redemptive-Historical View." In *Biblical Hermeneutics: Five Views*, edited by Stanley E. Porter and Beth M. Stovell, 89–110. Downers Grove, IL: InterVarsity, 2012.

———. "Some Epistemological Reflections on 1 Cor 2:6-16." *Westminster Theological Journal* 57 (1995) 103–4.

Geehan, E. R., ed. *Jerusalem and Athens: Critical Discussions on the Philosophy and Apologetics of Cornelius Van Til*. Phillipsburg, NJ: Presbyterian and Reformed Publishers, 1980.

Giles, Kevin. "Evangelicals and the Doctrine of the Trinity." *Evangelical Quarterly* 80 (2008) 323–38.

———. *Trinity and Subordinationism*. Downers Grove, IL: InterVarsity, 2002.

Gillespie, Thomas W. "Biblical Authority and Interpretation: The Current Debate on Hermeneutics." In *A Guide to Contemporary Hermeneutics*, edited by Donald K. McKim, 192–219. Eugene, OR: Wipf & Stock, 1986.

Goldsworthy, Graeme. *Christ-Centered Biblical Theology: Hermeneutical Principles and Principles*. Downers Grove, IL: InterVarsity, 2012.

———. *Gospel-Centered Hermeneutics: Foundations and Principles of Evangelical Biblical Interpretation*. Downers Grove, IL: InterVarsity, 2006.

———. "Ontological and Systematic Roots of Biblical Theology." *Reformed Theological Review* 62 (2003) 152–64.

Green, Garrett. *Theology, Hermeneutics, and Imagination: The Crisis of Interpretation at the End of Modernity*. Cambridge: Cambridge University Press, 2000.

Green, Joel B. "Modernity, History, and the Theological Interpretation of the Bible." *Scottish Journal of Theology* 54 (2001) 308–29.

———. "Practicing the Gospel in a Post-Critical World: The Promise of Theological Exegesis." *Journal of the Evangelical Theological Society* 47 (2004) 387–97.

———. *Practicing Theological Interpretation: Engaging Biblical Texts for Faith and Formation*. Grand Rapids: Baker, 2011.

———. "Scripture and Theology: Failed Experiments, Fresh Perspectives." *Interpretation* 56 (2002) 5–20.

Greene, Colin J. D. "In the Arms of Angels: Biblical Interpretation, Christology, and the Philosophy of History." In *Renewing Biblical Interpretation*, edited by Craig Bartholomew, Colin Greene, and Karl Möller, 198–239. Grand Rapids: Zondervan, 2000.

Greidanus, Sidney. *Preaching Christ from the Old Testament*. Grand Rapids: Eerdmans, 1999.

Grenz, Stanley J. *A Primer on Postmodernism*. Grand Rapids: Eerdmans, 1996.

Grondin, Jean. *Introduction to Philosophical Hermeneutics*. Translated by Joel Weinsheimer. Yale: Yale University Press, 1997.

Gruenler, Royce G. "A Response to the New Hermeneutic." In *Hermeneutics, Inerrancy, and the Bible*, edited by Earl D. Radmacher and Robert D. Preus, 559–89. Grand Rapids: Zondervan, 1984.
———. *The Inexhaustible God: Biblical Faith and the Challenge of Process Theism*. Grand Rapids: Baker, 1983.
———. *Meaning and Understanding: The Philosophical Framework for Biblical Interpretation*. Grand Rapids: Zondervan, 1991.
———. "The New Hermeneutic." In *Evangelical Dictionary of Theology*, edited by Walter A. Elwell, 829–31. 2nd ed. Grand Rapids: Baker, 2001.
Gunton, Colin. *The One, the Three, and the Many*. Oxford: Clarendon, 1993.
———. *The Triune Creator: A Historical and Systematic Study*. Edinburgh: Edinburgh University Press, 1998.
———. *Yesterday and Today: A Study of Continuities in Christology*. Grand Rapids: Eerdmans, 1983.
Hakkenburg, Michael A. "The Battle Over the Ordination of Gordon H. Clark." In *Pressing Toward The Mark*, edited by Charles Dennison and Richard C. Gamble, 329–50. Philadelphia: OPC, 1986.
Halsey, Jim S. *For Such a Time as This: An Introduction to the Reformed Apologetic of Cornelius Van Til*. Phillipsburg, NJ: P&R Publishing, 1976.
Harrington, Daniel J. "Biblical Hermeneutics in Recent Discussion: New Testament." In *A Guide to Contemporary Hermeneutics*, edited by Donald K. McKim, 13–20. Eugene, OR: Wipf & Stock, 1986.
Harrisville, Roy A. *Pandora's Box Opened: An Examination and Defense of Historical-Critical Method and Its Master Practitioners*. Grand Rapids: Eerdmans, 2014.
Hasker, William. *Metaphysics: Constructing a Worldview*. Downers Grove, IL: InterVarsity, 1983.
Hays, Richard B. *Echoes of Scripture in the Letters of Paul*. New Haven: Yale University Press, 1989.
———. "Reading the Bible with the Eyes of Faith." *Journal of Theological Interpretation* 1 (2007) 5–21.
Heidegger, Martin. *Being and Time*. Translated by J. Macquarrie and J. Robinson. Oxford: Blackwell, 1962.
———. *An Introduction to Metaphysics*. Translated by Ralph Manheim. New Haven: Yale University Press, 1959.
Henry, Carl F. H. *Fifty Years of Protestant Theology*. Boston: W. A. Wilde, 1950.
———. *God Who Stands and Stays. God, Revelation and Authority*. Vol. 5. Waco, TX: Word, 1982.
Hirsch, E. D. *Aims of Interpretation*. Chicago: University of Chicago, 1976.
———. "Meaning and Significance Reinterpreted." *Critical Inquiry* 11 (1984) 202–25.
———. "Transhistorical Intentions and Persistence of Allegory." *New Literary History* 25 (1994) 549–67.
———. *Validity in Interpretation*. New Haven: Yale University Press, 1967.
Hodge, A. A. *Evangelical Theology: Lectures on Doctrine*. Carlisle, PA: Banner of Truth, 1990.
Hodge, Charles. *Systematic Theology*. 3 vols. Grand Rapids: Eerdmans, 1973.
Hoekema, Anthony A. *The Bible and the Future*. Grand Rapids: Eerdmans, 1979.
Hoeksema, Herman. *The Clark-Van Til Controversy*. Hobbs, NM: Trinity Forum, 1995.

Hoffecker, W. A. "Schleiermacher, Friedrich Daniel Ernst." In *Evangelical Dictionary of Theology*, edited by Walter A. Elwell, 1064–66. 2nd ed. Grand Rapids: Baker, 2001.

Holmes, Arthur F. "Language, Logic, and Faith." In *Jerusalem and Athens: Critical Discussions on the Philosophy and Apologetics of Cornelius Van Til*, edited by E. R. Geehan, 428–38. Phillipsburg, NJ: Presbyterian & Reformed, 1980.

Horne, Charles M. "Van Til and Carnell—Part II." In *Jerusalem and Athens: Critical Discussions on the Philosophy and Apologetics of Cornelius Van Til*, edited by E. R. Geehan, 369–79. Phillipsburg, NJ: Presyterian & Reformed, 1980.

Horton, Michael S. "A Stoney Jar: The Legacy of Karl Barth for Evangelical Theology." In *Engaging with Barth*, edited by David Gibson and Daniel Strange, 346–81. Nottingham: Apollos, 2008.

———. "Consistently Reformed: The Inheritance and Legacy of Van Til's Apologetic." In *Revelation and Reason: New Essays in Reformed Apologetics*, edited by K. Scott Oliphint and Lane G. Tipton, 131–48. Phillipsburg, NJ: Presbyterian & Reformed, 2007.

Howard, Roy J. *Three Faces of Hermeneutics: An Introduction to Current Theories of Understanding*. Berkeley: University of California Press, 1982.

Huelin, Scott. "Toward a Theological Ontology of Textual Meaning." *Christians Scholar's Review* 34 (2005) 217–33.

Hughes, Philip Edgcumbe. "Crucial Passages for Christian Apologetics." In *Jerusalem and Athens: Critical Discussions on the Philosophy and Apologetics of Cornelius Van Til*, edited by E. R. Geehan, 131–40. Phillipsburg, NJ: Presbyterian & Reformed, 1980.

———. "The Truth of Scripture and the Problem of Historical Relativity." In *Scripture and Truth*, edited by D. A. Carson and John D. Woodbridge, 173–94. Grand Rapids: Baker, 1992.

Hunt, Jason Bennett. "An Introduction to Cornelius Van Til and His Doctrine of God." MTh diss., University of Wales, Lampeter, 2010.

———. "Bavinck and the Princetonians on Scripture: A Difference in Doctrine or Defense?" *Journal of the Evangelical Theological Society* 53 (2010) 317–33.

Ingraffia, Brian D. "Ontotheology and the Postmodern Bible." In *Renewing Biblical Interpretation*, edited by Craig Bartholomew, Colin Greene, and Karl Möller, 284–306. Grand Rapids: Zondervan, 2000.

Jacobsen, Douglas. "The Rise of Evangelical Hermeneutical Pluralism." *Christian Scholar's Review* 16 (1987) 325–35.

Jeanrond, Werner G. *Text and Interpretation as Categories of Theological Thinking*. Translated by Thomas J. Wilson. Eugene, OR: Wipf & Stock, 1986.

Jenson, R. W. "Scripture's Authority in the Church." In *The Art of Reading Scripture*, edited by E. F. Davis and R. B. Hays, 27–37. Grand Rapids: Eerdmans, 2003.

Johnson, Eric J. "Can God Be Grasped By Reason?" In *God Under Fire*, edited by Douglas F. Huffman and Eric L. Johnson, 71–103. Grand Rapids: Zondervan, 2002.

Johnson, John F. "Philosophical Presuppositions: Response." In *Hermeneutics, Inerrancy, and the Bible*, edited by Earl D. Radmacher and Robert D. Preus, 523–31. Grand Rapids: Zondervan, 1984.

Johnson, W. S. "Karl Barth." In *Dictionary of Major Bible Interpreters*, edited by Donald Mckim, 161–67. Downers Grove: InterVaristy, 2007.

Jue, Jeffery K. "*Theologia Naturalis*: A Reformed Tradition." In *Revelation and Reason: New Essays in Reformed Apologetics*, edited by K. Scott Oliphint and Lane G. Tipton, 168–89. Phillipsburg, NJ: Presbyterian & Reformed, 2007.

Juhl, P. D. "Playing with Texts: Can Deconstruction Account for Critical Practice?" In *Criticism and Critical Theory*, edited by Jeremy Hawthorn, 59–72. London: Edward Arnold, 1984.

Kaiser, Walter C., Jr. "A Response to Authorial Intention and Biblical Interpretation." In *Hermeneutics, Inerrancy, and the Bible*, edited by Earl D. Radmacher and Robert D. Preus, 443–46. Grand Rapids: Zondervan, 1984.

———. "Legitimate Hermeneutics." In *A Guide to Contemporary Hermeneutics*, edited by Donald K. McKim, 111–41. Eugene, OR: Wipf & Stock, 1986.

———. "The Meaning of Meaning." In *An Introduction to Biblical Hermeneutics: The Search for Meaning*, edited by Walter C. Kaiser and Moisés Silva, 37–61. Grand Rapids: Zondervan, 1994.

———. "Response to Bock." In *Three Views of the New Testament Use of the Old Testament*, edited by Kenneth Berding and Jonathan Lunde, 152–58. Grand Rapids: Zondervan, 2008.

———. "The Single Intent of Scripture." In *The Right Doctrine from the Wrong Texts?*, edited by G. K. Beale, 55–68. Grand Rapids: Baker, 1994.

———. "Single Meaning, Unified Referents." In *Three Views of the New Testament Use of the Old Testament*, edited by Kenneth Berding and Jonathan Lunde, 45–89. Grand Rapids: Zondervan, 2008.

———. *Toward an Exegetical Theology: Biblical Exegesis for Preaching and Teaching*. Grand Rapids: Baker, 1981.

Kaiser, Walter C., and Moisés Silva, *An Introduction to Biblical Hermeneutics: The Search for Meaning*. Grand Rapids: Zondervan, 1994.

Kant, Immanuel. *Critique of Pure Reason*. 2nd ed. Translated by J. M. D. Meiklejohn. New York: Everyman's Library, 1978.

———. *Prolegomena: To Any Future Metaphysics That Will Be Able to Present Itself as a Philosophy & the Christian Faith*. Translated by Peter G. Lucas. Reprint. Manchester University Press, 1971.

Karlberg, Mark W. Review of *Cornelius Van Til: An Analysis of His Thought*, by John M. Frame. *Mid-America Journal of Theology* 9 (1993) 297–308.

Kelly, Douglas F. *Systematic Theology: Volume One*. Scotland, UK: Mentor, 2008.

Klein, William W., Craig L. Blomberg, and Robert L. Hubbard, eds. *Introduction to Biblical Interpretation*. Revised and enlarged ed. Nashville: Thomas Nelson, 2004.

Klooster, Fred T. *The Incomprehensibility of God in the Orthodox Presbyterian Conflict*. Franeker: T. Weaver, 1951.

Knudsen, Robert D. "Crosscurrents." *Westminster Theological Journal* 35 (1973) 303–14.

Köstenberger, Andreas J. K. "Aesthetic Theology—Blessing or Curse? An Assessment of Narrative Theology." *Faith & Mission* 15 (1998) 27–44.

Köstenberger, Andreas J., and Richard D. Patterson, *Invitation to Biblical Interpretation: Exploring the Hermeneutical Triad of History, Literature, and Theology*. Grand Rapids: Kregel, 2011.

Köstenberger, Andreas J. "Of Professors and Madmen: Currents in Contemporary New Testament Scholarship." *Faith & Mission* 23 (2006) 3–18.

Krabbendam, Henry. "Cornelius Van Til: The Methodological Objective of Biblical Apologetics." *Westminster Theological Journal* 57 (1995) 125–44.

———. "The New Hermeneutic." In *Hermeneutics, Inerrancy, and the Bible*, edited by Earl D. Radmacher and Robert D. Preus, 533–58. Grand Rapids: Zondervan, 1984.

Kruger, Michael J. *Canon Revisited: Establishing the Origins and Authority of the New Testament Books*. Wheaton, IL: Crossway, 2012.

Kuhn, Thomas S. *The Structure of Scientific Revolutions*. 2nd ed. Chicago: University of Chicago Press, 1970.

Kunjummen, Raju D. "The Single Intent of Scripture." *Grace Theological Journal* 7 (1986) 81–110.

Kurka, Robert C. "*Before* 'Foundationalism': A More Biblical Alternative to the Grenz/Franke Proposal for Doing Theology." *Journal of the Evangelical Theological Society* 50 (2007) 145–65.

LaCugna, Catherine Mowry. *God for Us: The Trinity and Christian Life*. San Francisco: Harper, 1991.

Larkin, William J., Jr. *Cultural and Biblical Hermeneutics: Interpreting and Applying the Authoritative Word in a Relativistic Age*. Eugene, OR: Wipf & Stock, 1998.

LaSor, W. S. "Prophecy, Inspiration, and Sensus Plenior." *Tyndale Bulletin* 29 (1978) 49–60.

———. "The *Sensus Plenior* and Biblical Interpretation." In *A Guide to Contemporary Hermeneutics*, edited by Donald K. McKim, 47–64. Eugene, OR: Wipf & Stock, 1986.

Lategan, Bernard C. "Reference: Reception, Redescription, and Reality." In *Text and Reality: Aspects of Reference in Biblical Texts*, edited by Bernard C. Lategan and Willem S. Vorster, 67–93. Atlanta: Scholars, 1985.

Laughery, Gregory J. *Living Hermeneutics in Motion: An Analysis of Paul Ricoeur's Contribution to Biblical Hermeneutics*. New York: University Press of America, 2002.

Leithart, Peter J. *Deep Exegesis: The Mystery of Reading Scripture*. Waco, TX: Baylor University Press, 2009.

Leschert, Dale. "A Change of Meaning, Not a Change of Mind: The Clarification of a Suspected Defection in the Hermeneutical Theory of E. D. Hirsch, Jr." *Journal of the Evangelical Theological Society* 35 (1992) 183–87.

Letham, Robert. *The Holy Trinity*. Phillipsburg, NJ: Presbyterian & Reformed, 2004.

———. Review of *A New Systematic Theology of the Christian Faith*, by Robert L. Reymond. *Westminster Theological Journal* 62 (2000) 314–19.

Lewis, Gordon R. "Van Til and Carnell—Part I." In *Jerusalem and Athens: Critical Discussions on the Philosophy and Apologetics of Cornelius Van Til*, edited by E. R. Geehan, 349–61. Phillipsburg, NJ: Presbyterian and Reformed Publishing, 1980.

Lillback, Peter A. "The Infallible Rule of Interpretation of Scripture: The Hermeneutical Crisis and the Westminster Standards." In *Resurrection and Eschatology: Essays in the Honor of Richard B. Gaffin Jr*, edited by Lane G. Tipton and Jeffrey C. Waddington, 283–339. Phillipsburg, NJ: Presbyterian & Reformed, 2008.

Lints, Richard. *The Fabric of Theology: A Prolegomenon to Evangelical Theology*. Grand Rapids: Eerdmans, 1993.

———. "Two Theologies Or One? Warfield and Vos on the Nature of Theology." *Westminster Theological Journal* 54 (1992) 235–53.

Loder, James and W. Jim Neidhardt. *The Knight's Move: The Relational Logic of the Spirit in Theology and Science*. Colorado Springs: Helmer & Howard, 1982.

Longenecker, Richard N. *Biblical Exegesis in the Apostolic Period*. 2nd ed. Grand Rapids: Eerdmans, 1999.

———. "Major Tasks of an Evangelical Hermeneutic." *Bulletin for Biblical Research* 14 (2004) 45–58.

———. "Negative Answer to the Question." In *The Right Doctrine from the Wrong Texts?*, edited by G. K. Beale, 375–86. Grand Rapids: Baker, 1994.

———. "Who is the Prophet Talking About? Some Reflections on the New Testament's Use of the Old." In *The Right Doctrine from the Wrong Texts?*, edited by G. K. Beale, 375–86. Grand Rapids: Baker, 1994.

Lunde, Jonathan. "An Introduction to Central Questions in the New Testament Use of the Old Testament." In *Three Views of the New Testament Use of the Old Testament*, edited by Kenneth Berding and Jonathan Lunde, 7–41. Grand Rapids: Zondervan, 2008.

Lundin, Roger. "Interpreting Orphans: Hermeneutics in the Cartesian Tradition." In *The Promise of Hermeneutics*, edited by Roger Lundin, Clarence Walhout, and Anthony C. Thiselton, 1–64. Grand Rapids, Mich.: Eerdmans, 1999.

Macleod, Donald. *The Person of Christ*. Downers Grove, IL: InterVarsity, 1998.

Macquarrie, John. "Heidegger's Earlier and Later Work Compared." *Anglican Theological Review* 49 (1967) 3–16.

Madueme, Hans. "Theological Interpretation After Barth." *Journal of Theological Interpretation* 3 (2009) 143–56.

Maier, Gerhard. *The End of the Historical-Critical Method*. St. Louis: Concordia, 1977.

Marshall, I. Howard. "Evangelicals and Hermeneutics." In *Beyond the Bible: Moving From Scripture to Theology*, edited by I. Howard Marshall, Kevin J. Vanhoozer, and Stanley E. Porter, 11–32. Grand Rapids: Baker, 2004.

McCartney, Dan G. "The New Testament's Use of the Old Testament." In *Inerrancy and Hermeneutic: A Tradition, A Challenge, A Debate*, edited by Harvie M. Conn, 101–16. Grand Rapids: Baker, 1988.

McCartney, Dan, and Charles Clayton. *Let the Reader Understand: A Guide to Interpreting and Applying the Bible*. 2nd ed. Phillipsburg, NJ: P&R Publishing, 2002.

McIntire, C. T. "The Ongoing Task of Christian Historiography" In *A Christian View of History?*, edited by George Marsden and Frank Roberts, 51–74. Grand Rapids: Eerdmans, 1975.

McKim, Donald K., ed. *A Guide to Contemporary Hermeneutics: Major Trends in Biblical Interpretation*. Eugene, OR: Wipf & Stock, 1986.

McKnight, Edgar V. *Post-Modern Use of the Bible: The Emergence of Reader Oriented Criticism*. Nashville: Abingdon, 1988.

McQuilken, Robertson and Bradford Mullen. "The Impact of Postmodern Thinking on Evangelical Hermeneutics." *Journal of the Evangelical Theological Society* 40 (1997) 69–82.

Merrick, James R. A. "Giving God Hermeneutical Glory: Biblical Interpretation as if God Mattered." *Journal of Theological Interpretation* 2 (2008) 293–302.

Mickelsen, Berkeley. *Interpreting the Bible*. Grand Rapids: Eerdmans, 1963.

Moberly, R. W. L. "What is Theological Interpretation of Scripture?" *Journal of Theological Interpretation* 3 (2009) 161–78.

Molnar, Paul D. *Divine Freedom and the Doctrine of the Immanent Trinity: In Dialogue with Karl Barth and Contemporary Theology*. New York: T. & T. Clark, 2002.

———. "The Function of the Immanent Trinity in the Theology of Karl Barth." *Scottish Journal of Theology* 42 (1989) 367–99.
Montgomery, John Warrick. "Once Upon an A Priori." In *Jerusalem and Athens: Critical Discussions on the Philosophy and Apologetics of Cornelius Van Til*, edited by E. R. Geehan, 380–92. Phillipsburg, NJ: Presbyterian & Reformed, 1980.
Moo, Douglas J. "The Problem of Sensus Plenior." In *Hermeneutics, Authority, and Canon*, edited by D. A. Carson and John D. Woodbridge, 179–211. Grand Rapids: Zondervan, 1986.
Moore, Stephen D. *Literary Criticism and the Gospels: The Theoretical Challenge*. New Haven: Yale University Press, 1989.
Moritz, Thorsten. "Critical but Real: Reflecting on N.T. Wright's *Tools for the Task*." In *Renewing Biblical Interpretation*, edited by Craig Bartholomew, Colin Greene, and Karl Möller, 172–95. Grand Rapids: Zondervan, 2000.
Muether, John R. *Cornelius Van Til: Reformed Apologist and Churchman*. Phillipsburg, NJ: Presbyterian and Reformed Publishing, 2008.
Muller, Richard. *The Divine Essence and Attributes*. In Vol. 3, *Post-Reformation Dogmatics*. Grand Rapids: Baker, 2003.
———. *Prolegomena to Theology*. In Vol. 1, *Post-Reformation Dogmatics*. Grand Rapids: Baker, 2003.
———. *The Triunity of God*. In Vol. 4, *Post-Reformation Dogmatics*. Grand Rapids: Baker, 2003.
Nash, Ronald. "Gordon Clark's Theory of Knowledge." In *The Philosophy of Gordon Clark*, edited by R. H. Nash, 125–75. Philadelphia: P&R Publishing, 1968.
———. *The Word of God and the Mind of Man*. Grand Rapids: Zondervan, 1982.
Neusner, Jacob. *The Rabbinic Traditions about the Pharisees Before 70*. 3 Vols. Leiden: Brill, 1971.
Noll, Mark A. *Between Faith and Criticism: Evangelicals, Scholarship, and the Bible in America*. San Francisco: Harper & Row, 1986.
Notaro, Thom. *Van Til and the Use of Evidence*. Phillipsburg, NJ: Presbyterian & Reformed, 1980.
Oliphint, Scott. "The Consistency of Van Til's Methodology." *Westminster Theological Journal* 52 (1990) 27–49.
———. *Covenantal Apologetics: Principles & Practice in Defense of Our Faith*. Wheaton, IL: Crossway, 2013.
———. *God with Us: Divine Condescension and the Attributes of God* Wheaton, IL: Crossway, 2012.
———. *Reasons for Faith: Philosophy in the Service of Theology*. Phillipsburg, NJ: Presbyterian & Reformed, 2006.
Orthodox Presbyterian Church. "Minutes of the Eleventh General Assembly." May 16–19, 1944. https://opcgaminutes.org/wp-content/uploads/2018/04/1944-GA-11.pdf.
———. "Minutes of the Fourteenth General Assembly." May 22–28, 1947. https://opcgaminutes.org/wp-content/uploads/2018/04/1947-GA-14.pdf.
———. "Minutes of the Fifteenth General Assembly." May 13–19, 1948. https://opcgaminutes.org/wp-content/uploads/2018/04/1948-GA-15.pdf.
———. "Minutes of the Thirteenth General Assembly." May 21–28, 1946. https://opcgaminutes.org/wp-content/uploads/2018/04/1946-GA-13.pdf.

———. "Minutes of the Twelfth General Assembly." May 17–23, 1945. https://opcgaminutes.org/wp-content/uploads/2018/04/1945-GA-12.pdf.

Ortlund, Gavin. "Wholly Other or Wholly Given Over? What Van Til Missed in His Criticism of Barth." *Presbyterion* 35 (2009) 35–52.

Osborne, Grant R. "Genre Criticism—Sensus Literalis." *Trinity Journal* 4 (1983) 1–27.

———. *The Hermeneutical Spiral: A Comprehensive Introduction to Biblical Interpretation*. Downers Grove, IL: InterVarsity, 2006.

Ovey, Michael J. "A Private Love? Karl Barth and the Triune God." In *Engaging with Barth*, edited by David Gibson and Daniel Strange, 198–231. Nottingham: Apollos, 2008.

Oxenhandler, Neal. "Ontological Criticism in America and France." *Modern Language Review* 55 (1960) 17–23.

Packer, J. I. "A Response to the New Hermeneutic." In *Hermeneutics, Inerrancy, and the Bible*, edited by Earl D. Radmacher and Robert D. Preus, 559–71. Grand Rapids: Zondervan, 1984.

———. "Biblical Authority, Hermeneutics, and Inerrancy." In *Jerusalem and Athens: Critical Discussions on the Philosophy and Apologetics of Cornelius Van Til*, edited by E. R. Geehan, 141–53. Phillipsburg, NJ: Presbyterian & Reformed, 1980.

———. *"Fundamentalism" and the Word of God*. Reprint. Grand Rapids: Eerdmans, 1974.

———. "Infallible Scripture and the Role of Hermeneutics." In *Scripture and Truth*, edited by D. A. Carson and John D. Woodbridge, 321–56. Grand Rapids: Baker, 1992.

Palmer, Donald. *Looking at Philosophy*. 4th ed. New York: McGraw Hill, 2006.

Palmer, Richard. *Hermeneutics: Interpretation Theory in Schleiermacher, Dilthey, Heidegger and Gadamer*. Evanston, IL: Northwestern University Press, 1969.

———. "On the Transcendability of Hermeneutics." In *Hermeneutics: Questions and Prospects*, edited by Gary Shapiro and Alan Sica, 84–95. Amherst: University of Massachusetts, 1984.

———. Review of *Validity in Interpretation*, by E. D. Hirsch. *Journal of the American Academy of Religion* 36 (1968) 243–46.

Pannenberg, Wolfhart. *The Apostles' Creed in the Light of Today's Questions*. Translated by Margaret Kohl. London: SCM Press, 1972.

———. *Metaphysics and the Idea of God*. Translated by Philip Clayton. Grand Rapids: Eerdmans, 1990.

Payne, Philip Barton. "The Fallacy of Equating Meaning with the Human Author's Intention." In *The Right Doctrine from the Wrong Texts?*, edited by G. K. Beale, 70–81. Grand Rapids: Baker, 1994.

Perrin, Nicholas. "Some Reflections on Hermeneutics and Method: A Reply to Guy Waters." *Westminster Theological Journal* 68 (2006) 139–46.

Pike, Kenneth L. *Linguistic Concepts: An Introduction to Tagmemic*. Lincoln: University of Nebraska Press, 1982.

Pinnock, Clark H. "The Philosophy of Christian Evidences." In *Jerusalem and Athens: Critical Discussions on the Philosophy and Apologetics of Cornelius Van Til*, edited by E. R. Geehan, 420–25. Phillipsburg, NJ: Presbyterian & Reformed, 1980.

Plantinga, Alvin C. *Where the Real Conflict Lies: Science, Religion, and Naturalism* Oxford: Oxford University Press, 2011.

Plantinga, Cornelius, Jr. "The Three/Oneness Problem of the Trinity." *Calvin Theological Journal* 23 (1998) 37–53.
Poirier, John C. "Theological Interpretation and Its Contradistinctions." *Tyndale Bulletin* 60 (2009) 106–18.
———. "Why I'm Still Afraid: A Response to James K. A. Smith's *Who's Afraid of Postmodernism*." *Westminster Theological Journal* 69 (2007) 175–84.
Polanyi, Michael. *Knowing and Being: Essays by Michael Polanyi*. Edited by Marjorie Grene. Chicago: University of Chicago Press, 1969.
———. *Personal Knowledge*. Chicago: University of Chicago Press, 1958.
Porter, Stanley E., and Beth M. Stovell. "Introduction: Trajectories in Biblical Hermeneutics." In *Biblical Hermeneutics: Five Views*, edited by Stanley E. Porter and Beth M. Stovell, 9–24. Downers Grove, IL: InterVarsity, 2012.
Porter, Stanley E., and Jason C. Robinson. *Hermeneutics: An Introduction to Interpretive Theory*. Grand Rapids: Eerdmans, 2011.
Poythress, Vern S. "Analysing a Biblical Text: What Are We After?" *Scottish Journal of Theology* 32 (1979) 319–31.
———. "Biblical Studies: Kinds of Biblical Theology." *Westminster Theological Journal* 70 (2008) 129–42.
———. "Canon and Speech Act: Limitations in Speech-Act Theory, with Implications for a Putative Theory of Canonical Speech-Acts." *Westminster Theological Journal* 70 (2008) 337–54.
———. "Christ the Only Savior of Interpretation." *Westminster Theological Journal* 50 (1988) 305–21.
———. "Dispensing with Merely Human Meaning: Gains and Losses from Focusing on the Human Author, Illustrated by Zephaniah 1:2–3." *Journal of the Evangelical Theological Society* 57 (2014) 481–99.
———. "Divine Meaning of Scripture." *Westminster Theological Journal* 48 (1986) 241–79.
———. *God-Centered Interpretation*. Phillipsburg, NJ: Presbyterian & Reformed, 1999.
———. "God's Lordship in Interpretation." *Westminster Theological Journal* 50 (1988) 27–64.
———. *In the Beginning Was the Word: Language—A God-Centered Approach*. Wheaton, IL: Crossway, 2009.
———. "Kinds of Biblical Theology." *Westminster Theological Journal* 70 (2008) 129–42.
———. "Multiperspectivalism and the Reformed Faith." In *Speaking the Truth in Love: The Theology of John M. Frame*, edited by John J. Hughes, 173–200. Phillipsburg, NJ: Presbyterian & Reformed, 2009.
———. "Philosophical Roots of Phenomenological and Structuralist Literary Criticism." *Westminster Theological Journal* 41 (1978) 165–71.
———. "The Presence of God Qualifying Our Notions of Grammatical-Historical Interpretation: Genesis 3:15 as a Test Case." *Journal of the Evangelical Theological Society* 50 (2007) 87–103.
———. "Presuppositions and Harmonization: Luke 23:47 As a Test Case." *Journal of the Evangelical Theological Society* 56 (2013) 499–509.
———. *Redeeming Philosophy*. Wheaton, IL: Crossway, 2014.
———. *Redeeming Science: A God-Centered Approach*. Wheaton, IL: Crossway, 2006.

———. "Reforming Ontology and Logic in Light of the Trinity: An Appraisal of Van Til's Idea of Analogy." *Westminster Theological Journal* 57 (1995) 187–219.

———. "Rethinking Accommodation in Revelation." *Westminster Theological Journal* 76 (2014) 143–56.

———. Review of *Text, Church, and World: Biblical Interpretation in Theological Perspective*, by Francis Watson. *Westminster Theological Journal* 57 (1995) 475–77.

———. Review of *Is There a Meaning in This Text?*, by Kevin J. Vanhoozer. *Westminster Theological Journal* 61 (1999) 125–28.

———. "Science and Hermeneutics: Implications of Scientific Method for Biblical Interpretation." In *Foundations of Contemporary Interpretation*, edited by Moisés Silva, 431–531. Grand Rapids: Zondervan, 1996.

———. "Structuralism and Biblical Studies." *Journal of the Evangelical Theological Society* 21 (1978) 221–37.

———. *Symphonic Theology*. Phillipsburg, NJ: Presbyterian & Reformed, 1987.

———. "Three Modern Myths in Interpreting Genesis 1." *Westminster Theological Journal* 76 (2014) 321–50.

———. "Truth and Fullness of Meaning: Fullness Versus Reductionist Semantics in Biblical Interpretation." *Westminster Theological Journal* 67 (2005) 211–27.

———. *Understanding Dispensationalists*. 2nd ed. Phillipsburg, NJ: Presbyterian & Reformed, 1987.

———. "Why Must Our Hermeneutics be Trinitarian?" *The Southern Baptist Journal of Theology* 10 (2006) 96–98.

Pratt, Richard L., Jr. *Every Thought Captive: A Study Manual for the Defense of Christian Truth*. Phillipsburg, NJ: Presbyterian & Reformed, 1979.

———. *He Gave Us Stories*. Phillipsburg, NJ: Presbyterian & Reformed Publishing, 1990.

Preus, Robert D. "Unity of the Bible: Response." In *Hermeneutics, Inerrancy, and the Bible*, edited by Earl D. Radmacher and Robert D. Preus, 671–90. Grand Rapids: Zondervan, 1984.

Provan, Iain. "How Can I Understand, Unless Someone Explains It to Me? (Acts 8:30-31): Evangelicals and Biblical Hermeneutics." *Bulletin for Biblical Research* 17 (2007) 1–36.

Provan, Iain, V. Philips Long, and Tremper Longman III. *A Biblical History of Israel*. Louisville: Westminster John Knox, 2003.

Provence, Thomas E. "The Sovereign Subject Matter: Hermeneutics in the *Church Dogmatics*." In *A Guide to Contemporary Hermeneutics*, edited by Donald K. McKim, 241–62. Eugene, OR: Wipf & Stock, 1986.

Rae, Murray A. "Creation and Promise: Towards a Theology of History." In *"Behind" the Text: History and Biblical Interpretation*, edited by Craig Bartholomew et al., 267–99. Grand Rapids: Zondervan, 2003.

Rahner, Karl. *The Trinity*. Translated by Joseph Donceel. New York: Crossroad Publishing Company, 1970.

Ramm, Bernard. *Protestant Biblical Interpretation: A Textbook of Hermeneutics*. Grand Rapids: Baker, 1970.

Raschke, Carl. *The Next Reformation: Why Evangelicals Must Embrace Postmodernity*. Grand Rapids: Baker, 2004.

Reymond, Robert. *The Justification of Knowledge: An Introductory Study in Christian Apologetic Methodology*. Nutley, NJ: Presbyterian & Reformed, 1976.

---. *A New Systematic Theology of the Christian Faith.* 2nd ed. Nashville: Thomas Nelson, 1998.

Richardson, Kurt Anders. *Reading Karl Barth: New Directions for North American Theology.* Grand Rapids: Baker, 2004.

Ricoeur, Paul. *Conflict of Interpretations.* Evanston, IL: Northwestern University Press, 1974.

---. *Essays on Biblical Interpretation.* Edited by Lewis S. Mudge. Philadelphia: Fortress, 1980.

---. *Hermeneutics and the Human Sciences.* Edited and Translated by John B. Thompson. New York: Cambridge University Press, 1981.

---. *Interpretation Theory: Discourse and the Surplus of Meaning.* Fort Worth: Texas Christian University Press, 1976.

---. "World of the Text, World of the Reader." In *A Ricoeur Reader: Reflection and Imagination,* edited by Mario J. Valdés, 491–97. London: Harvester Wheatsheaf, 1991.

Ridderbos, Herman. *Redemptive History and the New Testament Scriptures.* Translated by H. De Jongste. Phillipsburg, NJ: Presbyterian & Reformed, 1968.

Robbins, John. *Cornelius Van Til: The Man and the Myth.* Jefferson, MD: Trinity Foundation, 1986.

Roberts, Wesley A. "Cornelius Van Til." In *Dutch Reformed Theology,* edited by David F. Wells, 71–86. Grand Rapids: Baker, 1989.

Rogerson, J. W. *W. M. L. de Wette: Founder of Modern Biblical Criticism: An Intellectual Biography.* Journal for the Study of the Old Testament: Supplement Series 126. Sheffield: Sheffield Academic, 1992.

Roth, Robert Paul. "Theological Fantasy: An Experiment in Narrative Hermeneutics and Ontology." *Word and World* 5 (1985) 258–68.

Rushdoony, Rousas. *The Biblical Philosophy of History.* 2000. Reprint. Vallecito, CA: Ross House, 1969.

---. *By What Standard? An Analysis of the Philosophy of Cornelius Van Til.* Fairfax, VA: Thoburn, 1958.

---. "The One and the Many Problem—The Contribution of Van Til." In *Jerusalem and Athens: Critical Discussions on the Philosophy and Apologetics of Cornelius Van Til,* edited by E. R. Geehan, 339–48. Phillipsburg, NJ: Presbyterian & Reformed, 1980.

---. *The One and the Many: Studies in the Philosophy of Order and Ultimacy.* Fairfax, VA: Thoburn, 1978.

Schleiermacher, Friederich D. E. *The Christian Faith.* Edited by H. R. Mackintosh and J. S. Stewart. Berkeley: Apocryphile, 2011.

---. *Hermeneutics: The Handwritten Manuscripts.* Edited by Heinz Kimmerle. Translated by James Duke and Jack Forstman. Missoula: Scholars, 1977.

Schorske, Carl E. *Thinking with History: Explorations in the Passage to Modernism.* Princeton: Princeton University Press, 1998.

Scott, J. Julius, Jr. "Some Problems in Hermeneutics for Contemporary Evangelicals." *Journal of the Evangelical Theological Society* 22 (1979) 67–77.

Searle, John R. *Expression and Meaning: Studies in the Theory of Speech Acts.* Cambridge: Cambridge University Press, 1979.

---. *Speech Acts: An Essay in the Philosophy of Language.* Cambridge: Cambridge University Press, 1969.

Shannon, Nathan D. "Christianity and Evidentialism: Van Til and Locke on Facts and Evidence." *Westminster Theological Journal* 74 (2012) 323–53.

———. "His Community, His Interpretation." Review of *Who's Community? Which Interpretation?*, by Merold Westphal. *Westminster Theological Journal* 72 (2010) 415–25.

Silva, Moisés. "The Case for Calvinistic Hermeneutics." In *An Introduction to Biblical Hermeneutics*, edited by Walter C. Kaiser and Moisés Silva, 251–69. Grand Rapids: Zondervan, 1994.

———. "God, Language and Scripture: Reading the Bible in the Light of General Linguistics." In *Foundations of Contemporary Interpretation*, 193–279. Grand Rapids: Zondervan, 1996.

———. "Has the Church Misread the Bible?" In *Foundations of Contemporary Interpretation*, 11–90. Grand Rapids: Zondervan, 1996.

———. "Law in the New Testament: Dunn's New Synthesis." *Westminster Theological Journal* 53 (1991) 339–53.

———. "The New Testament Use of the Old Testament: Text Form and Authority." In *Scripture and Truth*, edited by D. A. Carson and John D. Woodbridge, 147–65. Grand Rapids: Baker, 1992.

Singer, C. Gregg. "A Philosophy of History." In *Jerusalem and Athens: Critical Discussions on the Philosophy and Apologetics of Cornelius Van Til*, edited by E. R. Geehan, 328–38. Phillipsburg, NJ: Presbyterian & Reformed, 1980.

———. "The Problem of Historical Interpretation." In *Foundations of Christian Scholarship: Essays in the Van Til Perspective*, edited by Gary North, 53–73. Vallecito, CA.: Ross House, 1976.

Smith, James K. A. *The Fall of Interpretation: Philosophical Foundations for a Creational Hermeneutic*. Downers Grove, IL: InterVarsity, 2000.

Smith, Ralph. *Paradox and Truth: Rethinking Van Til on the Trinity*. Moscow, ID: Canon, 2002.

Snodgrass, Kline. "The Use of the Old Testament in the New." In *The Right Doctrine from the Wrong Texts?*, edited by G. K. Beale, 29–51. Grand Rapids: Baker, 1994.

Sontag, Frederick. "The Metaphysics of Biblical Studies." *Journal of the Evangelical Theological Society* 35 (1992) 189–92.

Soulen, Richard N., and R. Kendall Soulen. *Handbook of Biblical Criticism*. 3rd ed. Louisville: Westminster John Knox, 2001.

Sparks, Kenton L. *God's Words in Human Words: An Evangelical Appropriation of Critical Biblical Scholarship*. Grand Rapids: Baker, 2008.

Sproul, R. C., John Gerstner, and Arthur Lindsley. *Classical Apologetics*. Grand Rapids: Zondervan, 1984.

Stein, Robert H. "The Benefits of an Author-Oriented Approach to Hermeneutics." *Journal of the Evangelical Theological Society* 44 (2001) 451–66.

Steinmetz, David C. "The Superiority of Precritical Exegesis." In *A Guide to Contemporary Hermeneutics*, edited by Donald K. McKim, 65–77. Eugene, OR: Wipf & Stock, 1986.

Stiver, D. R. "Paul Ricoeur." In *Dictionary of Major Bible Interpreters*, edited by Donald K. McKim, 865–70. Downers Grove, IL: InterVarsity, 2007.

Stoker, Hendrik G. "Reconnoitering the Theory of Knowledge of Prof. Dr. Cornelius Van Til." In *Jerusalem and Athens: Critical Discussions on the Philosophy and*

Apologetics of Cornelius Van Til, edited by E. R. Geehan, 25–71. Phillipsburg, NJ: Presbyterian & Reformed, 1980.
Stott, John. *Evangelical Truth: A Personal Plea for Unity, Integrity, and Faithfulness*. Downers Grove, IL: InterVarsity, 1999.
Sutanto, Nathaniel Gray. "Covenantal Apologetics and Common-Sense Realism: Recalibrating the Argument." *Journal of the Evangelical Theological Society* 57 (2014) 777–91.
Tate, W. Randolph. *Biblical Interpretation: An Integrated Approach*. 3rd ed. Peabody, MA: Hendrickson, 2008.
Taylor, James E. *Introducing Apologetics: Cultivating Christian Commitment*. Grand Rapids: Baker, 2006.
Terry, Milton S. *Biblical Hermeneutics: A Treatise on the Interpretation of the Old and New Testament*. 1885. Reprint. Grand Rapids: Zondervan, 1947.
Thiselton, Anthony C. "Authority and Hermeneutics: Some Proposals for a More Creative Agenda." In *A Pathway Into Holy Scripture*, edited by Philip E. Satterthwaite and David F. Wright, 107–41. Grand Rapids: Eerdmans, 1994.
———. "Communicative Action and Promise in Interdisciplinary, Biblical, and Theological Hermeneutics." In *The Promise of Hermeneutics*, edited by Roger Lundin, Clarence Walhout, and Anthony C. Thiselton, 133–239. Grand Rapids: Eerdmans, 1999.
———. *The First Epistle to the Corinthians*. New International Greek Testament Commentary. Grand Rapids: Eerdmans, 2000.
———. *Hermeneutics: An Introduction*. Grand Rapids: Eerdmans, 2009.
———. *The Hermeneutics of Doctrine*. Grand Rapids: Eerdmans, 2007.
———. "The New Hermeneutic." In *A Guide to Contemporary Hermeneutics*, edited by Donald K. McKim, 78–107. Eugene, OR: Wipf & Stock, 1986.
———. *New Horizons in Hermeneutics*. Grand Rapids: Zondervan, 1992.
———. Review of *Rendering the Word in Theological Hermeneutics: Mapping Divine and Human Agency*, by Mark Alan Bowald. *Journal of Theological Studies* 60 (2009) 588–89.
———. "Speech-Act Theory and the Claim that God Speaks: Wolterstorff's *Divine Discourse*." *Scottish Journal of Theology* 50 (1997) 97–110.
———. *The Two Horizons: New Testament Hermeneutics and Philosophical Description with Special Reference to Heidegger, Bultmann, Gadamer, and Wittgenstein*. Grand Rapids: Eerdmans, 1980.
———. "The Use of Philosophical Categories in New Testament Hermeneutics." *Churchman* 82 (1973) 87–100.
Thomas, Robert L. "Current Hermeneutical Trends: Toward Explanation or Obfuscation?" *Journal of the Evangelical Theological Society* 39 (1996) 241–56.
———. *Evangelical Hermeneutics: The New Versus the Old*. Grand Rapids: Kregel, 2002.
Thompson, Mark D. *A Clear and Present Word: The Clarity of Scripture*. Edited by D. A. Carson. Downers Grove, IL: InterVarsity, 2006.
Thompson, Richard P. "Scripture, Christian Canon, and Community: Rethinking Theological Interpretation Canonically." *Journal of Theological Interpretation* 4 (2010) 253–72.
Tinker, Michael. "John Calvin's Concept of Divine Accommodation: A Hermeneutical Corrective." *Churchman* 118 (2004) 325–58.

Tipton, Lane G. "The Function of Perichoresis and the Divine Incomprehensibility." *Westminster Theological Journal* 64 (2002) 289–306.
———. "Incarnation, Inspiration, and Pneumatology: A Reformed Incarnational Analogy." https://opc.org/os.html?article_id=109.
———. "The Triune Personal God: Trinitarian Theology in the Thought of Cornelius Van Til." PhD diss., Westminster Theological Seminary, 2004.
Torrance, Thomas F. *The Christian Doctrine of God: One Being Three Persons*. New York: T. & T. Clark, 1996.
———. *Karl Barth, Biblical and Evangelical Theologian*. Edinburgh: T. & T. Clark, 1990.
———. Review of *The New Modernism*, by Cornelius Van Til. *Evangelical Quarterly* 19 (1947) 144–49.
———. *Theological Science*. Edinburgh: T. & T. Clark, 1996.
———. *Trinitarian Perspectives: Toward Doctrinal Agreement*. Edinburgh: T. & T. Clark, 1988.
Torres, Joseph Emmanuel. "Perspectives on Multiperspectivalism." In *Speaking the Truth in Love: The Theology of John M. Frame*, edited by John J. Hughes, 111–36. Phillipsburg, NJ: Presbyterian & Reformed, 2009.
Tracy, David. *Blessed Rage for Order: The New Pluralism in Theology*. New York: Seabury, 1975.
———. "Literary Theory and Return of the Forms for Naming and Thinking God in Theology." *Journal of Religion* 74 (1994) 302–19.
Treier, Daniel J. "Biblical Theology and/or Theological Interpretation." *SJT* 61 (2008) 16–31.
———. *Introducing Theological Interpretation of Scripture: Recovering a Christian Practice*. Grand Rapids: Baker, 2008.
———. *Virtue and the Voice of God: Toward Theology as Wisdom*. Grand Rapids: Eerdmans, 2006.
Trimm, Charlie. "Evangelicals, Theology, and Biblical Interpretation: Reflections on the Theological Interpretation of Scripture." *Bulletin for Biblical Research* 20 (2010) 315–29.
Trueman, Carl. "It Ain't Necessarily So." *Westminster Theological Journal* 65 (2003) 311–15.
Turretin, Francis. *Institutes of Elenctic theology*. Edited by James T. Dennison, Jr. Translated by George Musgrave Giger. 3 vols. Phillipsburg, NJ: Presbyterian & Reformed, 1992.
Twombly, Charles C. *Perichoresis and Personhood*. Eugene, OR: Wipf & Stock, 2015.
van Asselt, Willem J. "The Fundamental Meaning to Theology: Archetypal and Ectypal Theology." *Westminster Theological Journal* 64 (2002) 319–36.
Vander Stelt, John. *Philosophy and Scripture: A Study in Old Princeton and Westminster Theology*. Mariton, NJ: Mack, 1978.
VanGemeren, Willem A. "Prophets, the Freedom of God, and Hermeneutics." *Westminster Theological Journal* 52 (1990) 79–99.
Vanhoozer, Kevin J. "A Lamp in the Labyrinth: The Hermeneutics of 'Aesthetic' Theology." *Trinity Journal* 8 (1987) 25–56.
———. "A Person of the Book? Barth on Biblical Authority and Interpretation." In *Karl Barth and Evangelical Theology: Convergences and Divergences*, edited by Sung Wook Chung, 26–59. Grand Rapids: Baker, 2008.

———. *Biblical Narrative in the Philosophy of Paul Ricoeur: A Study in Hermeneutics and Theology*. Cambridge: Cambridge University Press, 1990.

———. *The Drama of Doctrine: A Canonical Linguistic Approach to Christian Theology*. Louisville: Westminster John Knox Press, 2005.

———. "Exegesis and Hermeneutics." In *New Dictionary of Biblical Theology*, edited by T. Desmond Alexander et al., 52–64. Downers Grove, IL: InterVarsity, 2000.

———. *First Theology: God, Scripture, and Hermeneutics*. Downers Grove, IL: InterVarsity, 2002.

———. "Four Theological Faces of Biblical Interpretation." In *Reading Scripture With the Church*, edited by A. K. M. Adam et al., 131–42. Grand Rapids: Baker, 2006.

———. "Imprisoned or Free? Text, Status, and Theological Interpretation in the Master/Slave Discourse of Philemon." In *Reading Scripture With the Church*, edited by A. K. M. Adam et al., 51–94. Grand Rapids: Baker, 2006.

———. "Introduction: What Is Theological Interpretation of the Bible?" In *Dictionary for Theological Interpretation of the Bible*, edited by Kevin J. Vanhoozer, 19–25. Grand Rapids: Baker, 2005.

———. *Is There a Meaning in This Text?* Grand Rapids: Zondervan, 1998.

———. "Lost in Interpretation? Truth, Scripture, and Hermeneutics." *Journal of the Evangelical Theological Society* 48 (2005) 89–114.

———. "Paul Ricoeur." In *Dictionary for Theological Interpretation of the Bible*, edited by Kevin J. Vanhoozer, Craig G. Bartholomew, and Daniel J. Treier, 692–95. Grand Rapids: Baker, 1995.

Van Huyssteen, J. Wentzel. *Essays in Postfoundationalist Theology*. Grand Rapids: Eerdmans, 1997.

van Inwagen, Peter. *Metaphysics*. 2nd ed. Dimensions of Philosophy Series. Boulder: Westview Press, 2002.

Van Til, Cornelius. *A Christian Theory of Knowledge*. Phillipsburg, NJ: Presbyterian & Reformed, 1969

———. *An Introduction to Systematic Theology*. 2nd ed. Edited by William Edgar. Phillipsburg, NJ: Presbyterian & Reformed, 2007.

———. "Antitheses in Education." In *Foundations of Christian Education*, edited by Dennis E. Johnson, 3–24. Phillipsburg, NJ: Presbyterian & Reformed, 1990.

———. "Bavinck the Theologian." *Westminster Theological Journal* 24 (1961) 48–64.

———. *The Case for Calvinism*. Philadelphia: Presbyterian & Reformed, 1975.

———. *Christ and the Jews*. Philadelphia: Presbyterian & Reformed, 1968.

———. *Christian Apologetics*. 2nd ed. Edited by William Edgar. Phillipsburg, NJ: Presbyterian & Reformed, 2003.

———. "The Christian Scholar." *Westminster Theological Journal* 21 (1959) 147–78.

———. *Christian Theistic-Ethics*. Phillipsburg, NJ: Presbyterian & Reformed, 1980.

———. *Christian Theistic-Evidences*. Phillipsburg, NJ: Presbyterian & Reformed, 1978.

———. *Christianity and Barthianism*. Phillipsburg, NJ: Presbyterian & Reformed, 1962.

———. *Christianity and Idealism*. Philadelphia: Presbyterian & Reformed, 1955.

———. *Common Grace and the Gospel*. Nutley, NJ: Presbyterian & Reformed, 1977.

———. *Common Grace and the Gospel*. 2nd ed. Edited by K. Scott Oliphint. Phillipsburg, NJ: Presbyterian & Reformed, 2015.

———. "Covenant Theology." In Vol. 1, *Twentieth Century Encyclopedia of Religious Knowledge*, edited by Lefferts A. Loetscher, 306. Grand Rapids: Baker, 1955.

———. "Creation: The Education of Man—A Divinely Ordained Need." In *Foundations of Christian Education*, edited by Dennis E. Johnson, 43–63. Phillipsburg, NJ: Presbyterian & Reformed, 1990.

———. *The Defense of the Faith*. 4th ed. Edited by K. Scott Oliphint. Phillipsburg, NJ: Presbyterian & Reformed, 2008.

———. *The Doctrine of Scripture*. Philadelphia: den Dulk Christian Foundation, 1967.

———. "Evil and Theodicy." In *The Works of Cornelius Van Til, 1895-1987*. Edited by Eric H. Sigward. Logos Library System. 1997. CD-ROM.

———. *The God of Hope*. Phillipsburg, NJ: Presbyterian & Reformed, 1978.

———. *The Great Debate Today*. Nutley, NJ: Presbyterian & Reformed, 1971.

———. "Has Karl Barth Become Orthodox?" *Westminster Theological Journal* 16 (1954) 135–81.

———. *The Intellectual Challenge of the Gospel*. Phillipsburg, NJ: Tyndale Press, 1953.

———. "Introduction." In *The Inspiration and Authority of the Bible*, by Benjamin Breckenridge Warfield, 3–68. Phillipsburg, NJ: Presbyterian & Reformed, 1948.

———. *Is God Dead?* Philadelphia: Presbyterian & Reformed, 1966.

———. *Karl Barth and Evangelicalism*. Philadelphia: Presbyterian & Reformed, 1964.

———. "My Credo." In *Jerusalem and Athens: Critical Discussions on the Philosophy and Apologetics of Cornelius Van Til*, edited by E. R. Geehan, 1–21. Phillipsburg, NJ: Presbyterian & Reformed, 1980.

———. "Nature and Scripture." In *The Infallible Word*, edited by N. B. Stonehouse and Paul Woolley, 263–301. Phillipsburg, NJ: Presbyterian & Reformed, 1967.

———. *The New Hermeneutic*. Phillipsburg, NJ: Presbyterian & Reformed, 1969.

———. *The New Modernism: An Appraisal of the Theology of Barth and Brunner*. Philadelphia: Presbyterian & Reformed, 1946.

———. *Paul at Athens*. Philadelphia: Presbyterian & Reformed, 1954.

———. *Pierre Teilhard de Chardin: Evolution and Christ*. Nutley, NJ: Presbyterian & Reformed, 1966.

———. *The Psychology of Religion*. Phillipsburg, NJ: Presbyterian & Reformed, 1971.

———. *The Reformed Pastor and Modern Thought*. Phillipsburg, NJ: Presbyterian & Reformed, 1971.

———. Review of *Religion in the Making*, by Alfred North Whitehead. *Princeton Theological Review* 25 (1927) 336–38.

———. *The Sovereignty of Grace: An Appraisal of G. C. Berkouwer's View of Dordt*. Philadelphia: Presbyterian & Reformed, 1969.

———. *A Survey of Christian Epistemology*. Philadelphia: Presbyterian & Reformed, 1969.

———. *The Theology of James Daane*. Grand Rapids: Eerdmans, 1954.

———. *Toward a Reformed Apologetic*. Philadelphia: N.p., 1972.

———. *Why I Believe in God*. Philadelphia: Committee on Christian Education of the OPC, 1948.

Vermes, Geza. "The Qumran Interpretation of Scripture in Its Historical Setting." *Annual of Leeds University Oriental Society* 6 (1966–1968) 85–97.

Virkler, Henry A. *Hermeneutics: Principles and Processes of Biblical Interpretation*. Grand Rapids: Baker, 1981.

Voelz, James W. *What Does This Text Mean? Principles of Biblical Interpretation in a Post-Modern World*. 2nd ed. Saint Louis: Concordia, 2003.

Vos, Geerhardus. *Biblical Theology*. Carlisle, PA: Banner of Truth, 1948.

———. "The Idea of Biblical Theology." In *Redemptive History and Biblical Interpretation: The Shorter Writings of Geerhardus Vos*, edited by Richard B. Gaffin, Jr., 3–24. Phillipsburg, NJ: Presbyterian and Reformed Publishing, 1980.

———. *Redemptive History and Biblical Interpretation: The Shorter Writings of Geerhardus Vos*. Edited by Richard B. Gaffin, Jr. Phillipsburg, NJ: Presbyterian & Reformed Publishing, 1980.

Walhout, Clarence. "Narrative Hermeneutics." In *The Promise of Hermeneutics*, edited by Roger Lundin, Clarence Walhout, and Anthony C. Thiselton, 65–132. Grand Rapids: Eerdmans, 2000.

Waltke, Bruce. *An Old Testament Theology*. Grand Rapids: Zondervan, 2007.

Ward, Timothy. *Words of Life: Scripture as the Living and Active Word of Life*. Downers Grove, IL: Intervarsity, 2009.

Warfield, Benjamin B. *Revelation and Inspiration*. In *The Works of Benjamin B. Warfield*. Vol. 1. Reprint. Grand Rapids: Baker, 2003.

———. *Selected Shorter Writings of Benjamin B. Warfield*. Edited by John E. Meeter. 2 Vols. Nutley, NJ: Presbyterian & Reformed, 1973.

———. *Studies in Theology*. Vol. 9 of *The Works of Benjamin B. Warfield*. Reprint. Grand Rapids: Baker, 2003.

Watson, Francis. "Authors, Readers, Hermeneutics." In *Reading Scripture with the Church*, edited by A. K. M. Adam et al., 119–23. Grand Rapids: Baker, 2006.

———. "The Old Testament as Christian Scripture." *Scottish Journal of Theology* 52 (1999) 227–32.

———. *The Open Text: New Directions for Biblical Studies?* London: SCM, 1993.

———. *Text, Church, and World: Biblical Hermeneutics in Biblical Perspective*. Grand Rapids: Eerdmans, 1994.

Weaver, Gilbert B. "Man: Analogue of God." In *Jerusalem and Athens: Critical Discussions on the Philosophy and Apologetics of Cornelius Van Til*, edited by E. R. Geehan, 321–27. Phillipsburg, NJ: Presbyterian & Reformed, 1980.

Webster, John. "Hermeneutics in Modern Theology: Some Doctrinal Reflections." *Scottish Journal of Theology* 51 (1998) 307–41.

Weeks, Noel K. "The Ambiguity of Biblical 'Background.'" *Westminster Theological Journal* 72 (2010) 219–36.

———. *Sufficiency of Scripture*. Edinburgh: Banner of Truth, 1988.

Weinsheimer, Joel. *Gadamer's Hermeneutics: A Reading of 'Truth and Method.'* New Haven: Yale University Press, 1985.

Wenkel, David H. "A Survey of Evangelical Criticisms of Protestant Fundamentalist Hermeneutics: 1994-2004." *Didaskalia* (Winter 2008) 113–27.

Westminster Confession of Faith. Glasgow, Scotland: Free Presbyterian, 2003.

Westphal, Merold. "In Defense of the Thing in Itself." *Kant-Studien* 59 (1968) 118–41.

———. "The Philosophical/Theological View." In *Biblical Hermeneutics: Five Views*, edited by Stanley E. Porter and Beth M. Stovell, 70–88. Downers Grove, IL: InterVarsity, 2012.

———. *Whose Community? Which Interpretation? Philosophical Hermeneutics for the Church*. Grand Rapids: Baker, 2009.

White, James Emery. *What is Truth?* Nashville: Broadman & Holman, 1994.

White, William, Jr. *Van Til: Defender of the Faith*. Nashville: Thomas Nelson, 1979.

Wolterstorff, Nicholas. *Divine Discourse: Philosophical Reflections on the Claim that God Speaks*. Cambridge: Cambridge University Press, 1995.

———. "The Importance of Hermeneutics for a Christian Worldview." In *Disciplining Hermeneutics: Interpretation in Christian Perspective*, edited by Roger Lundin, 25–47. Grand Rapids: Eerdmans, 1997.

———. "The Promise of Speech Act Theory for Biblical Interpretation." In *After Pentecost: Language and Biblical Interpretation*, edited by Craig Bartholomew, Colin Greene, and Karl Moller, 73–90. Grand Rapids: Eerdmans, 2001.

Wood, Donald. *Barth's Theology of Interpretation*. Burlington, VT: Ashgate, 2009.

Wright, Christopher J. "Interpreting the Bible Among the Religions of the World." *Themelios* 25 (2000) 35–54.

———. *The Mission of God: Unlocking the Bible's Grand Narrative*. Downers Grove, IL: InterVarsity, 2006.

Wright, N. T. *The Last Word: Beyond the Bible Wars to a New Understanding of the Authority of Scripture*. London: SPCK, 2005.

———. *The New Testament and the People of God*. Minneapolis: Fortress, 1992.

Wright, Stephen I. "Inhabiting the Story: the Use of the Bible in the Interpretation of History." In *"Behind" the Text: History and Biblical Interpretation*, edited by Craig Bartholomew et al., 492–517. Grand Rapids: Zondervan, 2003.

Yarbrough, Robert W. "Variation on a Theme: History's *nth* Great Hermeneutical Crisis." *Journal of the Evangelical Theological Society* 39 (1996) 443–55.

Zimmerman, Jens. *Recovering Theological Hermeneutics: An Incarnational-Trinitarian Theory of Interpretation*. Grand Rapids: Baker, 2004.

www.ingramcontent.com/pod-product-compliance
Lightning Source LLC
Chambersburg PA
CBHW050851230426
43667CB00012B/2240